OECD Development Pathways

Multi-dimensional Review of Peru

VOLUME I. INITIAL ASSESSMENT

OECD

DEVELOPMENT CENTRE

This work is published under the responsibility of the Secretary-General of the OECD. The opinions expressed and arguments employed herein do not necessarily reflect those of the OECD, its Development Centre or of their member countries.

This document and any map included herein are without prejudice to the status of or sovereignty over any territory, to the delimitation of international frontiers and boundaries and to the name of any territory, city or area.

Please cite this publication as:
OECD (2015), *Multi-dimensional Review of Peru: Volume I. Initial Assessment*, OECD Development Pathways, OECD Publishing, Paris.
http://dx.doi.org/10.1787/9789264243279-en

ISBN 978-92-64-24326-2 (print)
ISBN 978-92-64-24327-9 (PDF)

Series: OECD Development Pathways
ISSN 2308-734X (print)
ISSN 2308-7358 (online)

The statistical data for Israel are supplied by and under the responsibility of the relevant Israeli authorities. The use of such data by the OECD is without prejudice to the status of the Golan Heights, East Jerusalem and Israeli settlements in the West Bank under the terms of international law.

Photo credits: Cover © design by the OECD Development Centre.

Corrigenda to OECD publications may be found on line at: *www.oecd.org/about/publishing/corrigenda.htm*.

Foreword

Economic growth matters, but it is just one facet of development. Policy makers focus their attention on ensuring that their country's development path is sustainable and that the lives of their citizens improve. This requires reconciling economic, social and environmental objectives.

OECD Development Pathways is a new series that looks at multiple development objectives beyond an exclusive focus on growth. It recognises well-being as part and parcel of development and helps governments identify the main constraints to more equitable and sustainable growth by undertaking a multi-dimensional country review (MDCR). Governments trying to achieve economic, social and environmental objectives need to understand the constraints they face and develop comprehensive and well-sequenced strategies for reform that take into account the complementarities and trade-offs across policies. The MDCR methodology is based on quantitative economic analysis, as well as qualitative approaches including foresight and participatory workshops that involve actors from the private and public sectors, civil society, and academia.

The MDCR of Peru is the second review, following that of Uruguay, to be undertaken by the OECD in Latin America and represents the first report to be published as part of the 2015-16 Country Programme, signed between Peru and the OECD. It aims at delivering an overarching assessment, and is designed to help Peru formulate development strategies and identify and support the policy reforms needed to achieve further sustainable and inclusive development.

This review comes at a time when Peru faces new challenges to further the progress it has achieved in recent years. While the recommendations are intended primarily to support public policy action by Peru's national authorities, the findings are also useful for academics, the private sector and civil society.

The MDCRs are composed of three distinct phases: diagnosis, in-depth analysis of the main constraints to development, and implementation of reforms in the identified key areas. This phased approach allows for a progressive learning process about the country´s specific challenges and opportunities that culminates in a final synthesis report to inform reforms in Peru. This diagnostic report is the outcome of the first phase of the MDCR of Peru.

Acknowledgements

Multi-dimensional Country Reviews are the result of a collaborative effort of the OECD and the country under review. Work on this first phase of the Multi-dimensional Review of Peru was carried out jointly by the OECD's Development Centre, the OECD Economics Department, and the OECD Statistics Directorate, with support from the Ministry of Economy and Finance of Peru.

Mario Pezzini, Director of the OECD Development Centre, guided the review with crucial inputs from Martine Durand, OECD Chief Statistician, and Catherine Mann, OECD Chief Economist. The Multi-dimensional Country Review process is led by Jan Rielaender, Head of the MDCR Unit and Angel Melguizo, Head of the Latin America and Caribbean Unit, both at the OECD Development Centre. Marco Mira d'Ercole, Head of the Division on Household Statistics and Progress Measurement, and Conal Smith, Head of the Well-Being and Household Conditions Section, both at the OECD Statistics Directorate, provided supervision.

The review was co-ordinated by Sebastián Nieto Parra, with the support of Juan Vázquez Zamora (both OECD Development Centre) and drafted by Hande Inanc (OECD Statistics Directorate), Sebastián Nieto Parra, Eduardo Olaberria (OECD Economics Department) and Juan Vázquez Zamora. Deirdre Culley (OECD Development Centre) managed the Foresight and Visioning workshop. The review also benefited from contribution and research assistance from Laura Bermeo, Ariel Gruver, Guillaume Lecaros de Cossio, Sammy Libos and David López. Additional inputs were provided by Gérard Bonnis (OECD Environment Directorate), and Luis Martínez and Stephen Perkins (both at the International Transport Forum).

The team is grateful for the insightful comments made by Rolando Avendano, Paula Cerutti, Céline Colin, Nicola Harrington, Juan de Laiglesia, Ania Jankowska, Lahra Liberti, Adrien Lorenceau, René Orozco, José Ramón Perea, Caroline Tassot (OECD Development Centre), Bert Brys (OECD Centre for Tax Policy), José-Luis Álvarez-Galán (OECD Directorate for Education and Skills), Ian Forde and Emily Hewlett (OECD Directorate for Employment, Labour and Social Affairs), Gérard Bonnis and Simon Upton (OECD Environment Directorate), Anamaria de Crescenzio and Cristiana Vitale (OECD Directorate for Financial and Enterprise Affairs), José Antonio Ardavín and Jorge Carbonell (OECD Global Relations Secretariat), Apostolos Zampounidis (OECD Legal Directorate), Adam Ostry, Emma Cantera and Raffaele Trapasso (OECD Public Governance and Territorial Development Directorate), and Silvia Surescu (OECD Trade and Agriculture Directorate).

On the side of the Peruvian government, a special thanks goes to Alonso Segura, Minister of Economy and Finance, and Gonzalo Gutiérrez, former Minister of Foreign Affairs, who have launched this report together with the OECD Development Centre in Lima in February 2015. Various ministries and public agencies provided useful support during the authors' visit to Lima as well as throughout the production of the report. The role of the Ministry of Economy and Finance, the main counterpart for this report, was particularly valuable, both technically and analytically. Special thanks go to Javier Roca, José de La Rosa, Natalia Jordán and Karen Trujillo for all their support. The Peruvian Embassy in Paris, particularly Gonzalo Guillén and Catherine Vennard, members of the OECD Development Centre's Governing Board provided crucial support to the process. Other ministries and public agencies also contributed largely, namely: the Central Reserve Bank of Peru, the Ministry of Development and Social Inclusion, the Ministry of Education, the Ministry of Energy and Mining, the Ministry of Foreign Trade and Tourism, the Ministry of Environment, the Ministry of Health, the Ministry of Labour, the Ministry of Production, the Ministry of Transport and Communications, as well as with the National Centre for Strategic Planning (CEPLAN). Particular thanks go to the National Institute of Statistics (INEI) and to its Head, Mr. Alejandro Vilchez, for his invaluable support and all the relevant data shared with the authors. Finally, the team is grateful to all the participants of the workshop "Peru: vision and challenges" that brought together actors from a variety of sectors and was held in Lima in February 2015 to discuss the diagnostic phase of the report as well as the main development challenges of Peru.

Other institutions, agencies, international organisations and members from the civil society and the academia also gave useful support throughout the production process of the report: the private sector associations Sociedad Nacional de Industrias and the Sociedad Nacional de Minería, Petróleo y Energía; the research centres Centro de Investigación de la Universidad del Pacífico, the Centro de Investigaciones Sociales, Políticas, Económicas y Antropológicas from the the Pontificia Universidad Católica del Pacífico, and the Grupo de Análisis para el Desarrollo - GRADE; the NGOs Ciudadanos al Día, Enseña Perú, and Transparencia; and the Peru Country Offices of the Inter-American Development Bank, the International Labour Organization, and the World Bank. In addition, CAF (Development Bank of Latin America) and ECLAC (Economic Commission for Latin America and the Caribbean) have been very supportive for this MDCR through discussions and comments during the production of the report.

The team is grateful to Fiona Hinchcliffe and Sally Hinchcliffe for editing the manuscript and to the OECD Development Centre's Communications and Publications Unit, especially Delphine Grandrieux, Aida Buendia, Elizabeth Nash and Vanda Legrandgérard for their excellent support in editing, laying out and producing the report. Linda Smiroldo Herda, from the Director's Office of the Development Centre, made a notable contribution to improve the style and distil the main messages of this report.

Table of contents

Figures

Tables

Acronyms and abbreviations

BCRP	Banco Central de la Reserva del Perú (Central Reserve Bank of Peru)
BEPS	Base Erosion and Profit Shifting
BERD	Business Expenditure on Research and Development
CAF	Development Bank of Latin America
CEDLAS	Centro de Estudios Distributivos Laborales y Sociales (Center of Distributive, Labor and Social Studies)
CEPLAN	Centro Nacional de Planeamiento Estratégico (National Centre for Strategic Planning)
CITE	Technological Innovation Centre
CoG	Centre of Government
CONCYTEC	Consejo Nacional de Ciencia, Tecnología e Innovación Tecnológica (National Science and Technology Council)
CONSUCODE	Consejo Superior de Contrataciones y Adquisiciones del Estado (The Superior Council for Public Procurement and State Contracting)
ECI	Economic Complexity Indicator
ECLAC	Economic Commission for Latin America and the Caribbean
EIA	Estudios de Impacto Ambiental (Environmental Impact Assessment)
EIU	Economist Intelligence Unit
ENAHO	Encuesta Nacional de Hogares (National Households Survey)
FDI	Foreign Direct Investment
FIDECOM	Fondo de Investigación y Desarrollo para la Competitividad (Research and Development Fund for Competitiveness)
FINCyT	Fondo para la Innovación, Ciencia y Tecnología (Fund for Innovation, Science and Technology)
FOMITEC	Fondo Marco para la Innovación, Ciencia y Tecnología (Fund for Innovation, Science and Technology)
FTA	Free Trade Agreement
GDP	Gross Domestic Product
GRADE	Grupo de Análisis para el Desarrollo (Group for the Analysis of Development)
GVC	Global Value Chain
HEI	Higher Education Institutions
HHI	Herfindahl-Hirschman Index
ICTs	Information and Communication Technology
ILO	International Labour Organization
IMF	International Monetary Fund

INDECOPI	Instituto Nacional de Defensa de la Competencia y de la Protección de la Propiedad Intelectual (National Institute for the Defense of Competition and Protection of Intellectual Property)
INEI	Instituto Nacional de Estadística e Informática (National Institute of Statistics)
IPD	Institutional Profiles Database
ITF	International Transport Forum
KILM	Key Indicators of the Labour Market
LAC	Latin America and the Caribbean
LPI	Logistics Performance Index
MDCR	Multi-Dimensional Country Review
MEF	Ministerio de Economía y Finanzas (Ministry of Economy and Finance)
MEM	Ministerio de Energía y Minas (Ministry of Energy and Mining)
MINCETUR	Ministerio de Comercio Exterior y Turismo (Ministry of Foreign Trade and Tourism)
MinEdu	Ministerio de Educación (Ministry of Education)
MINSA	Ministerio de Salud (Ministry of Health)
MoE	Ministerio del Ambiente (Ministry of Environment)
MTC	Ministerio de Transportes y Comunicaciones (Ministry of Transport and Telecommunications)
OECD	Organisation for Economic Co-Operation and Development
OEFA	Organismo de Evaluación y Fiscalización Ambiental (Environmental Evaluation and Inspection Agency)
OSCE	Organismo Supervisor de Contrataciones del Estado (Supervisory Agency for Public Procurement)
OSIPTEL	Organismo Supervisor de Inversión Privada en Telecomunicariones (Supervisory Agency for Private Investment in Telecommunications)
OSITRAN	Organismo Supervisor de la Inversión en Infraestructura de Transporte de Uso Público (National Supervisory Agency for Investment in Public Transportation Infrastructure)
PCM	Presidencia del Consejo de Ministros (Presidency of the Council of Ministers)
PENX	Plan Estratégico Nacional Exportador (National Strategic Export Plan)
PISA	Programme for International Student Assessment
PMR	Product Market Regulation
PPP	Purchasing Power Parity
PRODUCE	Ministerio de la Producción (Ministry of Production)
PROJOVEN	Programa de Capacitación Laboral Juvenil (Program for Young People)
PRONABEC	Programa Nacional de Becas y Crédito Educativo (National Program of Scholarships and Educational Loan)
RCA	Revealed Comparative Advantage
SBS	Superintendencia de Banca, Seguros y AFP (Superintendency of Banking, Insurance and Private Pension Fund Administrators of Peru)
SEACE	Sistema Electrónico de Contrataciones del Estado (Electronic System of Government Procurement)
SEDLAC	Socio-Economic Database for Latin America and the Caribbean
SENACE	Servicio Nacional de Certificación Ambiental para las Inversiones Sostenibles (Service for Environmental Certification of Sustainable Investments)

SERNANP	Servicio Nacional de Áreas Naturales Protegidas por el Estado (Service for Natural Areas Protected by the State)
SME	Small and Medium-sized Enterprise
SNIP	Sistema Nacional de Inversión Pública (National Public Investment System)
SUNAT	Superintendencia Nacional de Aduanas y de Administración Tributaria (National Customs and Tax Administration)
TiVA	Trade in Value Added
TVET	Technical and vocational education and training
UIS	UNESCO Institute for Statistics
UNESCO	United Nations Educational, Scientific and Cultural Organization
VAT	Value Added Tax
VET	Vocational Education and Training
WDI	World Development Indicators
WHO	World Health Organization

Editorial

Peru has experienced extraordinary progress in the past two decades. Significant improvements in economic growth, well-being and poverty reduction have been observed since the introduction of macroeconomic reforms and more effective social programmes in the 1990s and 2000s. The country has raised its per-capita income level, reaching the status of an upper middle-income country, and an expanding middle class now represents around a third of the population.

Peru faces great challenges, however, if it is to continue on a sustainable and inclusive development path. Many gaps remain that result largely from its rather volatile economic and political history. These add to new challenges associated with the so-called "middle-income trap" (a situation where productivity growth stagnates after countries have reached middle-income status), and the emergence of a middle class with its own expectations, demands and vulnerability.

Large inequalities in income and quality of life across people and space, low productivity performance and widespread informality are three cross-cutting challenges that are particularly relevant for the country's future progress. In order to achieve sustainable and inclusive development, Peru will need to broaden the tax base and increase the effectiveness of taxation, as well as to strengthen its institutional frameworks and state legitimacy. This will enable the country to address further challenges such as promoting greater economic diversification, improving human capital formation (e.g. education, skills and health), addressing infrastructure and logistics gaps, tackling ineffective labour market regulation and strengthening social protection programmes.

Reforms are needed to achieve a more inclusive and sustainable path, and the OECD, together with other regional organisations, can support Peru's efforts. The country has embraced numerous policy initiatives to improve living conditions, but further progress demands additional reforms and innovative policy approaches to emerging challenges. This Multi-Dimensional Country Review (MDCR) helps meet these challenges. The first volume of the MDCR presents a diagnosis of some of the main impediments to development in Peru. Forthcoming volumes will present an in-depth analysis of the main constraints to inclusive development, accompanied by specific policy recommendations to carry out structural reforms and create the conditions for making reform happen. These analyses support Peru's own development agenda towards achieving a brighter future for its citizens.

Mario Pezzini
Director
OECD Development Centre

Martine Durand
OECD Chief Statistician
Director of Statistics Directorate

Catherine Mann
OECD Chief Economist
Head of the Economics Department

Facts and figures of Peru

(Numbers in parentheses refer to the OECD average)

The land, people and electoral cycle

Population (1 000 000)[e]	30.8	Official language	Spanish (Quechua, Aymara)[1]
Under 15 (%)[e]	28.3 (18)	Form of government	Constitutional republic
Over 65 (%)[e]	6.5 (16)	Last general election	April-June 2011
Population density (per km2)[e]	24 (37)	Next general election	April-June 2016
Life expectancy (years)[d]	75 (80)	Land area (km 2)	1 280 000

The economy

GDP, current prices (billion USD)[e]	202.9	In % of GDP:	
Latest 5-year average real GDP growth[e]	5.7 (1.8)	Exports of goods and services[e]	22.2 (53.7)
GDP per capita, PPP[e] (thousand, constant 2011 international USD)	11.5 (37.2)	Imports of goods and services[e]	23.8 (49.5)
GDP per capita[e] (thousand, current USD)	6.6 (38.4)	Exports composition: (% of total merchandise exports)	
Inflation rate[e]	3.2 (0.6)	Hard commodities	49.4
General government revenue (% of GDP)[e]	22.5 (42.8)	Agriculture	26.4
		Manufacture	24.2
General government total expenditure (% of GDP)[e]	22.4 (40.6)		
General government gross debt (% of GDP)[e]	20.7 (73.9)	GDP shares (%)[e]:	
		Primary	5.7 (2.5)
General government net borrowing (% of GDP)[e]	0.3 (2.2)	Secondary	34.4 (27.3)
		Tertiary	59.9 (70.2)
Foreign reserves (USD billion)[e]	60.5		
Current account balance (% of GDP)[e]	-4.05 (1.8)		

The labour market

Labour force participation (%)[e]	68.6 (70.6)	Unemployment rate (%)[e]	6 (8)
Males[e]	82 (79)		
Females[e]	64.5 (62)		
Employment rate (%)[e]	64.4 (65.7)	Youth unemployment rate (ages 15-24, %)[e]	14 (17.3)
Informal economy (as % of non-agricultural employment)[c]	68.8		

The environment

CO_2 emissions[b] (kg per 2005 PPP USD of GDP)	0.47	Renewables (% of total primary (i.e.) energy supply)[b]	24
		Forest area (% of land area)[a]	53.1

Social inclusion and innovation

Income inequality (Gini coefficient)[c]	45.3 (32)	Net enrolment rates	
Poverty headcount ratio[d] (at national poverty line, % of population)	23.9	Primary[d]	91.83 (96)
		Secondary[d]	76.28 (88)
		Tertiary (% gross)[a (d)]	40.64 (70)
Health expenditure, total (% of GDP)[d]	5.3 (9.3)	Education outcomes (PISA score, 2012)	
Public spending on education (% of GDP)[d (b)]	3.3 (5.2)	Reading	384 (496)
		Mathematics	368 (494)
		Science	373 (501)
School life expectancy (primary to tertiary, years)[a (d)]	13.1 (17)	Business enterprise R&D expenditure[c] (% of GDP)	0.05 (1.6)

Well-being [e]

(% of population who have or perceive)

% Satisfied with life	36.6 (58.2)	% Believes corruption is widespread in government	84.00 (65.45)
% Satisfied with affordable housing	40.19 (45.73)	% Satisfied with air quality	62.15 (75.50)
% Satisfied with personal health	72.75 (75.65)	% Satisfied with water quality	61.22 (68.02)
% with someone to count on	82.15 (79.81)	% Who feels safe walking alone at night	45.33 (60.28)

Notes:
a) Data for 2010.
b) Data for 2011.
c) Data for 2012.
d) Data for 2013.
e) Data for 2014.

1. According to Peru's Constitution Spanish is official in the areas where it is the predominant language, so are the Quechua and Aymara and other aboriginal languages.

Sources:

BCRP (2015), Central Bank of Peru Statistics, Banco Central de Reserva del Peru, http://www.bcrp.gob.pe/estadisticas.html
CEPAL (2015) CEPALSTAT (database), Economic Commission for Latin America and the Caribbean, http://estadisticas.cepal.org/cepalstat/WEB_CEPALSTAT/Portada.asp?idioma=i
Gallup Organisation (2015), Gallup World Monitor (database).
ILO (2015), ILOSTAT (database) Geneva, www.ilo.org/ilostat/faces/home/statisticaldata?_adf.ctrl-state=19ogkwb9t9_4&clean=true&_afrLoop=596941889745721.1
INEI (2015), Compendio Estadístico Perú 2015 (Peru in Figures 2015), Instituto Nacional de Estadística e Informática, Lima, http://www.inei.gob.pe/biblioteca-virtual/publicaciones-digitales
IMF (2015), World Economic Outlook Database, International Monetary Fund, April 2015 Edition, Washington DC
OECD (2013), Main Science and Technology Indicators Database, www.oecd.org/sti/msti; y OCDE forecasts based on RICYT.
UNESCO (2015) Institute for Statistics, Educational attainment, Mean years of schooling, http://data.uis.unesco.org/
UNDP (2013), Human Development Reports, http://hdr.undp.org/en/content/mean-years-schooling-adults-years
World Bank (2015), World Development Indicators (database), Washington, DC, http://data.worldbank.org.

Administrative regions of Peru

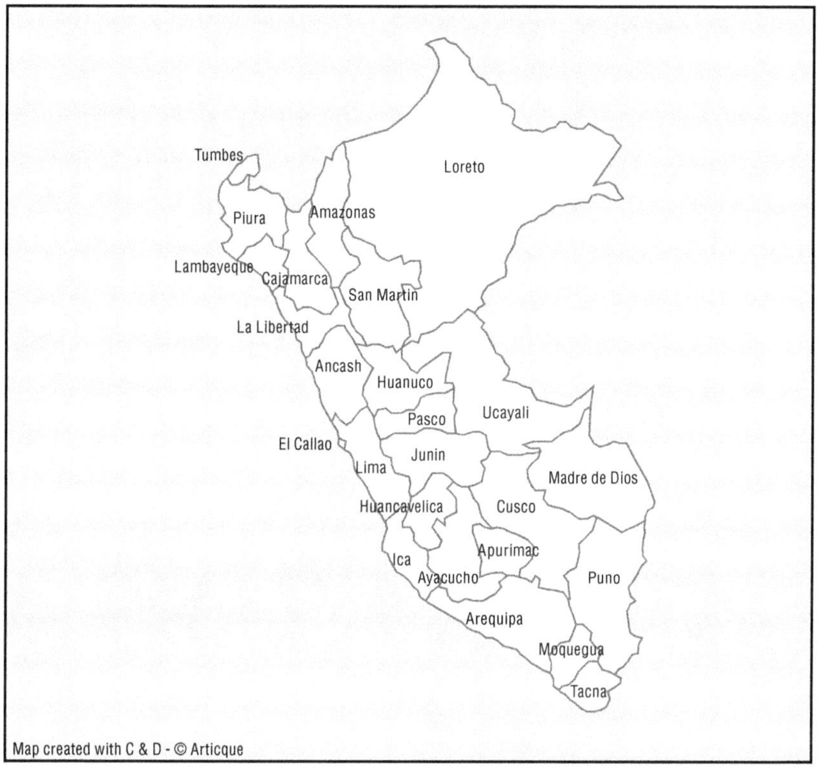

Executive summary

This document is the first report prepared in the context of the Multi-dimensional Country Review (MDCR) of Peru. The MDCR is undertaken to support Peru in achieving a sustainable path of development that continues to improve the well-being of its citizens and provide solid economic growth. The MDCR of Peru is being implemented in three phases, each leading to the production of a report. This first report aims to identify the main constraints on achieving sustainable and equitable improvements in well-being and economic growth. The second report will present in-depth analyses of the key policy areas identified in this first report in order to formulate recommendations for Peru. The final report will provide prioritisation, sequencing and a framework for measuring progress.

Peru has experienced considerable socioeconomic progress and improved well-being in the last two decades due to a combination of sound domestic policies and favourable external conditions. The country has recorded strong economic growth since the beginning of the 21st century, which has been accompanied by a significant reduction in poverty, from around 60% in 2004 to less than 24% in 2013. While inequalities remain large and relate not only to income but also to different dimensions of well-being, they have decreased. Sound macroeconomic policies, economic openness and effective social protection programmes are largely behind this success, which has also been fuelled by favourable external economic conditions.

However, in order to meet the middle-income challenge and strengthen the emerging middle class, Peru must overcome low productivity growth, large inequalities and high and widespread informality. Countries tend to face a prolonged slowdown at a certain level of development, commonly referred to as the middle-income trap. This phenomenon seems to be currently affecting Peru. The current drivers of growth, which are strongly reliant on labour, capital accumulation and on the commodity exporting sector, seem insufficient to sustain further socioeconomic progress. To unlock new drivers of lasting growth and improvements in social outcomes, Peru must find ways to boost productivity growth, and to reduce inequalities and informality. In addition, progress has expanded the size of the middle class, which now accounts for around a third of the population. Many in the middle class remain vulnerable and could slip back into poverty following any economic slowdown. In addition, this emerging middle class brings new and evolving demands, notably with regard to public services such as education, health and transportation.

A number of pathways for tackling these challenges across multiple dimensions emerge from the analysis and require a comprehensive approach. The analysis presented in this first volume of the OECD Multi-Dimensional Review of Peru shows that coherence and co-ordination of policies among a variety of social, economic and institutional dimensions are needed to tackle the constraints to development that the country still faces.

Despite improvements in access to both healthcare and education, the quality of these essential public services remains insufficient to meet the needs of citizens and the economy. Despite remarkable advances in providing health coverage to the most disadvantaged segments of the population, access to and trust in the healthcare system remain low and service quality is poor. Equitable access to quality education and formal jobs is critical for fostering social cohesion and improving economic performance. Secondary school students in Peru performed the lowest of all participating countries in the last 2012 PISA survey, showing that an average 15-year-old student in Peru is behind the average OECD student by the equivalent of 3 years of secondary schooling. There is ample room for more investment in education, and for a stronger focus on quality and performance through a greater emphasis on teaching, on policies at the classroom level and on pre-primary education, among other factors. Additionally, the pertinence of education is low; almost a third of Peruvian formal firms fail to find the workers with the skills they need, compared to close to 15% in OECD countries. This highlights the importance of focusing on a wider range of skills in the curriculum, including soft skills. It also means improving vocational education and training and mechanisms to better match the demand and supply of skills, including retraining workers throughout their working life and anticipating future skills demands.

Informality continues to dominate the world of work, holding back both job quality and productivity. The labour market is largely segmented, with poor working conditions, aggravated by significant inequalities by gender and socio-economic origin. Informality, at close to 60% of workers, is one of the highest in Latin America. Strong inequality defines both informality and working conditions. Young people with low education in rural areas are the worst affected, while higher education significantly reduces the likelihood of working in informality. The entrance into labour markets in Peru is more likely to take place through an informal job than a formal one, while informal workers are more likely to become jobless. Overly complex and burdensome labour regulations, high non-wage costs and the deficiencies in education and active labour market policies are some of the factors behind these poor outcomes.

Better jobs and continued socioeconomic progress require greater productivity and competitiveness. Low total factor productivity (TFP) explains close to 50% of the labour productivity gap between Peru and the United States. Furthermore, close to one half of all workers are employed in Peru's two less productive sectors: retail and restaurants, and agriculture. Peru needs increased economic diversification towards sectors with greater potential productivity gains, which can contribute to more value-added in exports. In that context, broad-based policies are necessary to foster productivity and competitiveness. In particular, more and better research and development, as well as the effective diffusion of new knowledge are required to close the innovation gap. To reduce transport costs, Peru should diversify transport modes and improve "soft" components of logistics, such as customs and the use of information and communications technology in the transport sector. Finally, despite recent improvements to reduce red tape and increase competition, room for improvement remains in areas such as contract enforcement and the administrative burdens for new businesses.

Improvements in the tax structure should complement a sound macroeconomic framework. The credible monetary and fiscal policies implemented in the past decade are key for inclusive development in Peru. Inflation rates and public debt are at low levels, increasing confidence among domestic and international investors. However, a more effective taxation system is needed to finance the existing socioeconomic gaps. The level of taxation at 18% of GDP remains low compared to OECD and Latin American countries (34% and 21%, respectively), and the taxation system does little to reduce inequalities and promote entrepreneurship and green growth. Major challenges are evident in the imbalance between direct and indirect taxes, the lack of progressivity in the tax system, the large tax expenditures as a proportion of total tax revenues and the low level of environment-related taxes.

Finally, to achieve the policy objectives required to boost inclusive development Peru needs stronger governance and greater state capacity to prioritise and implement. In particular, tackling corruption should both increase the trust citizens have in their government and build state legitimacy. This would boost tax morale and ease the political economy of tax reform. The governance of the judiciary and legislature should improve, while central government requires better co-ordination and enhanced leadership to drive long-term reforms. Much has been done to integrate the private sector in expenditures and investments, but better management of the process is needed to avoid inefficiencies and unexpected fiscal costs. At the sub-national level, the allocation of public resources and commodity revenues needs to be improved to address Peru's significant spatial inequalities, which are close to 20 percentage points higher than the OECD average. Local governments require more capacity to improve their policy making. Environmental regulations can be both powerful and efficiently administered and at the same time require better horizontal and vertical co-ordination of policies to promote green growth.

Chapter 1
Setting the scene: Towards greater well-being and stronger development in Peru

Peru has experienced significant improvements in growth, well-being and poverty reduction since the introduction of macroeconomic reforms, economic openness and more effective social programmes in the 1990s. However, the country still faces structural challenges if it is to escape the middle-income trap and consolidate its emerging middle class. The quantitative and qualitative analyses conducted as part of this Multi-dimensional Country Review offer a diagnosis of these barriers to sustainable and inclusive development. In particular, this chapter presents the results of the OECD well-being analysis, which paints a comprehensive picture of people's material living conditions and quality of life in Peru. It also summarises the main bottlenecks to inclusive development, studied in more depth in the chapters that follow. These include health, education and skills, the labour market, innovation, transport infrastructure and logistics, governance, and trust in institutions. These dimensions have considerable implications for the levels of productivity, inequalities and labour informality in Peru.

Peru has made extraordinary progress in recent decades, despite a rather volatile economic and political history. The country has gone through periods of economic crises which have significantly eroded its wealth, together with long episodes of political instability and social unrest that left deep marks on the country's institutional framework and in the memories of its people. This history explains to a large extent where Peru stands today and how, despite the recent encouraging progress, significant socio-economic challenges and gaps remain that are holding the country back on its pathway to inclusive and sustainable development.

This first volume of the OECD Multi-dimensional Country Review (MDCR) of Peru diagnoses the main barriers to sustainable and inclusive development (Box 1.1). Promoting equitable, inclusive and sustainable economic growth and improving the well-being of all citizens should be at the core of all national development strategies. Development strategies must take into account the multiplicity of development objectives and the means available for implementing public policy actions. The diagnostic analysis in this first report serves to identify the constraints hampering Peru's further development. The diagnosis focuses specifically on areas in which the country is lagging behind so as to identify actions to improve this performance.

Box 1.1. **The MDCR in the context of the OECD Country Programme with Peru**

In 2014, the OECD and Peru agreed to set out a joint Country Programme to support Peru in its reform agenda and improve its public policies in key priority areas. The Programme will facilitate Peru's adherence to OECD legal instruments, participation in OECD bodies and programmes, and effective implementation of OECD standards and best practices. Over two years (2015-16) the programme is and will be conducting a series of policy reviews and activities in five priority areas: removing barriers to growth, public governance, anti-corruption, human capital and the environment. The programme also includes workshops and capacity-building activities in areas such as tax policy, regulatory policy, and statistics.

This OECD Multi-dimensional Country Review (MDCR) is the first policy review of this Country Programme to be published. It is designed to help Peru formulate development strategies and identify and support the policy reforms needed to achieve further sustainable and inclusive development. This review is composed of three distinct phases:

- This first report aims to identify the main constraints on achieving sustainable and equitable improvements in well-being and economic growth.
- The second phase will further analyse the key constraints identified in this report in order to formulate policy recommendations that can be integrated into the development strategy of Peru.
- The final phase of the MDCR will provide support to the implementation of these recommendations.[1]

For each phase, a report is published and a series of workshops are organised. The MDCR methodology is based on quantitative economic analysis, as well as qualitative approaches including foresight and participatory workshops. Quantitative methods include standard approaches as well as a comparative analysis with a selection of countries, referred to here as the benchmark countries.

This introductory chapter explores well-being in Peru and summarises the key constraints on development. It starts with a review of economic developments of recent decades and summarises the main economic and social challenges in the context of an economy seeking to escape the so-called middle-income trap and reduce the vulnerability of its increasing middle class. It then presents the main results of the OECD well-being analysis, painting a comprehensive picture of people's material living conditions and quality of life. It also outlines the thematic areas which will be examined in greater detail in the chapters that follow. Finally, it concludes by summarising the key constraints for inclusive development in Peru.

Peru's recent progress marks the end of a tortuous path

The two and a half decades from the mid-1960s to the early 1990s represent for Peru a period of particular economic decline vis-à-vis most middle- and high-income countries. A combination of interventionist and protectionist policies and large microeconomic distortions, such as lack of competition in some markets and barriers to setting up formal businesses, undermined incentives to save and invest and led to a deterioration in Peru's economic potential. Private investment was at very low levels, with the ratio of exports to gross domestic product (GDP) falling dramatically and the fiscal budget in a significantly weak position.

The "lost decade" of the 1980s was Peru's worst economic period of the second half of the 20th century. GDP per capita decreased in real terms by more than 20%. Hyperinflation devastatingly eroded savings and wealth, and the country was battered by years of intense economic and social instability. The annual inflation rate was more than 50% throughout the decade, soaring to over 1 000% in both 1988 and 1989, and the annual fiscal deficit averaged more than 8.5% of GDP.[2] This explains in part why today, among the seven largest economies in Latin America (the others being Argentina, Brazil, Chile, Colombia, Mexico and Venezuela), GDP per capita in Peru has the largest gap with respect to OECD economies.

The 1990s represented a period of reforms aimed at modernising the economy, but challenges remained in the macroeconomic framework. These reforms included removing barriers to private investment. Investment and exports grew significantly during this period, and the fiscal deficit and inflation declined. Economic growth reached an average annual rate of almost 4% between 1991 and 1997. However, by the end of that decade, the government's expansionary fiscal policy, along with the creation of a number of tax exemptions, contributed to raising the fiscal deficit. In addition, the failure to implement an inflation targeting regime affected the credibility of the monetary regime. This decade was not without social unrest and terrorism-fuelled conflicts. Coupled with the international financial crisis and capital outflows in 1998, Peru was once again in a difficult position, and in need of deep and urgent structural reforms.

Following the macroeconomic instability at the end of the 1990s, Peru adopted key reforms to increase its credibility on both the monetary and fiscal fronts. The adoption of an inflation-targeting regime in 2002 to increase monetary stability, and the fiscal responsibility law of 1999 to strengthen public finances and reduce public debt, helped to boost investment and improve consumer confidence.

Since the beginning of the 21st century, Peru has experienced a period of extraordinary socio-economic progress. Between 2000 and 2014, economic growth reached an annual average rate of 5.3%. During this period, Peru's expansion in GDP was second only to Panama in the Latin American and Caribbean region, and well above the regional average of 3.1%. A sound and stable macroeconomic framework has been one of the main drivers of this expansion, coupled with a period of relative political stability. Favourable external conditions have also been key to this expansion, with high international commodity prices and relatively easy access to international finance. On the social side, the combination of high economic growth with a stronger emphasis on social policies and redistributive programmes have been crucial for reducing poverty rates and inequality, as well as for increasing the overall well-being of Peruvians.

New challenges are arising, such as escaping the middle-income trap and protecting the emerging middle class

Peru's recent period of high GDP growth helped it achieve upper middle-income status in 2008 but this success is not without its challenges. As suggested by recent economic-development literature, countries usually face a period of prolonged slowdown once they reach a certain level of income, in what is referred to as the "middle-income trap" (OECD/CAF/ECLAC, 2014). This phenomenon occurs when a country can no longer rely on its traditional drivers of growth (e.g. low labour costs, and the accumulation of labour as a major source of growth) to make further progress. This middle-income trap can be particularly hampering for the country's immediate growth and social prospects. Peru needs new drivers to sustain further growth. Escaping the trap will require increases in productivity and much greater diversification of the economy (OECD, 2014).

The emergence of Peru's middle class has been another distinctive feature of the recent period of socio-economic progress, but it also brings a whole set of new challenges. Between 2000 and 2012, the middle class jumped from 12.3% to 34.3% of the population (UNDP, 2014). This places greater demands on policies, as those in the middle class demand more and better public services and welfare provision. This is particularly challenging for a country like Peru, where improving public provision would entail raising tax revenues to finance them. However, the poor quality of public services has eroded the state's fiscal legitimacy, making it difficult to increase the fiscal burden. Another challenge is related to the increase in the size of those belonging to the "vulnerable" group, which increased from 33.8% to 40% (UNDP, 2014).[3] Despite the socio-economic progress achieved in recent years, many people in Peru are in an unstable situation in which they could easily slip back into poverty following any turbulence or slowdown in the economy.

In recent years, Peru has proposed a large number of policies to tackle the barriers to inclusive growth, but these need greater co-ordination and implementation to make reform happen. Several ministries and public-sector entities have presented valuable analysis on the current socio-economic challenges and set out objectives for the medium term. These include the *Agenda de Competitividad 2014-2018*, the *National Plan for Productive Diversification*, the *National Strategic Export Plan*, the *National Strategy on Development and Social Inclusion: "Incluir para Crecer"*, and the *Plan Bicentenario: El Perú hacia el 2021*. While these plans aim to tackle the main challenges in Peru, the country will need better co-ordination among public institutions to determine priorities, and a better connection between the budgeting process and these agendas to adopt and implement reforms for inclusive growth.

Peru's combination of good policies and favourable external conditions has led to improved overall well-being and better socio-economic conditions, but despite recent improvements, it cannot rest on its laurels. It still lags behind OECD economies and faces pressing socio-economic challenges. Income and spatial inequalities, informality and low productivity are affecting the prospect of inclusive growth. The country needs to embrace structural reforms to overcome the challenges associated with the middle-income trap, to improve living conditions and to promote greater well-being.

The multi-dimensional review methodology explores development from all perspectives

Development is multi-dimensional in the sense that it implies an aggregate improvement in a set of desirable outcomes, as opposed to progress along a single dimension. The OECD's Multi-dimensional Country Reviews analyse development challenges from a wide variety of perspectives, using a combination of tools: a gap analysis across a dashboard of indicators, detailed cross-country benchmarking with a set of comparator countries selected for Peru, and a visioning exercise.

The MDCR dashboard of indicators covers three broad areas: well-being, drivers of long-term growth, and structural characteristics and development dynamics. The well-being analysis plays a key role in determining not only "how's life in Peru?", but also in assessing development outcomes.

To accurately assess Peru's economic and social strengths and weaknesses, the MCDR goes beyond describing average outcomes and adopts a more analytical approach. The benchmarking exercise is thus based on both a gap analysis and a comparison with 14 comparator countries.[4] The choice of these countries is based on factors such as income per capita, size and structural characteristics of the country as well as the degree to which their successful policies could act as a role model for Peru. The comparator countries were selected in conjunction with the Ministry of Economy and Finance of Peru and include Australia, Brazil, Canada, Chile, Colombia, Costa Rica, Ecuador, Korea, Mexico, Norway, Panama, Portugal, South Africa and Turkey (see Annex 1.A1 for more detail). In addition to these countries, this review compares Peru to the Latin America and Caribbean (LAC) and OECD averages.

In addition to this quantitative dimension, the OECD MDCR methodology includes a series of participatory workshops. These workshops enable the OECD team to connect with diverse perspectives in Peru and to bring together different parts of Peruvian society to reflect on the challenges to inclusive and sustainable development, as well as on the context in which policy responses will be implemented. The participatory workshops serve as a platform for dialogue and ideas between the OECD team and Peruvian stakeholders to enhance understanding of local issues to test recommendations and ensure these are both targeted and pertinent. A multi-stakeholder participatory workshop was organised in Lima in February 2015 to gather perceptions on the main bottlenecks to inclusive development. Participants included actors from the private and public sectors, civil society, and academia (see Annex 1.A2 for the topics discussed in the workshop).

Using this combination of quantitative and qualitative techniques, this report identifies the main constraints for Peru's development. These constraints are summarised at the end of this chapter and discussed in detail in the rest of the report. An overview of well-being outcomes in Peru is presented below.

How's Life in Peru: An overview of well-being

Development is often considered synonymous with economic growth, and yet growth in GDP is only one element of development. If aggregate increases in productivity and material wealth do not produce meaningful gains in the well-being of a country's population, development has failed in both human and economic terms. Economic growth is only a means to an end – the sustainable and equitable improvement of people's lives. To comprehensively assess life within a country, it is necessary to go beyond macroeconomic indicators and monitor well-being across the many different areas that matter for citizens.

Part of the OECD MDCR benchmark analysis examined a range of well-being indicators in Peru. Well-being is multi-dimensional concept and can be difficult to define in isolation as it covers many areas of people's lives. However, the core idea is relatively intuitive: well-being encompasses those aspects of life that people would consider essential to meet one's needs, to pursue one's goals and to feel satisfied with life (Box 1.2).

Box 1.2. **Using the OECD's "How's Life" framework to measure well-being in developing countries**

The OECD has developed a framework for measuring well-being in OECD countries based on a number of national initiatives undertaken in several countries and several years of collaboration with experts and representatives from national governments (OECD, 2011). This "How's Life" framework has also been adapted to measure well-being in non-OECD countries, taking into account the literature on measuring development outcomes and embracing the realities of these countries. Its dimensions have been redefined to better match the availabilities of data, the priorities and critical concerns of these countries (Boarini, Kolev and McGregor, 2014).

This adjusted framework, like the original, measures well-being outcomes in two broad pillars. The first pillar, material conditions, comprises the dimensions of consumption possibilities, work, housing conditions and infrastructure. The second pillar, quality of life, comprises health status, education and skills, social connections, empowerment and participation, vulnerability and life evaluations, feelings and meaning, i.e. the main aspects of subjective well-being (Figure 1.1). These ten dimensions are used to measure current well-being; they are complemented with another set of indicators to measure the sustainability of current well-being in the future. The framework emphasises the importance of preserving the natural, human, economic and social resources that are essential for ensuring the well-being of future generations.

The OECD well-being framework is informed by a number of analytical principles. First, it is concerned with the well-being of individuals rather than aggregate economic conditions. Second, it focuses on well-being outputs rather than inputs, recognising that outcomes may be uncorrelated with the resources devoted to achieve them. Third, it emphasises the need to measure the distribution of well-being outcomes to identify inequalities across and within population groups. Finally, it considers both objective and subjective indicators, as people's own evaluations and feelings about their lives matter as much as the objective conditions in which they live (OECD, 2013).

Box 1.2. **Using the OECD's "How's Life" framework to measure well-being in developing countries** (*cont.*)

Figure 1.1. **OECD well-being framework for developing countries**

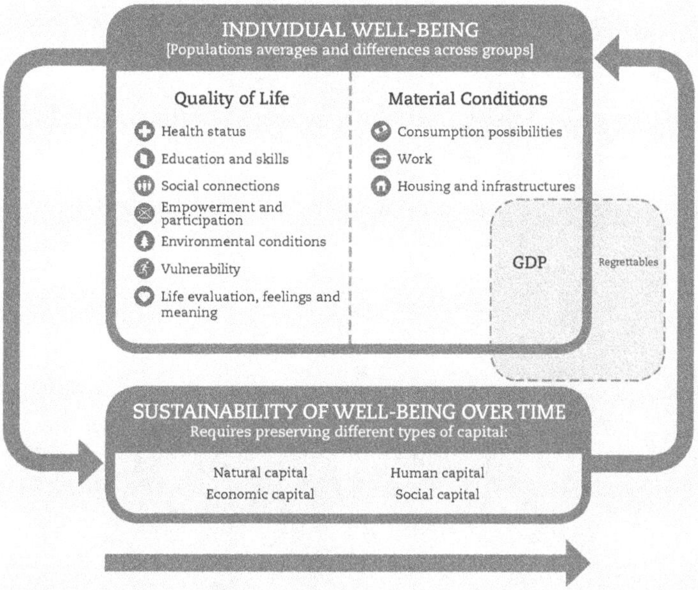

Source: OECD (2011), *How's Life?: Measuring Well-being*, OECD Publishing, Paris, http://dx.doi.org/10.1787/9789264121164-en; Boarini, R., A. Kolev and A. McGregor (2014), "Measuring well-being and progress in countries at different stages of development: Towards a more universal conceptual framework", *OECD Development Centre Working Papers*, No. 325, OECD Publishing, Paris, http://dx.doi.org/10.1787/5jxss4hv2d8n-en.

When it comes to well-being, Peru has areas of strengths and weaknesses. Peru performs reasonably well in the areas of consumption possibilities, social connections and life evaluations, but it underperforms in the areas of work, education and skills, and health (Figure 1.2). These latter areas are also characterised by remarkable inequalities across socio-demographic groups. Peru also displays weaknesses in terms of housing and infrastructure, environmental conditions, vulnerability, and empowerment and participation.

Incomes are reasonably good in Peru, but jobs can be precarious and living conditions poor

Given its level of economic development, Peru scores reasonably well for consumption possibilities. Gross national income (GNI) per capita captures the gross flow of income to individuals from earnings, self-employment and income from capital.[5] Peru's GNI is USD 11 280 per capita, which is around the expected level for countries with similar GDP per capita. Satisfaction with living standards is also reasonably high. Two out of three Peruvians say that they are satisfied with their living standards, while 58% report that they can either get by or live comfortably on their household income. Most Peruvians report they can meet their basic needs, with 63% reporting that they have enough money for food, and 84% for shelter.

Figure 1.2. **Current and expected well-being outcomes for Peru: Worldwide comparison**

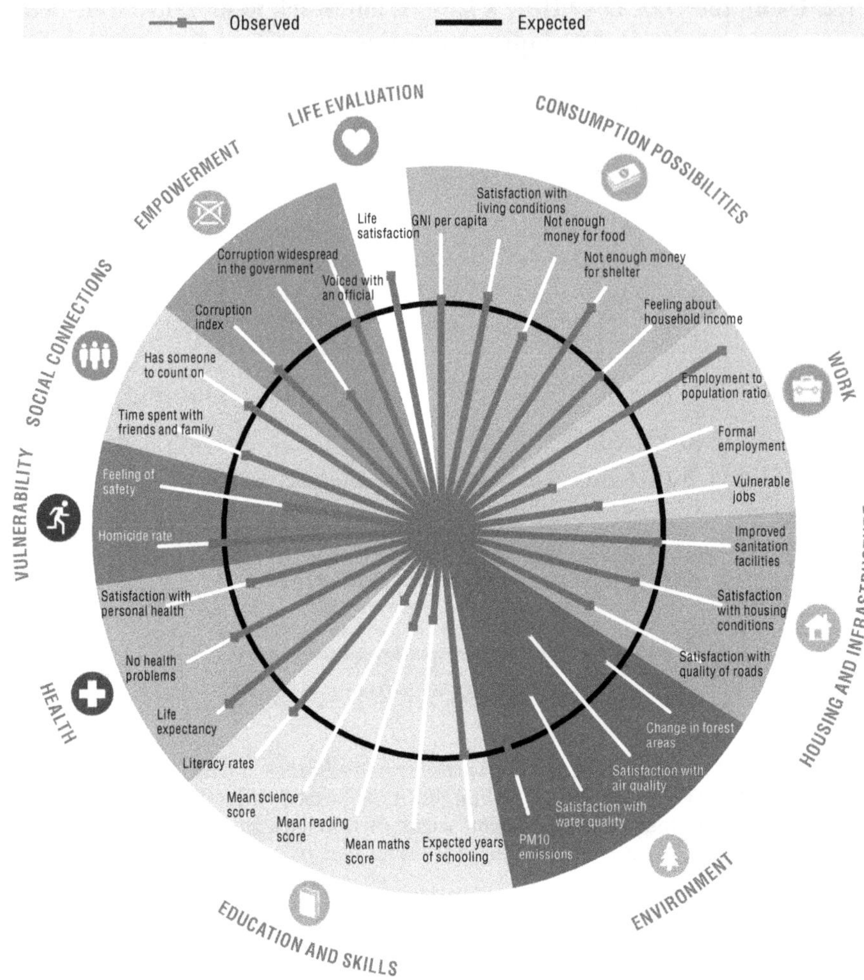

Note: This figure is based on running bivariate regressions where the indicator is the dependent variable and GDP per capita is the independent variable. The expected value of each indicator is then computed by taking the coefficient of the bivariate regression and applying it to the actual GDP per capita of the country. The country's observed results are then compared to the expected value for each indicator. The difference between the fitted values and the observed values is standardised by the standard deviation of the indicator. Standardising the size of the gap highlights those dimensions in which the performance of the country stands out. Expected values are calculated using all countries with a population over 1 million.

Sources: OECD calculations based on Gallup Organization (2014), *Gallup World Monitor* (database); UNDP (United Nations Development Programme) (2014), *International Human Development Indicators* (database), United Nations Development Programme, http://hdr.undp.org/en/data; UIS (UNESCO Institute for Statistics) (2013), UIS Data Centre (database), United Nations Educational, Scientific and Cultural Organisation, http://data.uis.unesco.org/ (accessed 15 January 2014); World Bank (2014), *World Development Indicators* (database), Washington, DC, http://data.worldbank.org; OECD PISA 2012 data; Transparency international (2014), Corruption Perceptions Index, http://www.transparency.org/cpi2014/results#myAnchor1

StatLink http://dx.doi.org/10.1787/888933265108

Labour force participation is high in Peru, but the quality of employment is remarkably low. The ratio of employment to population is 73% among individuals over the age of 15. However, Peru underperforms significantly in terms of the quality of employment. The share of informal employment in the Peruvian labour market (i.e. those who do not have the right to a pension or those in a firm with five or fewer employees, a non-professional self-employed, or a zero-income worker) is one of the highest in the world – around 70%, depending on the criteria used to define informality (see Chapter 2 for more details) – and very high for a country at Peru's level of economic development. Similarly, the share of those in vulnerable employment, i.e. unpaid family workers and own-account workers, is above what is expected from a country at Peru's level of economic development.

Access to decent housing and infrastructure is another key dimension of material conditions. Peru provides access to improved sanitation facilities to three-quarters of its population, with 73% of households having access in their house to sanitation facilities such as flush or pour flush toilet (to piped sewer system, septic tank and pit latrine), ventilated improved pit latrine, pit latrine with slab or composting toilet. This value is close to the expect level for Peru based on the experience of countries with similar GDP per capita. However, access to affordable housing and to decent highways and roads is problematic. Only 40% of Peruvians are satisfied with the availability of good and affordable housing and 44% are satisfied with the quality of the roads and highways (Chapter 3). These figures are slightly below what would be predicted in a country with a level of economic development similar to Peru, and highlight the need for more and better use of public finances (Chapter 4).

Key quality of life failings on health status, education and skills, and empowerment and participation are holding Peru back

Peru performs remarkably well in terms of life expectancy, but not so well in other aspects of health status. Good health is a major determinant of quality of life and a core dimension of well-being. In addition to its intrinsic value, it is vital for people's ability to work and participate in social life. Life expectancy at birth in Peru is 77 years (76 years for men and 79 years for women), 1.3 years longer than the world average. In this regard, Peru performs reasonably well given its level of economic development. Despite their relatively high life expectancy, however, one-quarter of Peruvians report being dissatisfied with their health conditions, which is 5 percentage points lower than the world average and below what is expected of a country with Peru's level of economic development.

Education and skills are also a major weakness. In terms of access to education, Peru performs as expected given its GDP per capita. Average years of schooling were 10.1 years in 2013. However, Peru's education outcomes suggest that the quality of its education is a major barrier. While the basic literacy skills of the adult population, i.e. percentage of the population ages 15 and older who can, with understanding, both read and write a short simple statement on their everyday life, are at an acceptable level (90%), the skills of 15-year olds are remarkably poor. Peru ranked at the bottom of the 65 middle and upper-income countries participating in the last round of the Programme for International Student Assessment (PISA). PISA measures the cognitive skills of 15- to 16-year olds in the areas of mathematics, reading and science, assessing their competencies when they reach the end of compulsory education.

Social connections in Peru are relatively strong. The ability to count on others in times of need and the amount of time people spend with friends and family are good proxies of the strength of people's close, personal networks. In Peru, 82% of the population says that they have at least one friend or a relative that they can turn to for help in time of need, slightly above the world average. The average time spent socially with friends and family on a typical day is 5.7 hours, slightly below the world average. These measures of social connections are close to the expected level for a country of Peru's level of economic development.

Peru has significant weaknesses in the area of empowerment and participation. Trust in government and institutions is relatively low and participation is similarly limited. According to Transparency International's Corruption Perception Index (Transparency International, 2014), which ranks countries based on how corrupt their public sector is perceived to be by business people and country analysts, Peru ranks just at the midline for countries where data are available. This is in line with its level of economic development. However, the Gallup World Monitor 2015 database suggests that perceived quality of government is remarkably low: 84% of the population think corruption is widespread in government and only 23% believe that elections are honest, levels that are below what would be expected given Peru's GDP per capita. Business people and citizens differ in their perceptions of the trustworthiness of Peruvian institutions, where business people place Peru higher than citizens. This discrepancy is probably due to business-friendly reforms made in the trade sectors, while plenty of room for improvement remains in public services. Turning to participation, just 19% of people have voiced their opinion to a public official, a proxy for citizens' channels of influence in formal institutions (lack of trust and perceptions of corruption are discussed in detail in Chapter 5).

Environmental conditions are close to the expected benchmark levels, but satisfaction with environmental quality is low. Environmental quality has an intrinsic value for individuals and is an important determinant of health and the sustainability of well-being. In objective measures, Peru's environment outcomes are close to what can be expected from a country with similar GDP per capita. For example, there has been a 3.3% reduction in forest area between 1990 and 2011, which is only slightly higher than expected. Similarly, air pollution is also at the expected level for a country with Peru's level of industrialisation. According to the World Bank, Peru's PM10 level (a measure of particulate matters up to 10 micrometres in size that have severe health effects) was 63 micrograms per cubic metre in 2013, which is slightly lower than would be expected. However, Peru does much worse on subjective measures of environmental conditions. Satisfaction with air quality and satisfaction with water quality (at around 40%) are both remarkably low compared to the benchmark outcome (environmental conditions are discussed in detail in Chapter 5).

Personal security is relatively high in Peru, but fear of crime remains widespread. In 2012 there were 9.6 homicides per 100 000 inhabitants, approximately what could be predicted given Peru's GDP per capita and close to the world average of 9.8 per 100 000. In contrast, people's perceived risk of safety is more widespread: in 2014 only 45% of Peruvians reported that they feel safe walking home alone at night, as opposed to 60% for the world average yet similar to 40% for Latin American average. This relatively high level of perceived insecurity could be related to an increase in homicide rates during the last decade, as well as to an increase in crime reporting.

Despite this complex reality, with areas of strong and poor performance, subjective well-being overall in Peru is above average. The way people experience and evaluate their own life outcomes provides essential information that cannot be obtained by objective measures alone. Subjective well-being reflects how people experience a set of circumstances and is as important as the circumstances themselves. It is based on the idea that people are the best judges of how their own lives are going (OECD, 2011). Using the Cantril Ladder, a measure which asks respondents to rate their lives as a whole on a scale of 1 to 10, average life satisfaction in Peru is 5.9, as compared to a world average of 5 and a Latin American average of 6. The high level of subjective well-being relative to the level that could be predicted based on the country's GDP per capita is a feature that Peru shares with most other Latin American countries.

Major bottlenecks to inclusive development

This report takes a holistic approach to determining the major bottlenecks to achieving sustainable and inclusive development in Peru. In particular, it looks at how well Peru is meeting the objectives of sustainable and equitable development and promoting citizens' well-being. It also examines how the underlying dynamics of the country's development process affect these objectives, and how they reinforce Peru's middle-income trap and the fragility of its middle class, hampering the country's prospects for continued progress towards inclusive development. The quantitative and qualitative analyses of well-being outcomes described above are complemented in this review by an in-depth analysis of the dimensions associated with inclusive development in Peru, which are the focus of the remaining chapters of the report. Chapter 2 assesses social challenges, including health, education and the labour market. Chapter 3 covers factors affecting productivity and competitiveness, such as economic diversification and sectoral productivity, innovation, infrastructure, and the business environment. Chapter 4 analyses macroeconomic stability from the monetary, fiscal and financial perspectives, as well as how well the taxation system is used to finance development. Finally, Chapter 5 focuses on governance and state capacity to boost inclusive development.

The analyses presented in this chapter (focused mainly on the general results of the OECD well-being framework) and in the rest of the chapters of this report, show that the major key constraints to sustainable and inclusive development in Peru are:

- Low quality of education, combined with large inequalities in access to education and performance across socio-economic groups.
- Poor levels of skills, which are not aligned with the needs of the labour market.
- Segmented and rigidly regulated labour markets, with unequal working conditions.
- Poor diversification of the economy into sectors that can create both more and better jobs and boost labour productivity and competitiveness.
- Low connectivity of the Peruvian economy due to high transport costs.
- Low levels of research and development spending which are holding back innovation.
- Limited state capacity at regional and national levels, leading to low trust and legitimacy.
- Structural weaknesses in the tax system which undermine progressivity and miss opportunities to fill educational, innovation and infrastructure gaps.

These constraints interact – and further reinforce – with three cross-cutting challenges in Peru which exacerbate the impact on the middle-income trap and the vulnerability of the middle class.

- High levels of informality, which dominate the labour market and stifle productivity. Inefficiencies on the demand and supply sides of the labour market should be tackled to boost inclusive growth.
- High levels of inequality, affecting social cohesion and equality of opportunities, and leaving many people in poverty. Inequalities appear at many different levels, from income, regional location, to gender and ethnic groups, among others.
- Low levels of productivity, which are a longstanding issue for the Peruvian economy. Rectifying these will be at the heart of a sustained growth process and the capacity to compete in global markets and to raise income levels for all.

The second phase of the Peru Multi-dimensional Country Review will complement OECD policy reviews conducted as part of the Country Programme with Peru (Box 1.1). These include a Skills Strategy Review, a Vocational Education and Training Review, an Environmental Performance Review, a Public Governance Review, and a Territorial Review. The second phase of Peru's MDCR will complement these reviews, and take forward the findings outlined in this present report, by focusing on three key areas for boosting inclusive development:

- Tackling informality in the labour market. Several dimensions, such as active labour policies and labour market regulation will be included in the analysis.
- Improving connectivity to foster competitiveness. Transport infrastructure and regulation, and logistics will be analysed as key factors to reduce transport costs in Peru.
- Promoting economic diversification and improving productivity. Better management of natural resources and policies to improve the productive structure of the Peruvian economy will be part of this study.

Notes

1. As in other Latin American economies, this final phase is particularly relevant in Peru given the complexity of both the political economy and the policy-making process to make reform happen (Dayton-Johnson et al., 2011).

2. In 1990, the inflation rate was even higher at over 7 400% year-on-year.

3. The vulnerable group is defined as the group that has 10% or more probability of falling back into poverty, following the definition in López-Calva and Ortiz-Juarez (2014).

4. The gap-based exercise benchmarks Peru against all countries with a population over a million. See note to Figure 1.2 for more detail of how the gaps are calculated.

5. Economy-wide and household level income measures can differ significantly, in terms of both levels and changes, particularly in countries that are relying heavily on natural resources and where a significant part of income from production is transferred abroad. Note that the ideal measure of household living standard is a measure of household net adjusted disposable income but since many developing countries lack such measure the report uses the Gross National Income.

References

Boarini, R., A. Kolev and A. McGregor (2014), "Measuring well-being and progress in countries at different stages of development: Towards a more universal conceptual framework", *OECD Development Centre Working Papers*, No. 325, OECD Publishing, Paris, http://dx.doi.org/10.1787/5jxss4hv2d8n-en.

Dayton-Johnson J., J. Londoño and S. Nieto-Parra (2011), "The process of reform in Latin America: A review essay", *OECD Development Centre Working Papers,* No. 304, OECD Publishing, Paris, http://dx.doi.org/10.1787/5kg3mkvfcjxv-en .

López-Calva, L.F. and E. Ortiz-Juarez (2014), "A vulnerability approach to the definition of the middle class", *Journal of Economic Inequality*, Vol. 12(1), pp. 23-47.

OECD (2014), *Perspectives on Global Development 2014: Boosting Productivity to Meet the Middle-Income Challenge*, OECD Publishing, Paris, http://dx.doi.org/10.1787/persp_glob_dev-2014-en.

OECD (2013), *OECD Guidelines on Measuring Subjective Well-being,* OECD Publishing, Paris, http://dx.doi.org/10.1787/9789264191655-en.

OECD (2011), *How's Life?: Measuring Well-being*, OECD Publishing, Paris, http://dx.doi.org/10.1787/9789264121164-en.

OECD/CAF/ECLAC (2014), *Latin American Economic Outlook 2015: Education, Skills and Innovation for Development*, OECD Publishing, Paris, http://dx.doi.org/10.1787/leo-2015-en.

UNDP (2014), *Perfil de Estratos Sociales en América Latina: Pobres, Vulnerables y Clases Medias*, UNDP (United Nations Development Programme), New York, www.sv.undp.org/content/dam/el_salvador/docs/vih-sida/Grupos_sociales_AL.pdf.

Annex 1.A1
The cross-country benchmarking exercise in Peru

No two countries face the same combination of development challenges or opportunities and therefore no perfect comparison country exists. The idea of creating a benchmark group is to allow comparative evaluation of Peru's performance over a variety of dimensions. The aim of the comparison is to draw upon a range of policy successes that relate to the multiple challenges and opportunities that Peru faces. The 14 benchmark countries selected have been used in the analysis of Phase I of the MDCR. Throughout the analysis, Peru will also be compared to the Latin America and Caribbean average and the OECD member average.

The 14 countries and a brief summary of their economic structures, strengths and particular relevance to Peru are described below. They were selected according to criteria that included their GDP per capita, the contribution of natural resources (particularly minerals) to GDP and the degree to which their successful economic policies could be relevant to Peru.

Eight of the countries are OECD members: Australia, Canada, Chile, Korea, Mexico, Norway, Portugal, and Turkey. Australia, Canada and Norway are included because of their important natural resource sectors; Portugal and Turkey in part because of their development path; and Korea as an example of a highly successful, export-based Asian economy. In addition to Chile and Mexico, five other Latin American and Caribbean countries are included: Brazil, Colombia, Costa Rica, Ecuador and Panama. Brazil and South Africa, both among the BRICS (Brazil, Russia, India, People's Republic of China and South Africa), are included because of their growing economic power and their mineral resources.

OECD members

Australia

The Australian economy is dominated by the service sector but its economic growth is primarily driven by the mining and agriculture sectors. Mining and mining-related industries contribute around 20% of GDP, with the service sector adding 69% in 2012. The Australian economy has displayed remarkable resilience to international turbulence; for more than 20 years in a row, it has experienced consistent economic growth and no recessions. Strong demand from People's Republic of China, Japan and other East Asian markets for commodities as well as sound macroeconomic policies have been important in maintaining Australia's growth.

Australia ranks very highly in terms of financial market development. According to the World Economic Forum and the Australian Securities Exchange, it has the 9th largest stock exchange in the world in terms of market capitalisation. In 2014, Australia had 32 companies listed in the Forbes 2000.

Canada

The Canadian economy is primarily composed of the service sector that employs around three-quarters of all Canadians. The oil and logging industries are also of considerable importance to the Canadian economy, as is the sizeable manufacturing sector. International trade has an important role in the economy, and this is related to the country's endowment of natural resources; in 2009, 58% of total exports were from agriculture, energy, forestry and mining. Only 4% of Canadians, however, are employed in these areas, and only 4% of GDP is generated by oil and gas revenues.

Canada is estimated to have the world's second largest oil reserves and despite decades of exploitation, its natural resources are not approaching exhaustion. This makes their level of export sophistication – which is higher than Norway's – even more impressive as diversification is often motivated by fear of dwindling resources.

Canada's natural resource endowment varies considerably between regions leading to different economic structures within the country and this contributes to its strong regionalism.

Chile

Chile is regarded as one of South America's most economically stable and prosperous countries. The largest sectors by GDP of the Chilean economy are mining (principally copper), business services, personal services and manufacturing. The Chilean copper industry has been supported both by progressive legislation and the country's good investment climate. Chile currently produces more than one-third of the global copper output. To negate the effects of the volatile international copper market on the Chilean economy, the government created a Copper Stabilisation Fund that collects a direct proportion of revenues when copper prices are high for use when prices fall.

The Chilean service industry has experienced rapid growth as a result of increased access to education and substantial advances in communications and information technology. The government has liberalised the service sector and entered into a number of free trade area agreements. As a result, Chile has been able to expand into the export market for services and specialise in maritime and aeronautical services, tourism, informatics, engineering and construction services, and health and education.

Chile is a highly competitive country, ranked 33 out of 144 countries by the 2014-15 *Global Competitiveness Report* as a result of its strong institutional setup, efficient government, well-functioning markets and a high level of domestic competition and openness to foreign trade.

Korea

Korea is a very successful, high-income market economy and is the ninth largest country in terms of value of international trade in the world. Its economy is largely based on exports of finished goods such as electronics, textiles, ships, automobiles and steel. In total, exports account for more than half of Korea's GDP.

Korea has excellent infrastructure and a sound macroeconomic environment that contribute to its international competitiveness. The country's high-quality education system is one of its particular strengths; in 2014, Korea had the highest gross enrolment rate in tertiary education in the world.

Mexico

Mexico is an export-orientated economy. Its manufacturing industry contributed 17.4% of GDP in 2012 and has benefited from free trade agreements with over 50 countries, including 20 years in the North American Free Trade Alliance (NAFTA). Since 2012, Mexico and Peru have been partners, along with Colombia and Chile, in the Pacific Alliance, which furthers free trade and promotes economic integration.

For its level of development, Mexico's level of business sophistication is relatively high. The country also benefits from a stable macroeconomic environment and a sound banking system. The current Mexican government has passed structural reforms targeting areas including labour, education, competition policy, the financial sector, telecommunications and the energy sector, and it is expected that these reforms will help improve productivity and growth.

Norway

Norway's economy is significantly dominated by the oil-related industries (oil and gas revenue contribute around 25% of GDP) and its citizens enjoy an exceptionally high standard of living relative to other European countries. Successive Norwegian governments have managed the country's natural resource wealth well and used it to further development outcomes, including establishing a strong welfare system. The country has a sovereign wealth fund generated by the exploitation of natural resources. The fund is invested abroad, shielding the economy from fluctuations in oil prices and removing excess liquidity from the economy.

In the last decade, the government has taken initiatives to promote the development of other "mainland industries" that are internationally competitive. These include creating nine "centres of expertise" and forming the Oslo Cancer Cluster. The objective of these initiatives is to encourage the expansion of the high-tech industry and also to encourage small-business growth as a way to create future jobs. Industries like manufacturing have been supported with new knowledge and technology to help reduce their dependence on the oil sector. Investments in education have contributed to Norway's high and growing levels of human capital and this also plays an important role in improving the competitiveness of non-oil sectors.

Portugal

The Portuguese economy was adversely affected by the financial crisis and its ranking on the World Economic Forum's Global Competitiveness Report has fallen notably. Portugal introduced reforms to increase its competitiveness, such as increasing market liberalisation and promoting educational attainment. It implemented labour market reforms, including improving employment protection to protect vulnerable workers. Portugal has also made substantial progress in expanding its tax base, an area Peru must similarly target.

Portugal benefits from an excellent transport infrastructure that includes an extensive network of high-quality roads, motorways and railways, seven major seaports, and three international airports.

Turkey

Turkey has experienced rapid economic growth recently with per capita income nearly tripling in the space of a decade. The country is a major producer and exporter of agricultural products, textiles, motor vehicles and construction material. In the past five years, foreign direct investment has risen from just over USD 1 billion to an average of USD 13 billion. Turkey also has a very successful business sector that is complemented by the country's intensely competitive domestic market.

Turkey benefits from a well-developed transport network, especially with respect to roads and air transport. The country's tourist sector has expanded rapidly, and according to the World Travel and Tourism Council, the sector contributed about 11% of Turkish GDP and supported 8% of jobs in 2012.

The Turkish financial sector displayed notable resilience during the global financial crisis; indeed, it was the only country in the OECD to not give public-sector support to its banking sector. According to the World Bank, the strength of the banking sector can be attributed to fundamental reforms that the country undertook after 2001.

BRICS comparison countries

Brazil

Brazil is the seventh largest economy in the world in both nominal GDP and purchasing power parity terms. Its population boom in the 1950s necessitated the country's green revolution and created a complex agribusiness sector. Brazil has been the world's largest producer of coffee for 150 years, but the relative prominence of the sector has declined as other sectors have developed. Coffee exports made up over half of Brazil's total exports in the 1960s; today, they contribute only around 2%.

The country's principal commodity export is still foodstuffs but metal exports, especially iron ore, are becoming increasingly important. Brazil has a significant supply of mineral resources including nickel, tin, copper and gold and these provide industrial raw materials and contribute to the country's export earnings. Brazil also has a large industrial sector with a variety of advanced manufacturing industries such as chemicals, computers, automobiles and aircraft.

Since 2007, Brazil's performance in the World Bank's Logistic Performance Index has increased markedly as a result of improved traceability and a fall in the cost of shipping goods. Brazil is ranked 57 out of 144 countries in the 2014-2015 *Global Competitiveness Index*. It scores particularly well in relation to innovation and the level of sophistication of its business community.

South Africa

Mining and, to an extent, agriculture have historically played an important role in the development of the South African economy. The country has successfully diversified into higher value-added sectors; by 2013, 70% of national GDP came from the tertiary sector.

South Africa's institutions are of high quality, particularly in relation to things like intellectual property protection, property rights and the efficiency of the legal framework for challenging and settling disputes. South Africa's financial market development is ranked seventh by the 2014-2015 *Global Competitiveness Report*. South Africa also has an efficient market for goods and services and quite high levels of business sophistication and innovation.

Latin American and Caribbean countries

In addition to Chile and Mexico (as OECD economies) and Brazil (as a BRICS country), there four other Latin American and Caribbean countries included in the benchmark group:

Colombia

Colombia has significant supplies of minerals and energy resources including the largest coal reserves in Latin America. In addition, the country has reserves of nickel, gold, silver, emeralds and platinum. Coffee was instrumental to the growth of the Colombian economy and promoted the development of its railways and communications infrastructure.

Colombia has taken measures to attract foreign direct investment including passing laws in many sectors in 1991 and 1992 designed to stimulate investment. The United States is Colombia's biggest investor and is principally involved in the petroleum sector, natural gas, coal mining, and the chemical and manufacturing industries.

Colombia is ranked 66 out of 144 countries in the 2014-2015 *Global Competitiveness Index*, performing particularly well in indicators of macroeconomic performance such as balanced public budget, low levels of public debt and controlled inflation. Colombia also scores well in terms of financial service sophistication and education enrolment. Improved infrastructure, logistics and customs service have contributed to a significant increase in the country's performance in the World Bank Logistic Performance Indicator in 2014.

Costa Rica

Over the past 25 years, Costa Rica has enjoyed steady economic growth as exports have risen and the country has gradually liberalised trade and opened itself to foreign investment.

Costa Rica has strong institutions and a high-quality education system that provides the country with a skilled labour force and contributes to a high rate of technological adoption and business sophistication. Related to these favourable conditions and the stable political environment, Costa Rica has one of the highest per capita rates of foreign direct investment in Latin America.

The Costa Rican economy benefits significantly from tourism; in 2013 the country welcomed more than 2.4 million visitors making it the most visited nation in Central America. Agriculture and electronics exports are also important drivers of the Costa Rican economy.

Ecuador

Ecuador has experienced strong economic growth since 2011, and this growth has translated into a reduction in poverty, reduced inequality and a growing middle class. This growth has been particularly favourable to the poor; between 2000 and 2011, the income of the poorest 40% increased by 8.8% in comparison to the national average of 5.7%.

Public-sector spending and investment as a percentage of national GDP have more than doubled since 2006, and a large amount of the extra resources have been devoted to developing energy, infrastructure, transportation and the social sectors. Ecuador's ranking in the Global Competitiveness Index has increased substantially in recent years as a consequence of infrastructure development, innovation and improved education quality.

Panama

In the last decade, Panama has experienced average annual growth rates of about 8% making it one of the fastest-growing economies in Latin America. Panama's economy is dominated by a successful service industry, particularly focused on banking, commerce and tourism which contribute nearly 80% of GDP.

Panama is ranked as the most competitive economy in Central America according to the 2014-15 *Global Competiveness Report* (it scores second in Latin America behind Chile). The country has impressive transport infrastructure with one of the best ports and airport networks in the survey. This allows it to be a major transport hub in the region. Foreign multinationals have set up corporations in the country, contributing to a high degree of technological adoption and well-developed financial markets.

Panama has implemented a number of policies aimed at tackling poverty and providing improved access to services. These include a conditional cash transfer programme known as *Red de Oportunidades* designed to help very poor mothers. It is estimated that this programme currently assists 357 000 people.

Annex 1.A2
MDCR workshop: Participatory process around inclusive development in Peru

The Ministry of the Economy and Finance and the Ministry of Foreign Affairs hosted the workshop for the MDCR's diagnostic phase, with the theme of "Peru: Vision and challenges". The workshop brought together more than 30 participants from a variety of sectors, notably government ministries, private sector representatives, trade unions, civil society and academia.

The workshop was divided into two sessions. The first session focused on Peru's vision and developmental objectives and participants' normative preferences for the future. Participants were divided into groups and were asked to develop narratives from citizens' perspectives of a Peru in 2030 where all policies had succeeded. Participants then extracted the different categories from their stories, which were subsequently clustered into policy areas.

The participants' general outlook on Peru's future was positive. Delivery of public services surfaced as a major theme, most notably quality and access to healthcare and education, which were perceived as key to economic development. Discussions focused on how to manage and finance public services in the future, with concerns over the impact of privatisation of access. Human rights, workers' rights and most notably gender equality emerged as major themes as participants discussed the treatment of women and opportunities in the labour force. Participants were also concerned about Peru's macroeconomic stability, and reflected on economic diversification, regional development, informality and infrastructure. Finally, the themes of governance, democracy and citizenship were cited broadly, with special focus on the role of institutions and the quality of democracy.

The second session focused on Peru's context. The exercise encouraged participants to consider how changes in Peru's environment and beyond could affect Peruvian development. The exercise provided participants' views on the opportunities and threats presented by technology and globalisation: from solving national challenges such as population ageing and energy supply, to handling increasing vulnerability through integration in competitive global markets. Participants also noted Peru's vulnerability to regional political developments.

The workshops also identified major themes for further research, and provided some insight into the challenges Peru faces in realising its developmental objectives. Most participants agreed that the delivery, quality and access to public services like education and infrastructure are key future challenges, alongside providing decent employment and wages. Peru's capacity to tackle informality, successfully diversify its economy, and build resilient social and judicial institutions will affect its ability to implement meaningful reform. These themes are perceived as key bottlenecks for inclusive development in Peru. They provide the basis for further discussion in Phase II of the MDCR, which will involve the use of scenarios based on the first workshop's thematic outputs.

Chapter 2
Social inclusion and sustainable development in Peru

This chapter focuses on three key aspects: health, education and skills, and work. Peru is underperforming relative to its upper-middle income status in these three areas, and they seem to be particularly important for the future well-being of Peruvians and essential for social inclusion. The access to the health system is unequal. Coverage in education has expanded widely, but quality remains poor across all levels and the most socio-economically disadvantaged, especially women and the rural and indigenous population, experience significant inequality. A mismatch between existing skills and the needs of the economy is a key barrier to development. Furthermore, informal employment is still widespread, albeit declining. To overcome the persistent inequalities, Peru needs to create the incentives to formalise the labour market extensively.

Improving the well-being of all is the ultimate development goal for any country, and requires a sustainable and inclusive approach: sustainable in terms of long-term viability and resilience; and inclusive in terms of allowing everyone to participate in the socio-economic progress brought by development.

Peru has made significant progress in social inclusion and sustainable development in recent years. However, large inequalities and high levels of poverty and vulnerability remain, with some structural constraints preventing the country from achieving further progress.

This chapter presents a diagnosis of these key constraints. It first presents an overview of recent trends in poverty and inequality levels, and the extent to which the period of economic expansion has promoted socio-economic inclusion. It then goes on to analyse three dimensions of well-being in which Peru seems to be particularly lagging behind according to the results of the well-being analysis and benchmarking exercise presented in Chapter 1: health, education and skills, and work. These three issues are of great importance as they are both means and ends. Good health has an intrinsic value for quality of life, but it also translates into human capital accumulation. Education and skills not only help individuals to participate in their society, but they also increase labour productivity. Similarly, good jobs and employment opportunities provide a financial livelihood for workers, while enabling them to use their productive capacities. Tackling these three areas will not only improve overall well-being in Peru, but also increase the level of human capital and productivity, hence paving the way for social inclusion and sustainable development.

Social progress is remarkable, but vulnerability and inequality remain

Peru's recent period of economic growth, which began in 2003, has seen an improvement in living standards and the reduction of inequality and poverty levels. From this point of view, its growth can be labelled as "inclusive", as it "creates opportunity for all segments of the population and distributes the dividends of increased prosperity, both in monetary and non-monetary terms, fairly across society", as stated in the OECD definition of inclusive growth (OECD, 2015a). However, there are significant nuances to this, as not all groups have benefitted equally, and inequalities and vulnerabilities are still a threat to social inclusion and development in the country.

Poverty reduction has been one of the main successes of the recent economic expansion

The past decade of economic expansion has been accompanied by remarkable progress in social inclusion and, in particular, in poverty reduction. The alleviation of poverty has been one of the most outstanding phenomena in the last decade across Latin America and the Caribbean region. Peru has been particularly successful in this respect, with poverty rates falling by half since 2001 to a level of around 24% in 2013, and with extreme poverty rates falling from close to 25% to around 5% in the same period (Figure 2.1). In addition, the poverty gap decreased from 21% in 2003 to 8.6% in 2012 (CEDLAS and World Bank, 2014).[1]

Yet despite this progress, poverty rates are high for certain groups and regions and vulnerabilities remain large. A great divergence exists between metropolitan Lima and the rest of the country, in particular in terms of aggregate levels of poverty. In addition, there are areas where the incidence of poverty is particularly high, such as the rural parts of the Andes, where around 53% of the population was still poor in 2013 (INEI, 2015).[2] Finally, poverty remains concentrated in population groups which are more difficult to target, such as the elderly, unemployed youth and working-age women, among others. This may complicate further reductions in poverty, as such groups may not benefit so easily from growth, unless specific, targeted policies are put in place (Martinez-Restrepo and Gray-Molina, 2013). Interestingly, while poverty in Latin America has stagnated since 2012, in Peru it has continued to decrease. However, the reasons behind this regional stalemate – the recent downslide in economic performance in the region (ECLAC, 2014) – could also negatively affect the reduction of poverty in Peru in the near future. Despite the sharp reduction in poverty rates, it remains uncertain whether those who escaped poverty are still vulnerable to falling back into it, and whether the conditions still exist for continued poverty reduction. A forthcoming study by the OECD Development Centre will be focused on one of the main vulnerable groups in Peru: youth. This *Youth Well-Being Policy Review* will be conducted in ten developing countries, including Peru, and will include the profiling of vulnerable youth, identifying the determinants of vulnerability and reviewing sectorial policies like health, education and employment.

Figure 2.1. **Poverty and extreme poverty in Peru 2001-13**

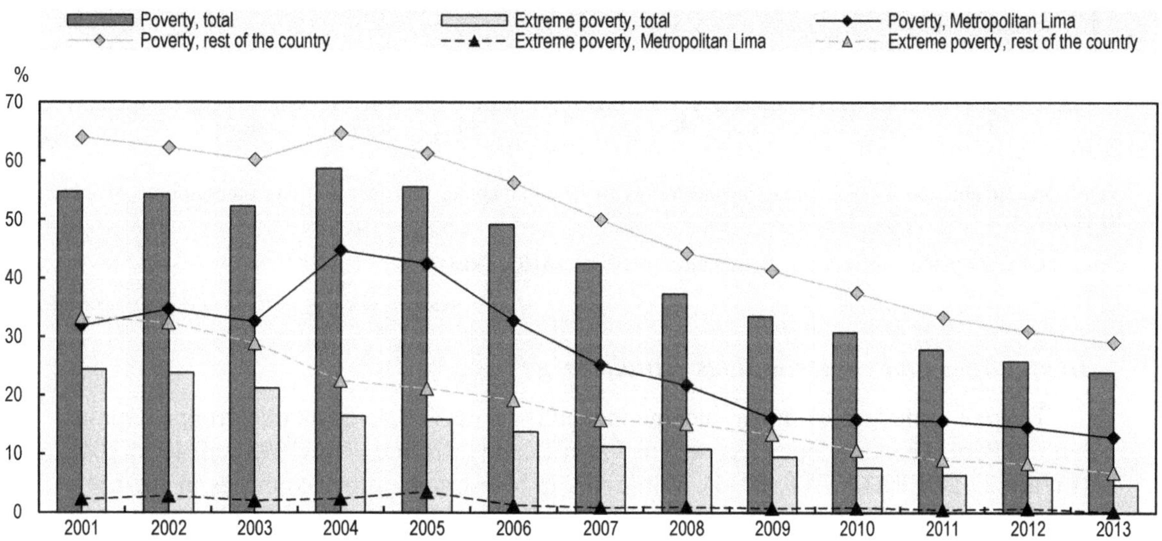

Note: 2013 data are estimates. According to INEI, total poverty includes individuals who belong to a household where either income or consumption per capita is less than the cost of a minimum basket of minimum and essential goods and services; extreme poverty includes those where this is below the value of a minimum basket of food.

Source: INEI (National Institute of Statistics).

StatLink http://dx.doi.org/10.1787/888933265112

Growth has been relatively more beneficial for the middle class

The evolution of income in this period shows that while economic growth has benefitted all income groups in absolute terms, it has been relatively more important for those in the middle class (Figure 2.2). This feature has been one of the main drivers of the expansion of the middle class in Peru in recent years; many of those who have been lifted out of poverty have now joined this group. This emergence of a middle class is one of the main features of Peru's recent history, and is also a regional phenomenon. Depending on the methodology employed, Peru's middle class increased between 10 percentage points and 20 percentage points in the past decade (Ferreira et al., 2013; Tornarolli, 2014). It is estimated that 34.3% of the population belongs to the middle class in Peru today. However, the heterogeneity in growth across income groups suggests that the gap between the poorest and the rest of society is widening and that growth has had an unequal impact across income groups.

Figure 2.2. **Incidence of growth in Peru across income percentiles, 2003-12**

Percentage annual growth of gross household income across income percentiles

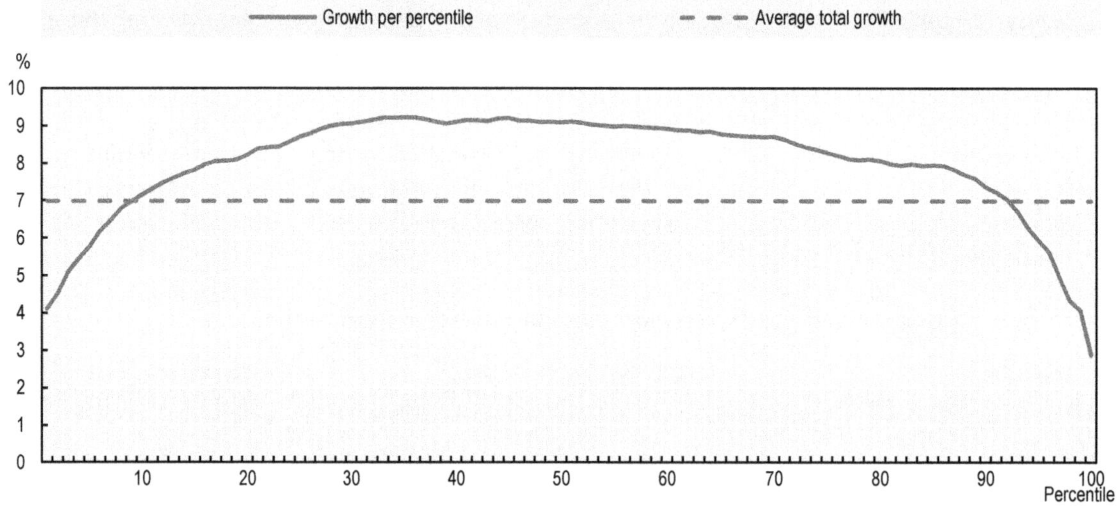

Note: Data at household level. Gross income refers to labour income, transfers and any other source of income, before taxes.

Source: OECD calculations based on household surveys (ENAHO, INEI).

StatLink *http://dx.doi.org/10.1787/888933265128*

Inequalities and vulnerabilities remain large

Despite some improvement, income inequality across socio-economic groups remains high in Peru. The Gini index has declined significantly, from 0.56 in 1998 to 0.45 in 2012 (Figure 2.3; CEPALSTAT, 2015). While this is below some other countries in the Latin America and Caribbean region, such as Mexico (0.48), Chile (0.51) and Colombia (0.53), inequality is still very high relative to OECD standards. The concentration of national income across income quintiles shows the persistence of large inequalities in the country (Figure 2.3). In this context, the impact of redistributive mechanisms, such as taxes and social transfers, seems inadequate (Chapter 4).

Overall, while socio-economic conditions have improved, large challenges remain in the pursuit of a sustainable development pattern that promotes inclusion and, ultimately, well-being for all. It is therefore critical to get to grips with some key constraints undermining further social inclusion and sustainable development. The results of the well-being analysis and the benchmarking exercise (Chapter 1) showed that Peru's performance in health, education and skills, and work is lower than one would expect given its income level. We explore these issues in the sections which follow.

Figure 2.3. **Gini coefficient (index) and income shares by quintiles (%), 1998-2012**

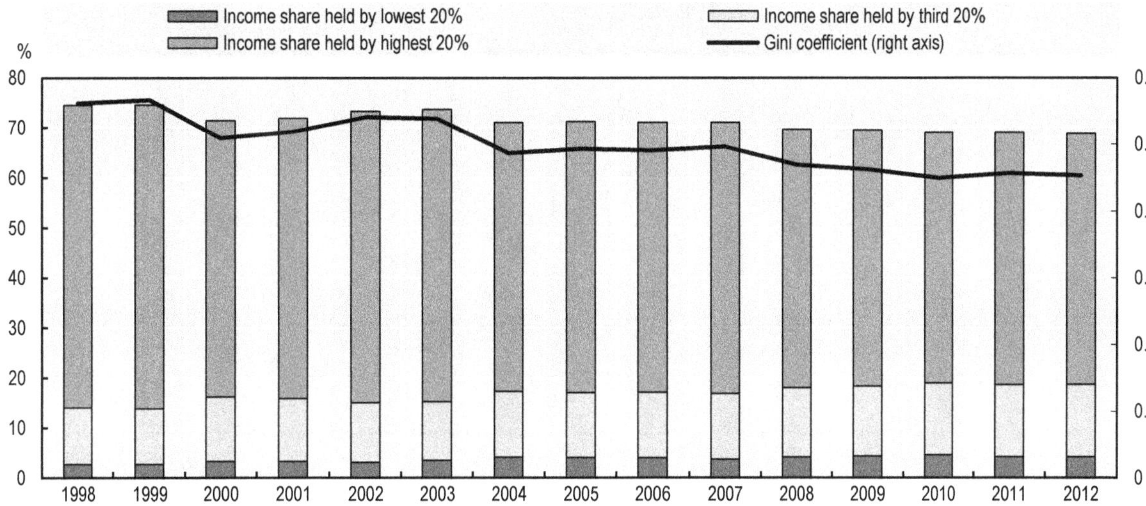

Source: World Bank (2015a), *World Development Indicators* (database), Washington, DC, http://data.worldbank.org.

StatLink http://dx.doi.org/10.1787/888933265134

Health is a necessary condition for development

Good health is key to well-being and directly related to quality of life. Disability, illness and disease hinder people's ability to participate fully in social life, the education system and the labour market, reducing their autonomy and control over their lives. Providing good quality and universal health service is a major item on Peru's development agenda. This section examines overall health outcomes in Peruvian society. Major challenges include the high number of years of life lived with disabilities, the relatively high rates of child mortality and large inequalities in access to insurance and good quality healthcare services.

As Chapter 1 shows health in Peru, in terms of life expectancy, appears relatively good, with only minimal gender differences. Average life expectancy at birth is 77 years (76 years for men and 79 years for women), which is relatively normal for countries at this level of economic development (Figure 2.4). Of the group of selected benchmark countries (described in Annex 1.A1 of Chapter 1), Peru's gender gap in life expectancy is the smallest (three years); in some countries – such as South Africa, Korea and Brazil – it is as much as seven years.

Despite the reasonable average life expectancy, most Peruvians do not live long healthy lives and child mortality is relatively high. The "disability adjusted life year" is an indicator of the gap between current health status and the ideal health situation in which the entire population lives to an advanced age, free from disease or disability (WHO, Global Health Estimates). Age standardised years lived with disability in Peru are higher than most of the benchmark countries, with 11.6 years lost every 100 years (Figure 2.5, Panel A). As for child mortality, for every 1 000 live births in Peru, 15 will die before reaching the age of 5. These figures put Peru behind many OECD members, as well as Costa Rica and Brazil (Figure 2.5, Panel B).

Figure 2.4. **Peruvians have relatively good life expectancy at birth, whatever their gender**

Years of age, 2013

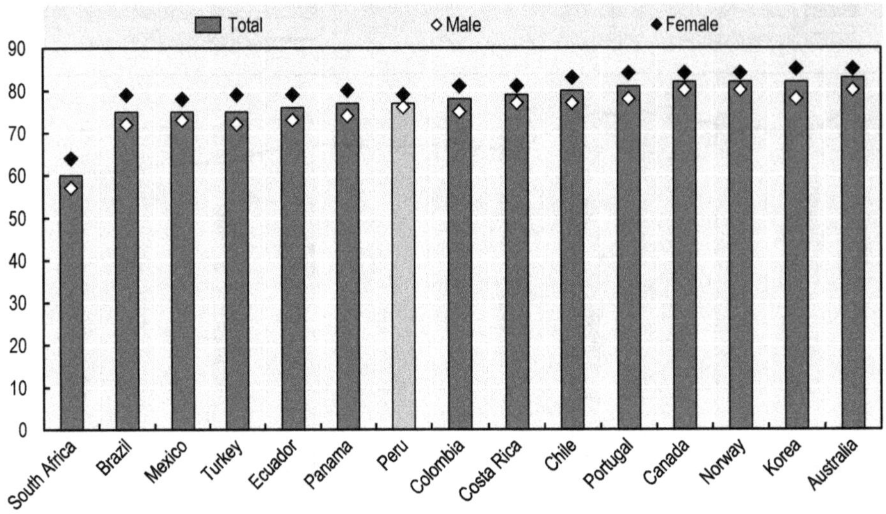

Source: OECD calculations based on the Global Health Observatory Data Repository of the World Health Organisation, http://apps.who.int/gho/data/ node.main.688.

StatLink http://dx.doi.org/10.1787/888933265142

Figure 2.5. **Healthy life and child mortality**

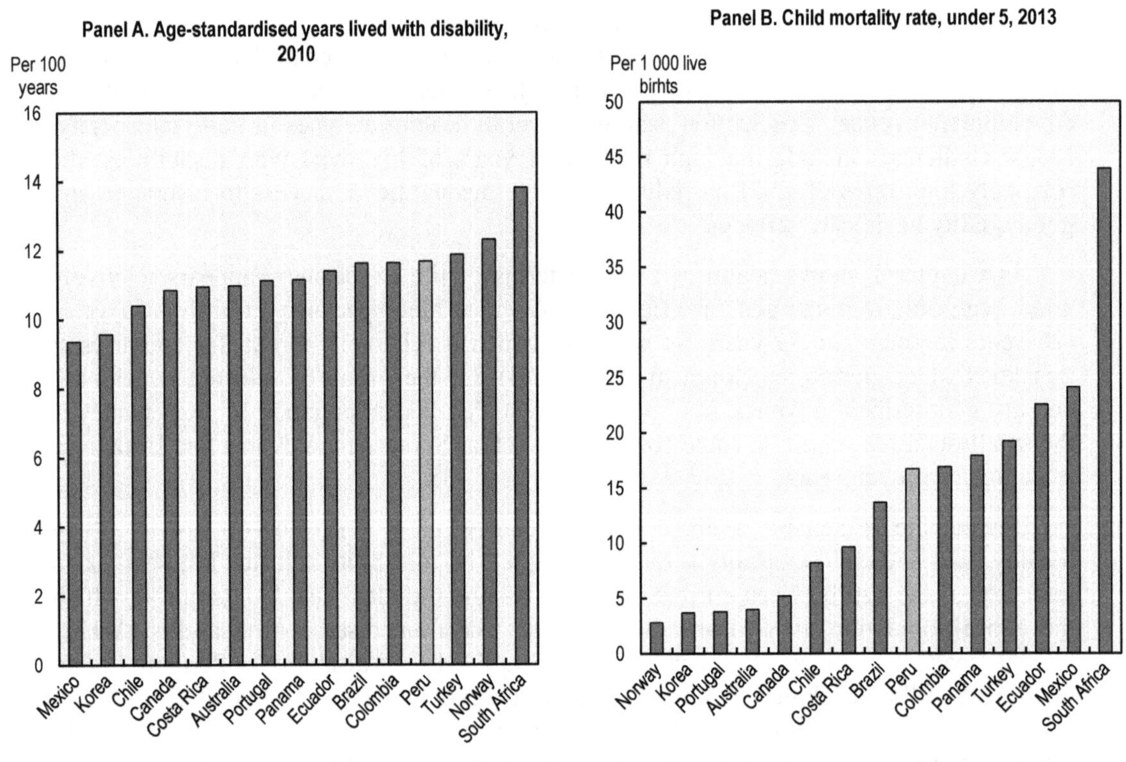

Note: Years lived with disability from Panel A are estimated by weighting the prevalence of different conditions based on severity.

Source: OECD calculations based on Global Burden of Disease Country Profiles of the Institute for Health Metrics and Evaluation for "Years Lived with Disability", and World Bank (2015a), *World Development Indicators* (database) for "Child Mortality Rate".

StatLink http://dx.doi.org/10.1787/888933265152

Peru does not do so well on self-reported health outcomes either. Compared to the other countries in the group, a relatively low proportion of the population (around 77%) report that they do not have any health problems that prevent them from doing things people their age can normally do (Panel A, Figure 2.6). This ranks Peru 5th from the bottom of the 15 benchmark countries. Peru also performs poorly in personal satisfaction with health (Panel B, Figure 2.6), with 75.6% of the population reporting they are satisfied with their personal health, only above Korea and Chile.

Figure 2.6. **Self-reported health among benchmark countries, 2014**

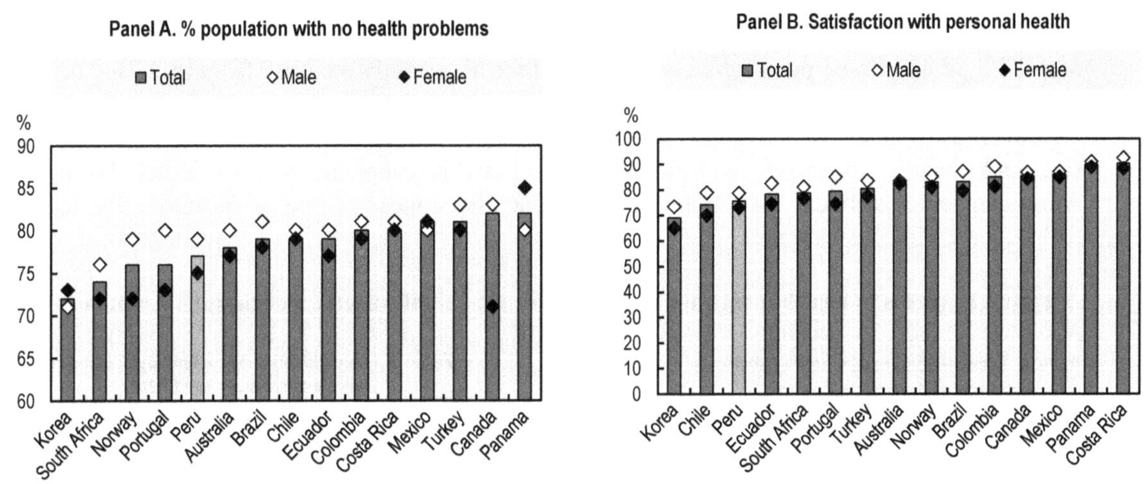

Note: Data for the "% of the population with no health problems" show the percentage of people responding "no" to the question "Do you have any health problems that prevent you from doing any of the things people your age normally can do?". Data for "Satisfaction with personal health" show the percentage of people responding "satisfied" to the question "Are you satisfied or dissatisfied with your personal health?".

Source: Gallup Organisation (2015), *Gallup World Monitor* (database).

StatLink http://dx.doi.org/10.1787/888933265162

Access to healthcare is increasing, but not yet universal

The health system is currently regulated by the General Health Law of 1997, and is divided into a universal public health sector and a private sub-sector. This law turned the state into a "subsidiary" agent rather than a "provider" agent (Mesa-Lago, 2005), allowing the affluent Peruvians to purchase healthcare from the market. The public health insurance system has three components: 1) *Sistema Integral de Salud* (SIS); 2) *Sistema Social de Salud* (EsSalud); and 3) *Sanidades de las Fuerzas Armadas y de la Policía Nacional* for police and army officers.

- The *Sistema Integral de Salud* is a non-contributory system that offers only basic medical care to a wide section of the population. It was created in 2001 by combining the *Seguro Escolar Gratuito* and *Seguro Materno Infantil* and aimed at covering all uninsured populations. In 2005, the coverage of SIS was extended to young adults over 17, and in January 2015 to all age groups. Since the SIS was designed to primarily serve those in poverty and workers in small and medium-sized enterprises (SMEs), it has made a tremendous impact in reducing inequalities in access to health services.

- EsSalud is a contributory health insurance programme and is obligatory for wage earners. Members of co-operatives and independent workers can also choose to join the EsSalud. EsSalud is a more comprehensive system than SIS and provides medical care for illnesses, accidents and maternity and subsidised medicines.
- *Sanidades de las Fuerzas Armadas y de la Policía Nacional* is funded from the Treasury, and like EsSalud, provides a wide range of healthcare services (Lavigne, 2013).

Access to health insurance has increased remarkably, especially thanks to the creation of the SIS, but Peru is still far from achieving universal coverage. The share of insured individuals was 36% in 2005 and increased to 62% in 2012. Among salaried workers, only 23% of employed people had health insurance as recently as 2005 (Figure 2.7). The coverage rate expanded significantly in 2008 and has continued to increase since then. However, as of 2013, 38% of those in employment and 4 out of 10 people overall in Peru still lack health insurance. Not surprisingly, Peru is outperformed by other Latin American and Caribbean countries: for example the coverage rate is around 80% in Colombia, Chile and Uruguay.

Figure 2.7. **Access to health insurance in Peru (over time) and selected benchmark countries**

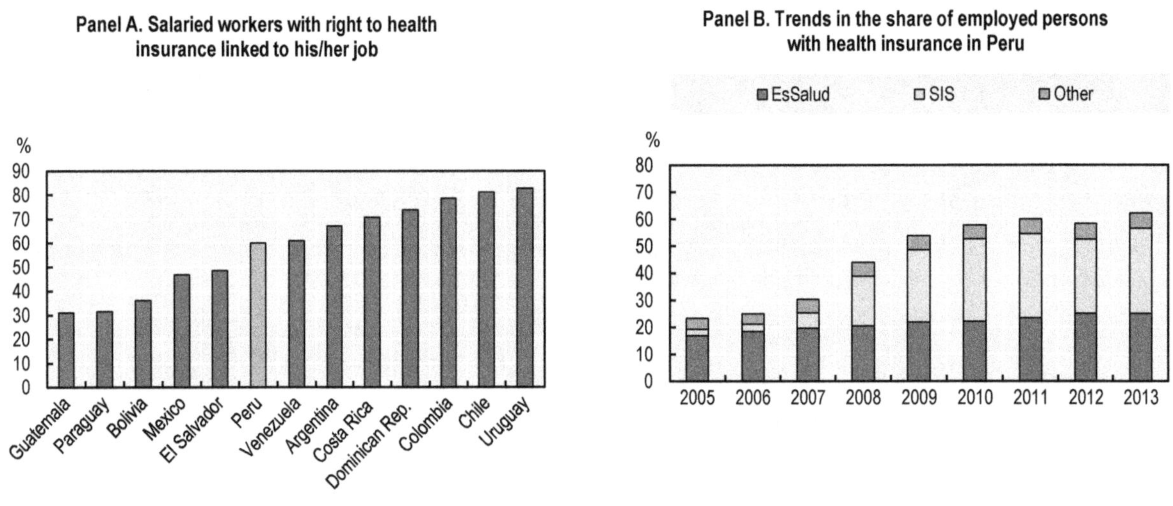

Note: Figures for benchmark countries are from the most recent year for which data are available. 2005 data for Paraguay, 2006 data for Venezuela, 2007 data for El Salvador, 2010 data for Mexico and Costa Rica, 2011 data for Guatemala, Bolivia, Peru, Dominican Republic, Colombia, Chile and Uruguay, and 2012 data for Argentina are used.

Source: CEDLAS and World Bank (2014), *Socio-Economic Database for Latin America and the Caribbean (SEDLAC)* (database), http://sedlac.econo.unlp.edu.ar/eng/index.php and Instituto Nacional de Estadística e Informática (INEI), Evaluación de los indicadores de empleo e ingresos por departamento (2013), http://www.inei.gob.pe/media/MenuRecursivo/publicaciones_digitales/Est/Lib1105/.

StatLink http://dx.doi.org/10.1787/888933265171

While both urban and rural populations now have better health insurance coverage, some discrepancies have emerged between the two. The share of those insured was more or less the same in urban and rural areas between 2005 and 2007. However, since 2008 the urban population is now more likely to have access to health insurance as a result of higher growth in access to the SIS in urban areas (Figure 2.8). The poorest populations do not have access to SIS services because they mainly live in remote locations that lack health services, widening the gap in access to health insurance among income groups.

Figure 2.8. **Evolution of the population affiliated to a health insurance scheme in Peru, 2005-12**

Percentage, by type of insurance and urban/rural population

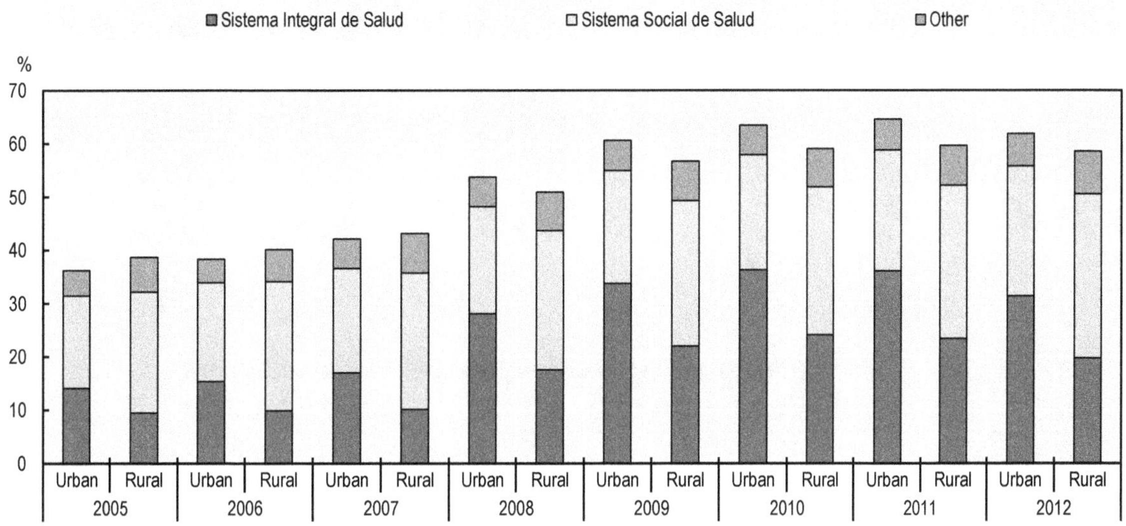

Note: "Other" category includes Seguro Privado de Salud, Entidad Prestadora de Salud, Seguro de las Fuerzas Armadas/Policiales, Seguro Universitario, and Seguro Escolar Privado.

Source: OECD calculations based on figures published by Evolución de los indicadores de empleo e ingresos por departamento, National Households Survey Data (ENAHO, Encuesta Nacional de Hogares) from INEI (National Institute of Statistics).

StatLink http://dx.doi.org/10.1787/888933265184

Despite a remarkable increase in access to health insurance in both urban and rural areas, geographical inequalities remain with respect to access to health and to health outcomes (Figure 2.9, and also discussed in Chapter 5). For instance, there are far fewer doctors per inhabitant in rural regions compared with urban ones. In Peru, on average one doctor attends to 568 persons, but there is a large variation across geographic regions. There are fewer than 350 inhabitants per doctor in Lima and Arequipa, whereas there are almost 5 times as many in Huancavelica, Huánuco, San Martín and Cajamarca. Because of the variation in health services, middle-class Peruvians typically prefer to pay for private healthcare services.

Moreover, indigenous people, especially women, have difficulties in accessing health centres and, once accessed, often receive discriminatory treatment (Mora-Bernasconi, 2006). The Ministry of Health adopted the *Estrategia Sanitaria Nacional Salud de los Pueblos Indígenas* in 2009 in order to tackle the health inequalities faced by indigenous people, prioritising the Amazonian region. This plan aims to increase public health services for these regions, and to give greater respect to traditional practices and traditional medicine of indigenous people through an intercultural approach.

Figure 2.9. **Health indicators across Peru's regions, 2012-13**

Panel A. Number of persons per doctor (2012)

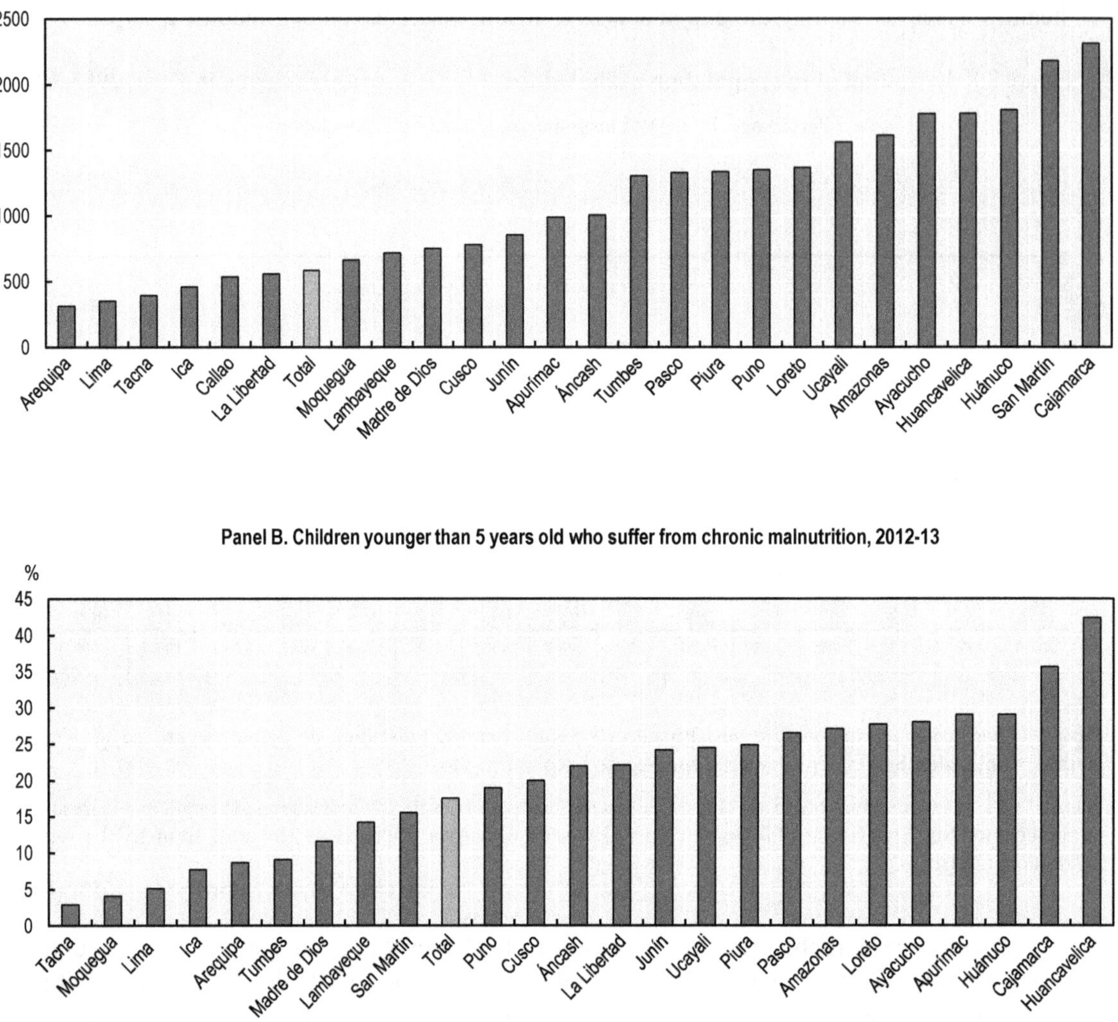

Sources: Data from Instituto Nacional de Estadística e Informática, Compendida Estadística Peru (2014). Figures for persons per doctor by regions are based on Ministry of Health (MINSA), and figures on chronic malnutrition among children come from Encuesta Demográfica y Salud Familiar.

StatLink http://dx.doi.org/10.1787/888933265198

Satisfaction with healthcare facilities is poor

Many Peruvians are dissatisfied with the level of accessibility and the quality of their healthcare services. The Gallup World Poll asks individuals each year whether they think healthcare services in their country are accessible to anyone who needs them, regardless of their economic situation. The share of Peruvians who believe anyone can access healthcare increased between 2006 and 2010 from 35% to 45%, reflecting the expansion of the SIS (Gallup, 2015). While there was a deterioration in people's perceptions of healthcare accessibility between 2010 and 2012, opinions improved in 2014 (Figure 2.10, Panel A). Despite the overall upward trend, international comparisons show that Peruvians are not as satisfied with their health-care system as other nations. Peru outperforms Turkey and Colombia but has fallen behind Chile, Mexico and Bolivia (where on average 43-50% of the population think healthcare is accessible), and particularly Costa Rica, Ecuador and Panama (where over 65% of the population are satisfied with the accessibility of healthcare services) (Figure 2.10, Panel B).

Figure 2.10. **Perceptions of the accessibility of healthcare services, 2006-14**

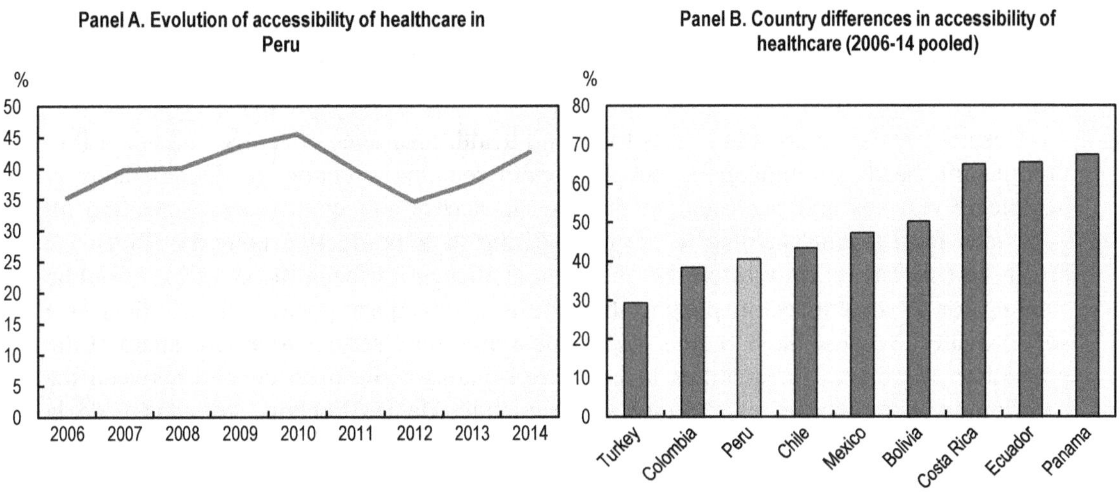

Note: Data for "perceptions of accessibility of healthcare" show the percentage of people responding "yes" to the question "Are healthcare services in this country accessible to any person who needs then, regardless of their economic situation, or not?".

Source: Gallup Organisation (2015), *Gallup World Monitor* (database).

StatLink *http://dx.doi.org/10.1787/888933265200*

Peruvians have very little confidence in their health-care and medical system. Between 2006 and 2010 (the most recent data available), only 48% of Peruvians had confidence in the health system, placing Peru behind all of the benchmark countries (Figure 2.11). For instance, confidence in the health system reached 63% in Colombia, 68% in Mexico and 73% in Costa Rica. Perhaps this is why many middle-income Peruvians prefer to pay for private healthcare.

Figure 2.11. **Confidence in health systems in benchmark countries, 2005-10**

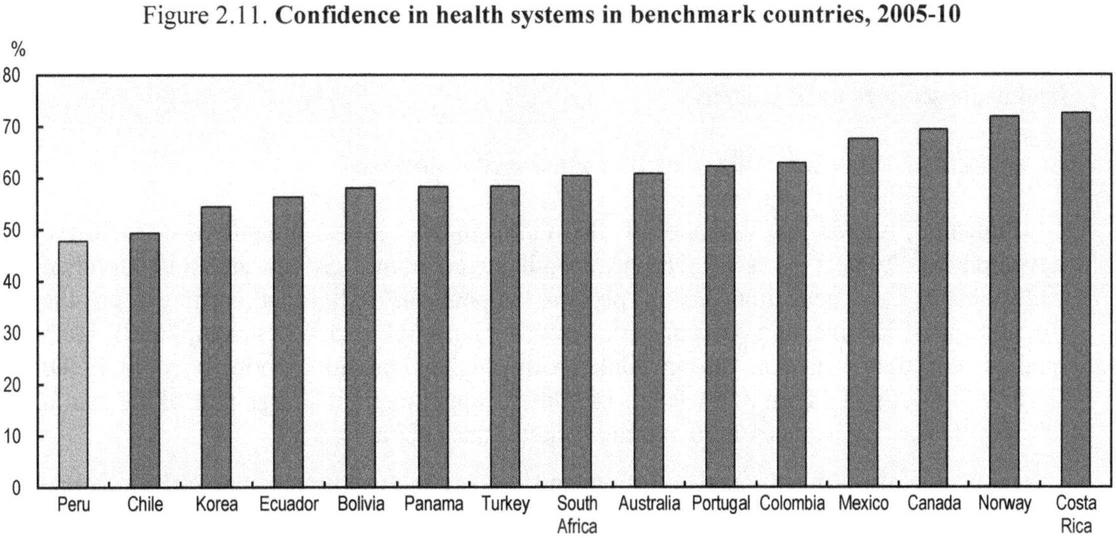

Note: Data for "confidence in health systems" show the percentage of people responding "yes" to the question "Do you have confidence in healthcare or medical systems?".

Source: Gallup Organisation (2015), *Gallup World Monitor* (database).

StatLink *http://dx.doi.org/10.1787/888933265214*

Health is still holding back Peru's economic development

Health and development are closely linked: a healthy population is a key to sustainable development. Good health can be viewed as capital; healthier individuals are capable of investing more in human capital accumulation and so are more productive, thus contributing to sustainable growth. Economic growth in turn can improve health: higher incomes can allow people to spend more on healthier diets, and technological advances help improve medical science.

Despite Peru's remarkable efforts to extend health insurance coverage and adapt it to the specific needs of indigenous people, health remains a challenge. Deficiencies in healthcare services and persistent inequalities in access and quality are preventing all Peruvians from leading healthy lives and realising their productive potential. Since the health system was recently reformed, the main challenge has been the shortage of public funding for the health sector, placing the state in a subsidiary position, rather than as a sole provider. Because the SIS aims to provide a minimum service to a wide share of the population, significant inequalities in healthcare quality have been created between the contributory beneficiaries of EsSalud and Sanidades de las Fuerzas Armadas y de la Policía Nacional and the non-contributory beneficiaries of the SIS. Peru needs to continue increasing health insurance coverage while improving the quality and accessibility of services provided via the SIS.

Effective health expenditure is crucial for ensuring that public resources produce gains in health outcomes. One crucial issue for the effectiveness of health spending is drug procurement. Drugs in Peru currently are free of charge only for specific groups covered by the SIS, while some treatments can be extremely costly, especially in the private sector (Seinfeld and La Serna, 2007; Meza-Cornejo, 2007). Drug procurement and the overall efficiency of the health system will be discussed in detail as part of the OECD's country programme with Peru which will include two thematic reviews. One of these will specifically focus on the Peruvian health system and in particular on the issue of universal health coverage. A second review will assess the current status and availability, as well as the underlying data infrastructure, of Peru's routinely reported health statistics. These reviews will be crucial for assessing the impact of reforms that the Peruvian government will implement in order to improve the quality and accessibility of healthcare services to all citizens.

Education is one of the main pillars of inclusive development

Education stands out as one of the main pillars of sustainable and inclusive development. As such, it is very relevant both for economic growth and for individual well-being. Good education has a positive impact on individual earnings, on the distribution of income, and on economic growth (Hanushek and Woessman, 2007). High quality education has a strong link with higher labour productivity (OECD/ CAF/ECLAC, 2014). Peru's low levels of human capital explain a large part of the gap in labour productivity between Peru and the United States (Chapter 3).

Education also affects social cohesion, and is a key factor in improving citizens' civic engagement, social interactions and democratic participation. Education is therefore an area of public policy where the traditional trade-off between equity and efficiency can be avoided, and is a strategic area for policy action. This section presents the evolution of access to and investment in education in Peru, and focuses on the main education challenges for the country: quality, which remains low; and the persistence of large inequalities in both access and performance.

Access to education in Peru has expanded significantly

Peru has experienced a large increase in access to education at all levels. A variety of indicators shows that the "quantity" of education held by the population in Peru has increased in recent years. The average number of years of education among 15-year olds reached 10.1 in 2013, up from 9.5 years in 2005 (INEI, 2015). Adult literacy rates (for 15-year olds and over) have also expanded, from 87.6% in 2004 to a projected rate of 94.5% for 2015 (UNESCO/UIS, 2015). But the main improvement has been the number of people participating in education, which has increased substantially at all levels in the last decade. However, gaps between Peru and OECD members still remain, particularly in secondary and tertiary education (Figure 2.12).

Figure 2.12. **Enrolment rates in different levels of education, 2012**

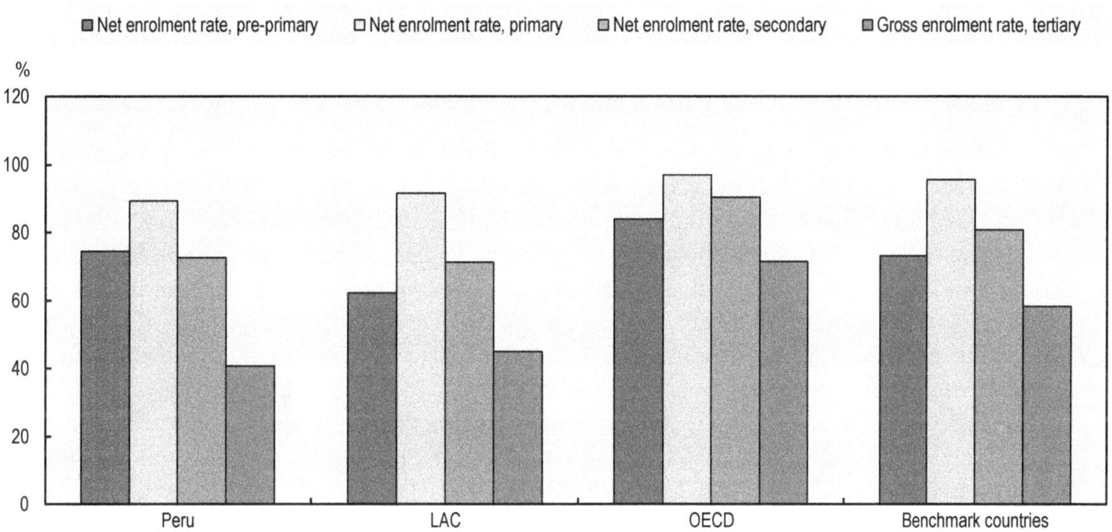

Note: Gross enrolment rates in tertiary education from Peru are from 2010.

Source: UNESCO/UIS (2015), UNESCO Institute for Statistics database, http://www.uis.unesco.org/Pages/default.aspx.

StatLink http://dx.doi.org/10.1787/888933265227

The last decade has seen remarkable progress in access to pre-primary education for children up to five years old. Net enrolment rates for those aged three to five reached around 77% by 2013, up from around 60% in 2005 (INEI, 2015). This is above the average for Latin America and the Caribbean (LAC), which averaged around 62% in 2012, but is still below the OECD average of 84% (Figure 2.12). This expansion has been partly supported by the provision of pre-primary education through formal settings, the *Centros de Educación Inicial* (CEIs), but particularly through non-formal community-based programmes called *Programas No Escolarizados de Educación Inicial* (PRONOEIs). These PRONOEIs have been in place for several decades, mainly serving children from rural and marginal urban areas, and have represented a lower-cost alternative for the government to expand access, given that the community provides most of the infrastructure (Woodhead et al., 2010). Private provision has also progressed in the field of pre-primary education (Woodhead et al., 2010). Overall, social programmes such as Juntos or Wawa Wasi have favoured access to early childhood care and education in Peru. More recently, the current administration has made children one of its public policy priorities. It has created the *Cuna Más* programme for the development of children aged three years old and under from poor areas; and *Qali Warma*, a school nutrition programme aimed at children in pre-primary and primary education.

Increased access to pre-primary education is of particular relevance given the importance of early childhood education for better child well-being and learning outcomes. The impact of pre-primary education on performance across the education cycle is highly significant, as shown by the performances of 15-year olds in the Programme for International Student Assessment (PISA). Secondary school children who have attended more than one year of pre-primary education outperform those who had not attended pre-primary education at all by the equivalent of more than one year of secondary schooling on average (OECD, 2013). In Peru, the advantage amounts to 1.3 years of schooling, the second largest difference of all the Latin American countries participating in the test (OECD, 2013). This performance gap persists even when taking into account the socio-economic status of the students, which can account for part of the discrepancy. Early childhood education also has a significant impact on the acquisition of non-cognitive skills (i.e. soft skills, such as motivation and perseverance), which are critical for the development of individuals within a society (OECD/ CAF/ECLAC, 2014).

Access to primary education is high, although it has decreased slightly and students still repeat years and drop out. Net enrolment rates in primary education were around 93% in 2013, similar to the Latin America and Caribbean average (91.5%), and slightly below the rate for OECD members of 97% (UNESCO/UIS, 2015; Figure 2.12). Levels of enrolment do not show significant discrepancies between urban and rural areas, or between girls and boys. The percentage of students that had to repeat a year of primary education decreased from 9.8% in 2002 to 4.8% in 2013 (ESCALE, 2015), leading to a decline in the proportion of over-age students from 18.8% in 2002 to 8.8% in 2013 (Ministerio de Educación, 2015). Dropout rates declined from 2.3% in 2004 to 1.1% in 2013 (ESCALE, 2015), and 80.3% of 12 and 13 year olds now complete their primary education, up from 67.2% in 2002 (UNESCO/UIS, 2015).

Secondary education is now accessed by almost 8 out of 10 students in Peru, although many leave before completion. Net enrolment rates have increased – from 68.1% in 2004 to around 76.2% in 2013 – slightly above the levels in the LAC region. However, Peru still remains behind the OECD, where access to secondary education reached around 90% in 2012 (UNESCO/UIS, 2015). The percentage of repeaters has decreased, from 5.6% in 2002 to 4.1% in 2013 (UNESCO/UIS, 2015). The percentage of dropouts is higher at secondary than other levels of education, despite a reduction from 11.0% in 2005 to 7.8% in 2013 (ESCALE, 2015). The reasons behind this dropout rate are diverse, and include the opportunity cost of staying in the education system – as opposed to working – and the need to support the income of the household. In fact, 39% of students aged 13 to 19 declared that the reason for dropping out was economic, while 17.4% claimed the reason was problems within the family. Around 10% blamed housework (ESCALE, 2015). The fall in dropout rates meant that 64.8% of those aged 18 and 19 completed their secondary education in 2013, up from 50.4% in 2005 (ESCALE, 2015). Finally, the transition to higher education was 32.9% in 2013, up from 22.9% in 2005 (ESCALE, 2015).

Access to tertiary education has expanded significantly. The expansion began in 1996 with the approval of the *Decreto Legislativo* 882, which liberalised higher education in the country. In 2002, the gross enrolment rate in tertiary education stood at 31.5%, but reached around 40.6% by 2010. This expansion has to a large extent been fuelled by newly created, or expanding, private higher education institutions. Just 45% of students were enrolled in private universities in 2004, but by 2012 the share had reached 66% (INEI, 2015). Despite this increase in access, only around 20% students aged 22-24 had completed tertiary education in 2013, up from 13.7% in 2005, and around 27% of those aged 25-34 (ESCALE, 2015).

Overall, Peruvian citizens are becoming more educated, with many more people reaching higher levels of education than in the past. In fact, the share of the population aged 15 and over with no schooling fell from 17% in 1980 to about 5% in 2010 (Figure 2.13). The share of the population with incomplete primary and secondary education also fell, showing that many more people now complete their studies. The largest increase was in the share of those who had completed secondary education, which jumped from around 14% of the adult population (aged 15 years and older) in 1980 to more than 37% in 2010. Those who had completed tertiary education also grew, from 7% to 12% between 1980 and 2010.

Figure 2.13. **Educational attainment for total population over 15 years old, 1980-2010**

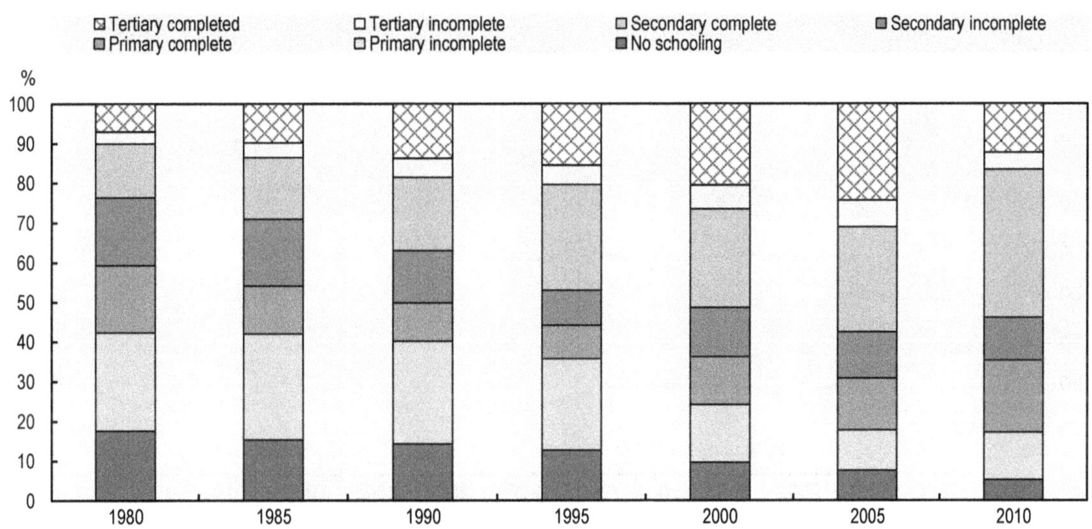

Source: OECD calculations based on Barro and Lee (2010), dataset.

StatLink http://dx.doi.org/10.1787/888933265234

Investment in education still lags behind regional and OECD levels

Investment in education has been persistently low in Peru, well below both OECD levels and those of other Latin American countries of similar levels of development. While the average share of gross domestic product (GDP) spent on education by governments was around 5.3% for the OECD and around 4.1% for LAC over the period 1999-2013, Peru recorded an average of 3% (Figure 2.14). A recent upsurge in spending – from 2.7% of GDP in 2011 to 3.3% in 2013 – indicates the stronger commitment by the current administration to invest in education. However, this indicator of expenditure may be somewhat distorted by the large expansion of Peru's GDP over the last decade. Other indicators, such as expenditure per student as a percentage of GDP per capita, confirm that Peru is still below the regional and OECD averages (Figure 2.15).

Peru still has much room to improve the education system by investing more financial resources, as well as making better use of resources spent. Peru's level of national income in purchasing power parity (PPP) terms is close to USD 12 000. According to the PISA results, a country's level of economic development is strongly related to its students' performance, but only up to a level of around USD 20 000 per capita GDP, beyond which higher national income no longer predicts educational performance (OECD, 2012a). Students performance is also closely linked to education expenditure, at least up to a level of around USD 8 000 (PPP) per student (Vegas and Coffin, 2015). Peru remains well below that level, with education expenditure at around USD 3 500 per student.

The efficiency of expenditure becomes more relevant after a certain level of expenditure has been reached, as shown by the large disparities in performance among countries with similar levels of educational expenditure (Vegas and Coffin, 2015). The capacity of education systems to absorb additional resources can limit the beneficial impacts of further investment in education.

Figure 2.14. **Expenditure on education as a percentage of GDP, 1999-2013**

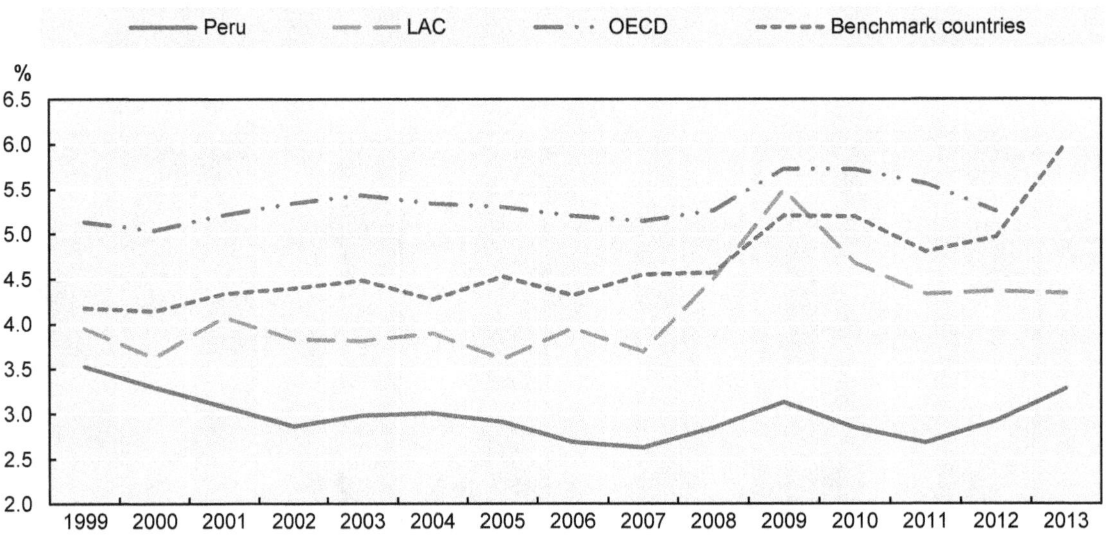

Source: OECD calculations based on UNESCO/UIS (2015), *UNESCO Institute for Statistics database*, http://www.uis.unesco.org/Pages/default.aspx.

StatLink http://dx.doi.org/10.1787/888933265247

A strong political consensus has emerged in recent years in Peru around the relevance of education for inclusive development. One of the commitments expressed in the *Acuerdo Nacional* refers to reaching a level of expenditure on education equivalent to 6% of GDP. Initially this was set as an objective for 2016 and now is referred to as a target for 2021, as stated in the National Education Project for 2021. In addition to this broader national strategy for education in the medium term, the current administration has set a number of priorities for educational policies. One is to close the gap in school infrastructure, which in Peru will cost an estimated 63 billion Peruvian soles (PEN), equivalent to USD 20 billion as of August 2015 (Ministerio de Educación, 2014). Given current spending trends, closing that gap would take almost two decades. To achieve this goal, the government is fostering both public-private partnerships and the programme *Obras por Impuestos*, which reduces tax payments for firms investing in school infrastructure. However, greater accountability in these programmes is needed at sub-national level to quantify the effectiveness of these investments on education outcomes (see Chapter 5).

Figure 2.15. **Expenditure on education per student as a percentage of GDP per capita, by level of education (2013 or latest year available)**

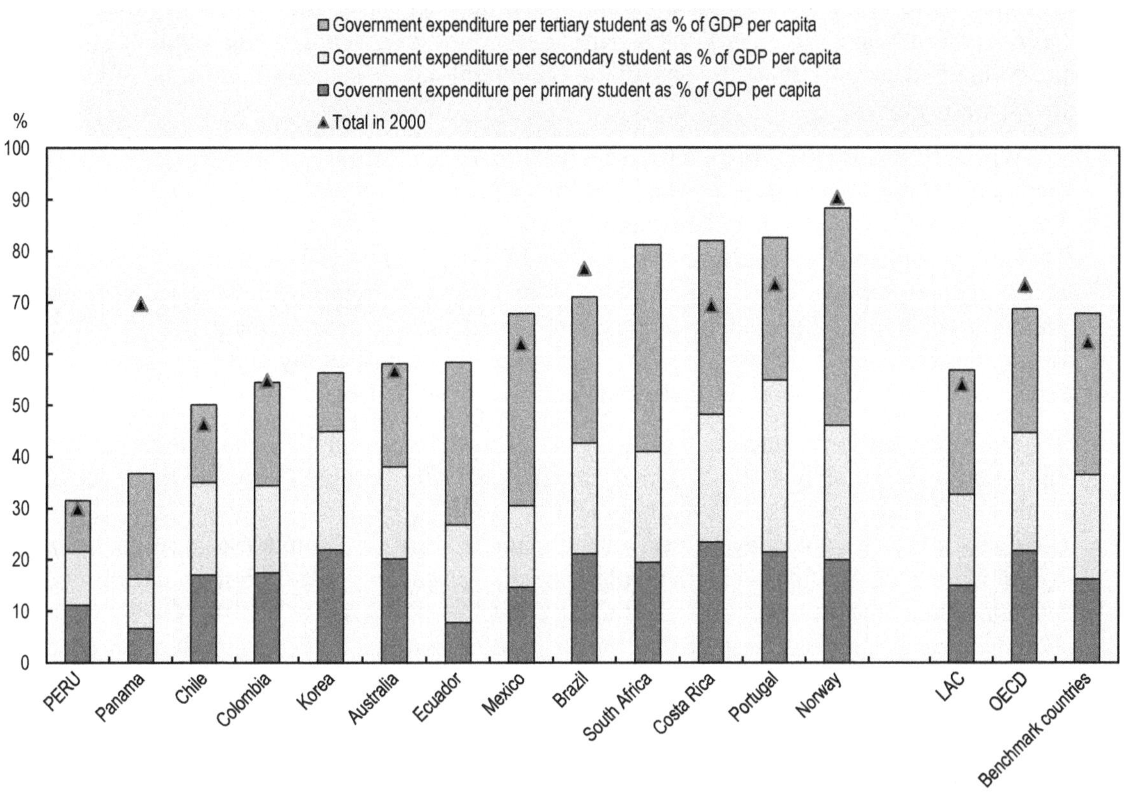

Source: OECD calculations based on UNESCO/UIS (2015), *UNESCO Institute for Statistics database*, http://www.uis.unesco.org/Pages/default.aspx.

StatLink http://dx.doi.org/10.1787/888933265255

Learning outcomes remain poor

Peru also faces the greater challenge of improving learning outcomes. The quality of Peru's education system remains poor at all levels of education. The increase in access to education has not been accompanied by similar improvements in quality, and in fact has sometimes occurred at the expense of quality. The performance of Peruvian students is generally lower than that of other countries with similar levels of development, and much worse than the OECD average. Low levels of quality translate into low relevance of education, thus discouraging students from pursuing or advancing their education.

Children do not receive a quality education at pre-primary level, which limits the positive impact that pre-primary education can have on the future performance of students. Indeed, at these early stages of education and development, poor education and care can do more harm than good (Schady, 2012). Comparable indicators on the quality of pre-primary education are scarce, but the pupil-to-teacher ratio can be illustrative, given the importance of the care, motivation and pedagogic work given by teachers at this early stage (UNESCO, 2013). In Peru in 2012 there was one teacher for every 18 students at pre-primary level, a similar ratio to the average for Latin America and the Caribbean, but well below the OECD, where there was on average one teacher for every 14 students (UNESCO/UIS, 2015). The quality of teachers is one of the main explanatory variables in the performance of students, and this is particularly true in early childhood education

(Verdisco and Ñopo, 2012). In general for Latin America and the Caribbean, however, teachers educating pre-primary children tend to receive less training, earn lower salaries and face more precarious labour conditions than teachers in higher levels of education (Verdisco and Ñopo, 2012). All this is particularly relevant given that interventions at this pre-primary stage are crucial to improving the overall performance of students all along the education cycle.

While the quality of primary education has improved, it still remains far below OECD members. The recent results of the TERCE (*Tercer Estudio Regional Comparativo y Explicativo*) study show that Peru has improved its performance in primary education. This analysis focuses particularly on the 3rd and 6th grade of primary school. It found that in the reading test for the 3rd grade, Peru had greatly improved on the results in the previous study in 2006, and now performs above the regional average for this test. Results in the 6th grade reading test have also improved significantly since 2006, but still remain slightly below the average regional performance (UNESCO, 2014).

The poor learning outcomes of students at age 15 reveal that the quality of the education they receive is limited and insufficient. The results from the PISA 2012 mathematics test placed Peru at the bottom among the 65 participating countries globally (OECD, 2013). An average 15-year-old student in Peru is behind the average Latin American student by the equivalent of 8 months of secondary schooling, and around 3 years behind the average OECD student (OECD/CAF/ECLAC, 2014). Given these PISA scores, it could be argued that the years of schooling of Peruvian students aged 15-19 are thus not equivalent to years of schooling in the OECD, as the knowledge transmitted in one year in Latin America is less than in one year in the OECD. In this sense, a clearer picture of the gap between Peru, the LAC region and the OECD can be seen if average years of schooling are adjusted by quality based on PISA 2012 scores (Figure 2.16). This shows that although Peruvian students aged 15-19 on average have more years of schooling than their peers in Latin American countries participating in PISA 2012, they are below the LAC average, and significantly below the OECD average, when adjusting for PISA scores.

The quality of higher education is far below international standards and highly fragmented. Many higher education institutions (HEIs) have emerged in the last 15 years, but this expansion has been accompanied by deterioration in quality (Castro and Yamada, 2013). This deterioration has been mainly driven by the influx of students from less educated backgrounds; the shift to a model in which teaching is the predominant focus – to the detriment of research and the creation of knowledge; the emergence of HEIs in weak regulatory environments; and a certain commercialisation of higher education in a context of a proliferation of private institutions, with less demanding student selection mechanisms. These are also the main drivers of the deterioration of quality of higher education across the LAC region (OECD, 2015b; Yamada et al., 2013). Both LAC universities and Peruvian ones perform poorly in international rankings. Only 12 LAC universities are included in the top 400 universities in the world, while Peru has no universities among the top 400 (QS University Rankings, 2015). Another sign of decline in the quality of higher education is the increase in underemployment –understood as those who are overeducated for their job position, who work for a non-professional job, or who earn less than a certain threshold- in Peru, which rose from 29% to 35% between 2004 and 2010, showing that labour markets perceive that the quality and relevance of the skills and competencies acquired in higher education fall short of their needs (Lavado et al., 2014).

Figure 2.16. **Average years of schooling (ages 15-19), unadjusted and adjusted for academic achievement using PISA scores**

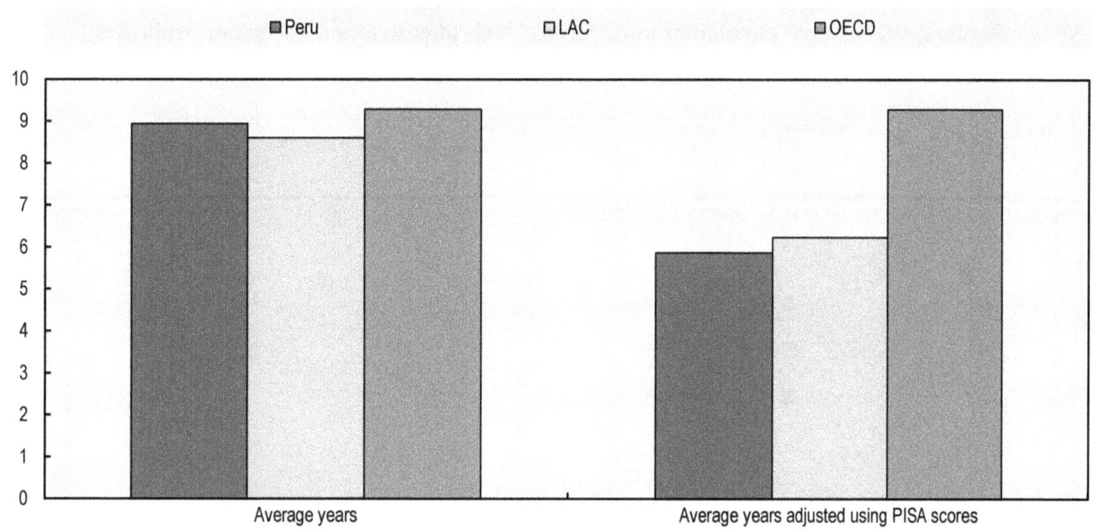

Note: LAC comprises Argentina, Brazil, Chile, Colombia, Costa Rica, Mexico, Peru and Uruguay, which are the countries in the region that participated in the PISA test in 2012.

Source: OECD calculations based on OECD/PISA 2012 database, and UNESCO/UIS (2015), *UNESCO Institute for Statistics database*, www.uis.unesco.org/Pages/default.aspx.

StatLink http://dx.doi.org/10.1787/888933265262

A University Law was passed in 2014 to strengthen the quality and relevance of Peru's higher education system. The law focuses on the quality of higher education, now managed by the Ministry of Education. This is especially relevant given that recent efforts to assure quality have not been particularly successful (Cuenca, 2015). One of the milestones of this law is the creation of the SUNEDU (*Superintendencia Nacional de Educación Superior Universitaria*). The main objectives of this body are to oversee and control the quality of universities, to grant permission to provide the service of university education, and to control and regulate the public funds given to universities to guarantee that they have been targeted toward improving quality.

The teaching profession in Peru at all levels of education faces many challenges that affect education quality. The problems suffered by the teaching profession have been one of the main factors behind the poor quality of education in Peru. These include inadequate teacher training, insufficient remuneration, and a regulatory framework that does not create incentives for professionalism (Rivero, 2010). In 2012, a law (*Ley de Reforma Magisterial*) was passed to reform the teaching profession and improve the quality of teachers. This reform aims to introduce more meritocratic criteria in teaching career development, better labour conditions, salaries linked to performance, and incentive schemes to promote continuous professional development. This is one of the main strategic areas of action for the current administration in the field of education.

Large inequalities remain in educational performance and access

Socio-economic factors remain strong determinants of an individual's access to education in Peru. Although access to primary education is broad and the differences are not significant at this level, the higher the level of education the wider the gap becomes.

The rates of access of different income quintiles show large disparities for secondary and tertiary education, a feature also seen across the LAC region (Figure 2.17).

Figure 2.17. **Rates of enrolment in different levels of education, by income quintiles, 2011 or latest year available**

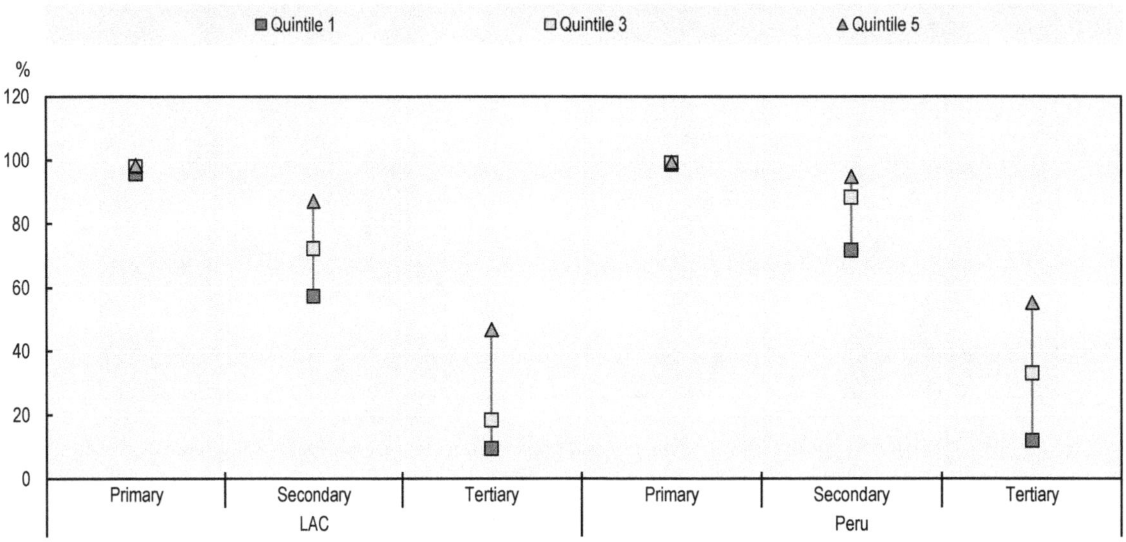

Note: LAC comprises Argentina, Brazil, Chile, Colombia, Costa Rica, Dominican Republic, Ecuador, El Salvador, Honduras, Mexico, Panama, Paraguay, Peru and Uruguay.

Source: OECD calculations based on CEDLAS and World Bank (2014).

StatLink *http://dx.doi.org/10.1787/888933265279*

Educational access and attainment are also determined by the student's ethnic origin, gender and rural/urban location. Although the impact of these factors has generally declined, ethnic origin remains a key factor in inequality. Both enrolment and completion rates at all levels of education are higher among white people than among Amazonians, the Quechua and Aymara population, and the Afro-descendent people, in that order (Castro and Yamada, 2011). The rates of enrolment in secondary education (among those aged 12 to 16) differ significantly between the urban population (89.1%) and the rural population (72.9%), although this is an improvement on 2005 when the respective rates were 81.8% and 57.3% (INEI, 2015). The urban population aged 25-34 had on average 12 years of education in 2013, significantly above the 7.9 year average for the rural population (ESCALE, 2015). The gender gap in urban areas has now closed, but for the rural population there is still a large difference in educational attainment between girls and boys. In 2013 women aged 25-34 in rural areas had completed on average 6.9 years of education compared with 8.7 years for men, while in urban areas the figures were 11.8 and 12.1 respectively (ESCALE, 2015).

The current administration has put measures in place to support access to higher education for the more socio-economically disadvantaged, and these will be key to the continued reduction of educational inequalities in the country. PRONABEC (*Programa Nacional de Becas y Crédito Educativo*) is the national organisation in charge of granting scholarships and educational loans to talented people without resources, in order to promote the formation of human capital and foster social inclusion. PRONABEC has recently put in place an important programme called Beca 18, a scholarship programme to support students coming from poor and extremely poor socio-economic backgrounds, who have excelled in secondary education. The programme supports their access to higher education and guarantees resources for successful completion and subsequent job preparation.

Figure 2.18. **Secondary-school performance and equity in education (PISA 2012)**

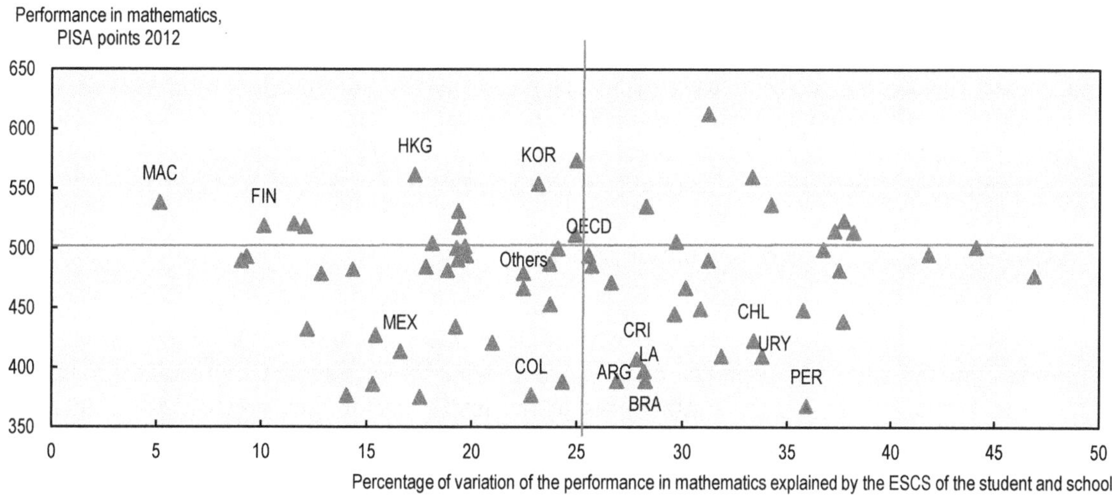

Note: Latin America ("LA" in the figure) comprises Argentina, Brazil, Chile, Colombia, Costa Rica, Mexico, Peru and Uruguay. "Others" comprise non-OECD and non-Latin American economies. The percentage change in mathematics performance explained by the economic, social and cultural status of students and schools is obtained from a student-level regression where the explanatory variables are the economic, social and cultural status of the student and that of the school.

Source: OECD/CAF/ECLAC (2014).

StatLink http://dx.doi.org/10.1787/888933265280

Peru also has large differences in educational performance, closely linked to different socioeconomic factors. According to the 2012 PISA results, students from the richest 25% households outperform those in the poorest 25% by the equivalent of around 2.5 years of secondary schooling. While the richest 25% show similar performance to an equivalent student in LAC, the poorest 25% perform well below an equivalent student in LAC (OECD/CAF/ECLAC, 2014). Around 36% of Peru's variation in performance between students is explained by the economic, social and cultural status (ESCS) of the students and the school, this being the highest percentage among Latin American countries participating in PISA (Figure 2.18). The ESCS largely explains the performance gaps between public and private schools. When the ESCS of students and schools is taken into account, students from private schools in Peru barely outperform those from public schools (OECD/CAF/ECLAC, 2014). School resources are another source of inequality. The correlation between a student's socio-economic status and the educational resources of his or her school is much stronger in Latin America than in the OECD, and this is particularly true for Peru, where the correlation (0.36) is the highest among the Latin American countries participating in PISA. In terms of gender, boys outperform girls by the equivalent of five and a half months of schooling (OECD/CAF/ECLAC, 2014). Cultural and linguistic diversity also has an impact. According to PISA 2012 scores, Peru has a mathematics performance gap equivalent to more than two years of schooling, between students who report speaking Spanish at home and students who report speaking Quechua (OECD/CAF/ECLAC, 2014).

Skills are another challenge to inclusive growth in Peru

Skills are a key dimension for promoting long-term inclusive growth. Skills are defined by the OECD as "the bundle of knowledge, attributes and capacities that can be learned and that enable individuals to successfully and consistently perform an activity or task and can be built upon and extended through learning" (OECD, 2012b). That is why skills matter, as they are directly related to productivity and to the capacity of a country to compete in a knowledge-based economy. Skills also drive economic dynamism; they increase the ability to innovate and to reap the benefits of technological progress, favouring participation in higher segments of the value chain. Finally, skills are also crucial from the perspective of socio-economic inclusion, as more and better skills favour the employability of individuals, while increasing their own job satisfaction.

Skills shortages can be a barrier to growth

In Peru, businesses are experiencing difficulties in finding the skills they need. About 28% of firms report they cannot find workers with the right skills. While this value is lower than the LAC region average (36%), it is well above the OECD average (17%) (World Bank, 2015b; Figure 2.19). Firms in the textile sector face greatest difficulties (one in three firms have trouble finding the skills they need), followed by the food sector (one in four) and the chemical sector (one in five) (World Bank, 2015b). Other surveys paint a more dismal picture; according to a 2014 Manpower survey, for example, approximately two out of three firms (67%) reported they could not find the skills they needed, making Peru a worse performer than Brazil and Argentina (63%), Panama (58%), Colombia (57%) and Mexico (44%) (Manpower, 2014). Around half of large firms reported difficulties hiring skilled workers, according to a sample of large firms whose revenues represented around 30% of Peru's GDP (Apoyo Consultoria, 2013).

Figure 2.19. **Firms identifying an inadequately educated workforce as a major constraint to their growth, 2010 or latest year available**

Percentages

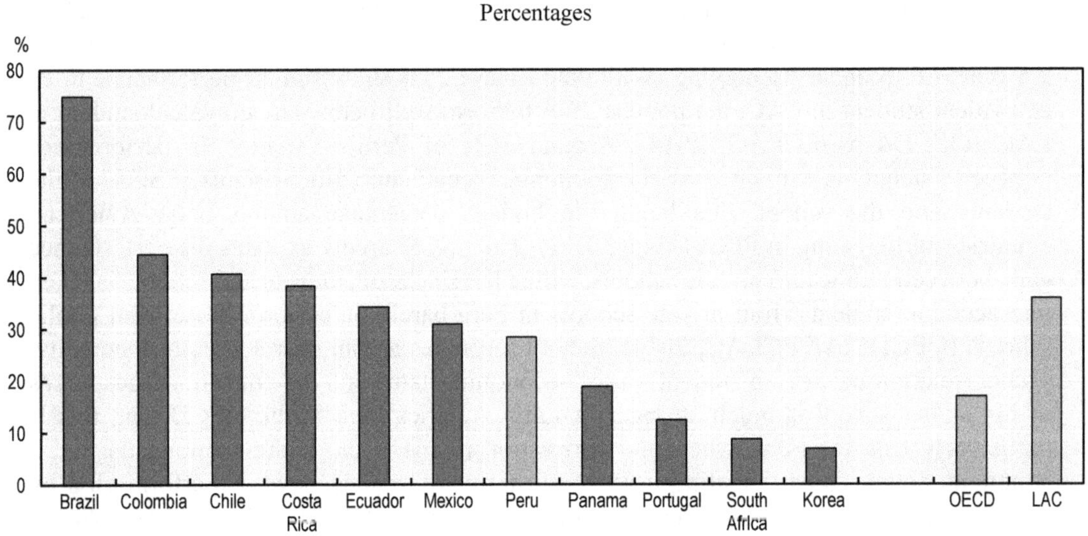

Source: World Bank (2015b), *Enterprise Surveys*, World Bank Group, www.enterprisesurveys.org/data, accessed on May 2015.

StatLink http://dx.doi.org/10.1787/888933265298

Skills mismatches are larger in middle-income economies like Peru than in low-income and OECD economies, suggesting that skills-related challenges are an important dimension of the middle-income trap (see Chapter 1). This phenomenon possibly stems from the transition in the production system of these countries towards sectors and tasks that demand more and better skills, while low quality education and training systems are holding back supply (OECD/ CAF/ECLAC, 2014).

These skill gaps represent a barrier to growth and labour participation and can lead to a situation in which jobs and economic activity become concentrated in low-skilled sectors. If firms cannot find the workforce they need, and fail to train their staff, they may either continue to operate at sub-optimal levels of productivity, or they may gradually adapt their investment decisions to the existing supply of skills, discarding investment initiatives that would require more complex, higher-level skills. In either case, the impact of an inadequate pool of skills on economic growth and productivity can be large. From a supply side perspective, if skills are not valued by employers then workers' incentives to invest in them declines. The effect on economic dynamism and the employability of the population can be pervasive. All in all, these dynamics can lead to a "low-skills trap", in which low skills deter economic activity while the scarcity of good jobs acts as a disincentive to skills formation.

In Peru, employment is concentrated in low and medium-skilled sectors, with only 18.6% of jobs requiring high skills and around 15% of the employed equipped with these (OECD/CAF/ECLAC, 2014). Although there are significant gaps between the demand and supply of skills in Peru, they have both been growing. Analysing the evolution of the demand and supply for skills in Peru is critical to better understanding their characteristics and the underlying forces behind the skills gaps.

The economy increasingly demands a broader set of skills

Demand in Peru is concentrated on generic skills, both cognitive skills and "soft", or socio-emotional skills – such as responsibility at work, the ability to work in teams under pressure and in a changing environment, and the ability to react to and solve problems (World Bank, 2011). Employers perceive these generic skills, which provide the basis for workers to learn more specific, work-related skills, to be particularly scarce in the country (World Bank, 2011). The lack of technical skills, experience and soft skills mean that employers find it hard to fill available positions (Manpower, 2013). These skills are relevant in some of the professions more demanded in Peru, such as security staff, sales technical agents and telephonists (MTPE, 2015).

The demand for skills in Peru has been increasing, with more highly skilled jobs now being created, assuming that the evolution of employment by level of education is an indicator of the demand for skills. The demand for highly-skilled workers, i.e. those who have completed higher education (both university and non-university) increased by 52% between 2004 and 2013. Demand for workers with low and medium skills, i.e. primary and secondary education, only increased by around 6%.[3]

The education and training system is not providing the right skills

Peru's system for building skills is of low quality and poorly matched to the demands of the labour markets. Skills are built through a variety of channels, one of the most important being the education system. In general, the evidence coming from studies like PISA is that Latin American students' skills are poor; this is confirmed by the scarcity of skills that firms report. But the challenge goes beyond that: not only is the overall quality of education poor, students do not focus on the subjects which employers demand. Fields like law, administration and accounting receive a large share of students (Figure 2.20), whereas labour markets in general demand more technical skills.

Figure 2.20. **Main university subjects studied in Peru, 2010**

Number of students

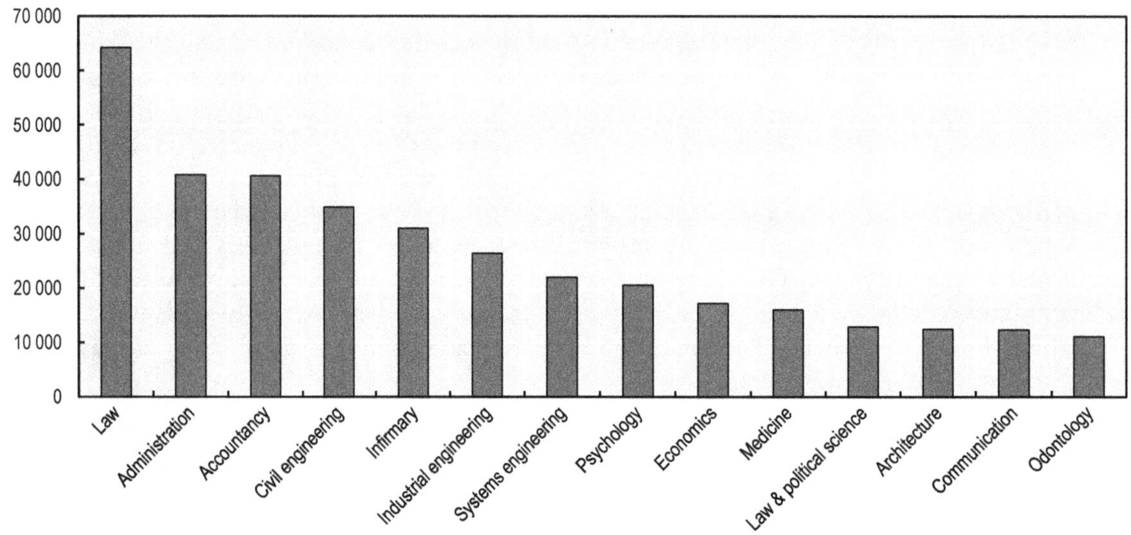

Source: ANR (2012), Asamblea Nacional de Rectores, Datos Estadísticos Universitario, Dirección de Estadística.

StatLink http://dx.doi.org/10.1787/888933265302

Technical and vocational education and training (TVET) is also not well regarded by society and has quality issues. TVET represents a powerful tool to train students in the type of skills that are directly applicable to jobs. A strong and dynamic TVET system is critical to improving the connection between the supply and demand of skills, and to support employability and productivity gains. Most of the TVET in Peru is offered by SENATI, a private institution created by industry to train workers in the skills it needs. However, the TVET system in Peru is of poor quality and is in many cases considered as inferior relative to university studies. Around 70% of students who finish secondary education and want to continue into higher education prefer to do so at university rather than within the TVET system. They consider university to be more complete and to offer a better quality education that is better connected to labour market demands (Alfageme and Guabloche, 2014; CAF, 2014). It is interesting to contrast this with the situation in emerging Asian economies. Here the opposite applies: TVET is much more valued by society and a much larger proportion of students follow that path, fuelling certain particularly dynamic sectors of the economy (Alfageme and Guabloche, 2014). One key recent effort to improve TVET in Peru is the PROJOVEN programme, which aims to provide professional training to young people aged 16-24. The importance of these issues is reflected in the OECD's Country Programme for Peru, which includes various reports on these themes: first, a vocational education and training review, focusing on the functioning of the VET system and on ways to improve it. Secondly, an "Investing in Youth" review, which will deal with issues related to the school-to-work transitions of youth and provide policy options to improve this. Finally, the Country Programme also includes an OECD Skills Strategy for Peru, which will provide a comprehensive assessment of the main skills challenges and needs in the country (Box 2.1).

Box 2.1. Better skills for better economic and social outcomes: Towards a skills strategy for Peru

Skills transform lives and drive economies. Effective skill development, activation and use are central to future economic and social development.

Peru's education system performs poorly, as illustrated by the PISA results, among other things. While this is just one of the explanatory factors of skills levels in a country, evidence from the demand side confirms that the skills developed are not relevant and do not match the demands of the production sector.

Investing in skills is one of the main policy strategies for pursuing development and economic growth. In a globalised and increasingly knowledge-based economy, the capacity of countries to compete is becoming more dependent on their ability to innovate and reap the benefits of technological progress, to add value to their goods and services, or to integrate their productive sector into higher segments of global value chains, among others.

In this context, the OECD is working with different countries to develop and implement skills strategies, which aim to provide countries with a strategic approach for building, maintaining and using their human capital to boost employment and economic growth, and promote social inclusion and participation.

The OECD works collaboratively with countries to develop a strategic assessment tailored to each country's specific skills challenges and needs. In particular, the Country Programme for Peru includes a skills strategy. The OECD Skills Strategy provides an overall framework for this work, focusing on: 1) developing relevant skills; 2) activating skills supply; 3) using skills effectively; and 4) strengthening the skills system.

Given the horizontal nature of skills challenges, a national skills strategy project needs to be designed together with all relevant government authorities and stakeholders. This means taking a whole-of-government approach, with dialogue and collaboration across ministerial portfolios, and engaging stakeholders to build a national consensus and commitment to action.

Source: OECD (2012b), *Better Skills, Better Jobs, Better Lives: A Strategic Approach to Skills Policies*, OECD Publishing, Paris, http://dx.doi.org/10.1787/9789264177338-en.

Inequalities persist in the labour market

Challenges remain also in the labour market. Many in the workforce still have low wages and rates of informal employment remain among the highest in the region. Inequalities persist between those with high and low levels of education as well as among geographical regions.

A well-functioning labour market is characterised by its ability to allocate jobs to those in search of work that match their skills. It pays workers a decent wage that is appropriate for their skills, protects them from social risks and ensures they can be re-employed without wage loss after spells of inactivity. Peru faces several challenges in improving the functioning of its labour market: a high share of informal work, poor job quality, lack of a comprehensive labour policy and weak law enforcement, and inefficient policies to reduce labour costs and provide both firms and workers with incentives to enter the formal sector. This section describes Peru's recent progress, and then reviews and evaluates these remaining challenges.

Recent progress in increasing labour-force participation has been remarkable

Labour-force participation has grown remarkably in Peru, with 12 million additional individuals joining the labour force between 1991 and 2013. The employment rate as a share of the population has increased from 56.6% to 73.3% (Figure 2.21). This increase was mainly driven by the rise in female labour-force participation and, to some extent, by the increase in youth employment. In 2013, Peru had the highest employment-to-population rate and the highest female employment rate among the benchmark countries.

Figure 2.21. **Employment trends in Peru and in comparison to benchmark countries**

(employment-to-population ratio)

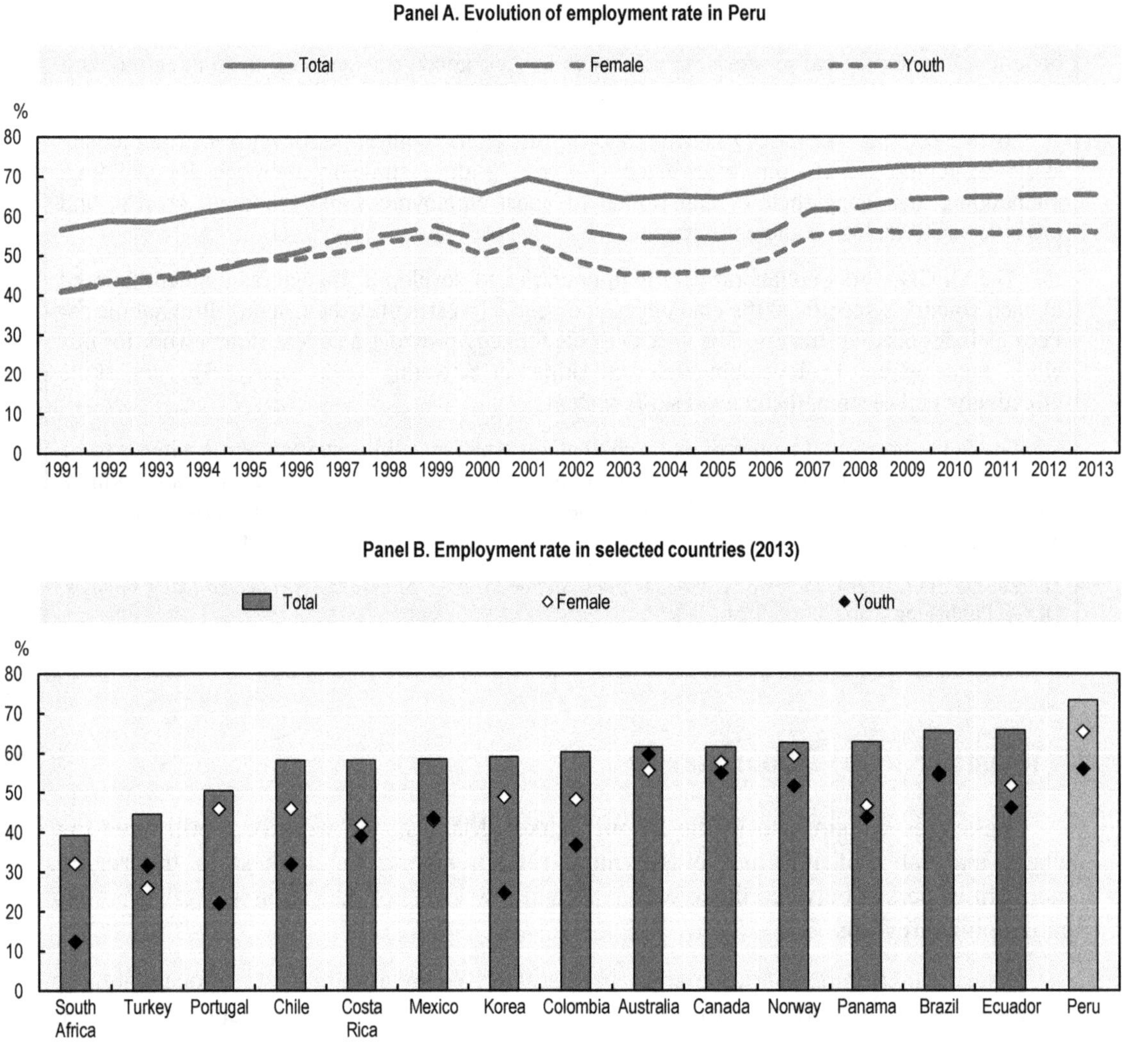

Source: ILO (2014), Key Indicators of the Labour Market, 8th Edition, International Labour Office, Geneva.

StatLink http://dx.doi.org/10.1787/888933265316

There has also been an improvement in time-related underemployment, which refers to the share of employed people who would like to work additional hours, and reflects the underutilisation of productive labour. Time-related underemployment declined in Peru from the early 2000s to 2012, with a short-lived increase in 2007. Despite this progress, in 2012 around 6% of working Peruvians were underemployed, which was higher than in other Latin American countries including Ecuador, Colombia, Costa Rica and Argentina (Figure 2.22).

Figure 2.22. **Time-related underemployment in Peru and in comparison to benchmark countries**

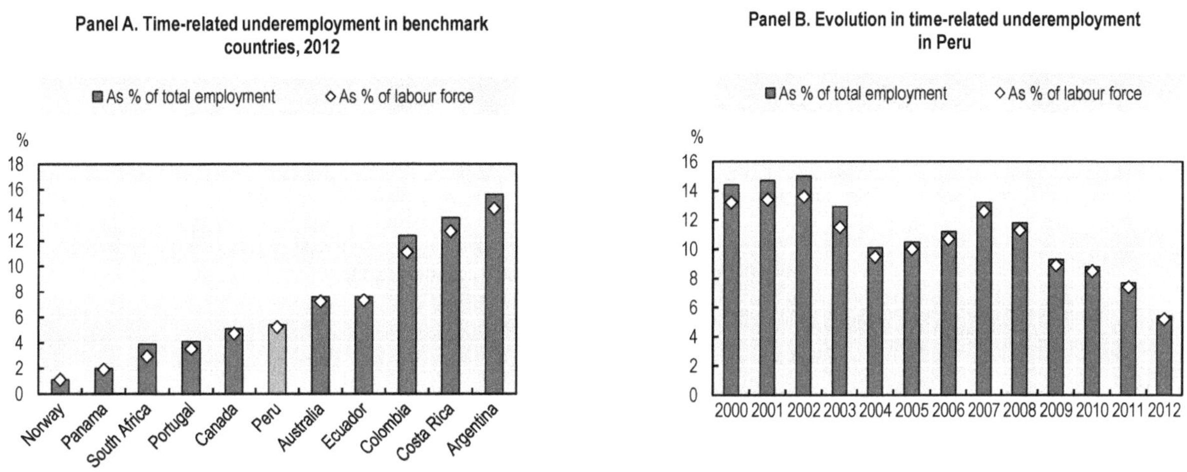

Source: ILO (2014), *Key Indicators of the Labour Market*, 8th Edition, International Labour Office, Geneva.

StatLink http://dx.doi.org/10.1787/888933265323

Peru's high employment rates are accompanied by low unemployment rates. At 3.9% they are among the lowest in the region as well as among the benchmark countries. After a period of fluctuation in the 1990s, the unemployment rate steadily declined between 2004 and 2013. Male and female unemployment trends have been similar, with slightly more women than men unemployed. At around 10%, youth unemployment has been approximately three times the total unemployment rate since 1990s (Figure 2.23) but is well below levels observed in most benchmark countries.

Peru's low unemployment rate reflects the fact that many individuals cannot afford to be jobless, rather than the efficiency of the labour market in allocating individuals to jobs. Because of the lack of a universal unemployment insurance system, many Peruvians are forced to accept the first job they are offered, which often prevents them from searching for a job in which they would be more productive and could earn higher wages. This is reflected by a very low incidence of long-term unemployment. The 2012 data show that, on average, an individual was unemployed for just 0.77 months in Peru, remarkably low compared with, for example, Brazil's average of 11.5 months or Australia's 9.3 months (Figure 2.24). Time spent unemployed varies with age, education and urbanisation. Prime-age workers (those aged 25 to 54 years old), older workers, those with high education and urban workers take longer to find a job when unemployed, but even for these groups' average unemployment duration is remarkably short compared to other countries. Many of the younger or lower-educated workers in Peru, and those in rural areas who do not have access to social security systems to support them during their job search, are more likely to take the first job available to them.

Figure 2.23. **Unemployment trends in Peru and in comparison to benchmark countries**

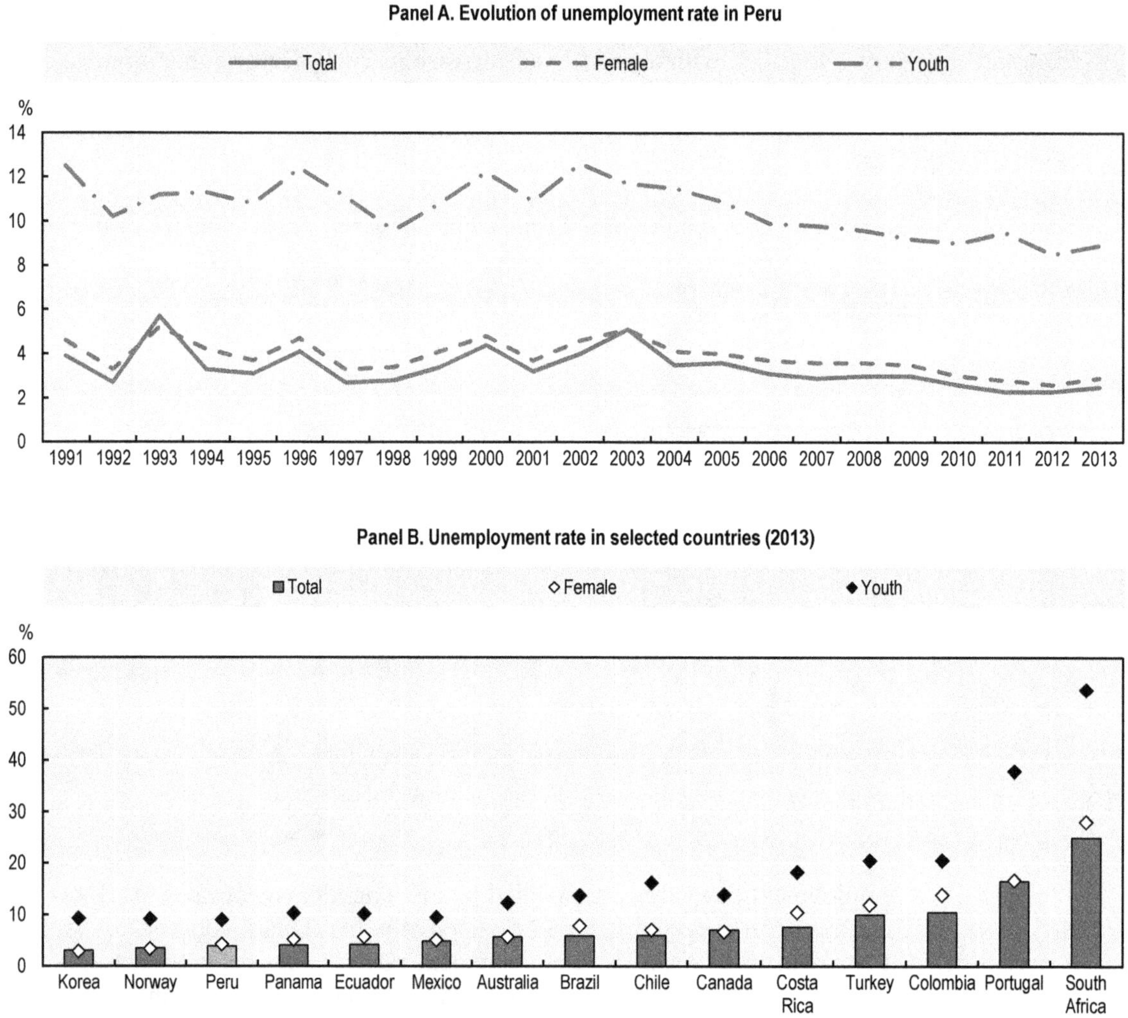

Source: ILO (2014), *Key Indicators of the Labour Market*, 8th Edition, International Labour Office, Geneva.

StatLink http://dx.doi.org/10.1787/888933265332

Peru's job loss rate is also generally low, although it is high for those in the informal employment. The overall size of the labour market and aggregate employment status are determined by the flows of workers moving from one status to another. Therefore it is crucial to analyse the labour market from a dynamic perspective. The degree of mobility between employment and joblessness effectively translates into income risk and entitlement to social assistance programmes. Figure 2.25 shows the probability of job losses among formal and informal workers from one year to another, calculated from 2009 and 2010 figures. It defines five states individuals can move into or out of: formal work, informal work, self-employment, unemployment and being out of the labour force. It shows that the probability of moving from formal employment to unemployment or out of the labour force is low in Peru. Only 3% of formal workers become unemployed and another 3% move out of the labour force each year. These figures are in direct contrast to countries like Turkey and South Africa, where job loss rates among formal workers are much higher. Informal workers overall are more likely to become jobless than formal workers. Yet Peru still has the lowest rate of transition from informal work to joblessness among the seven countries for which data are available.

Figure 2.24. **Unemployment duration among socio-demographic groups and among benchmark countries, 2012**

Months

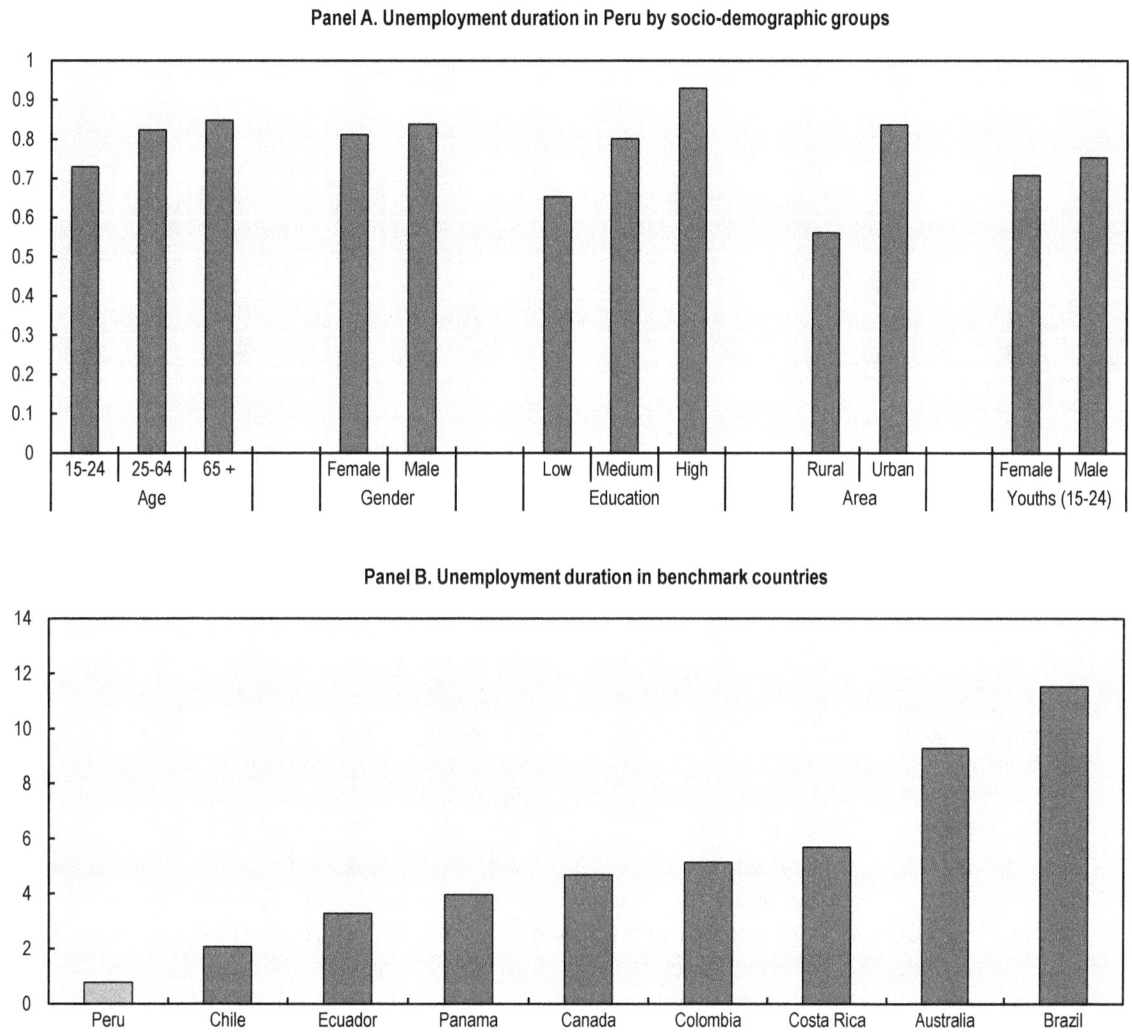

Sources: CEDLAS and World Bank (2014), *Socio-Economic Database for Latin America and the Caribbean (SEDLAC)* (database) for Latin American countries, http://sedlac.econo.unlp.edu.ar/eng/index.php and OECD unemployment statistics for Australia and Canada, http://stats.oecd.org/Index.aspx?DataSetCode=AVD_DUR.

StatLink http://dx.doi.org/10.1787/888933265340

Figure 2.25. **Job mobility trends in Peru and benchmark countries, 2009-10**

(*t-1* and *t*)

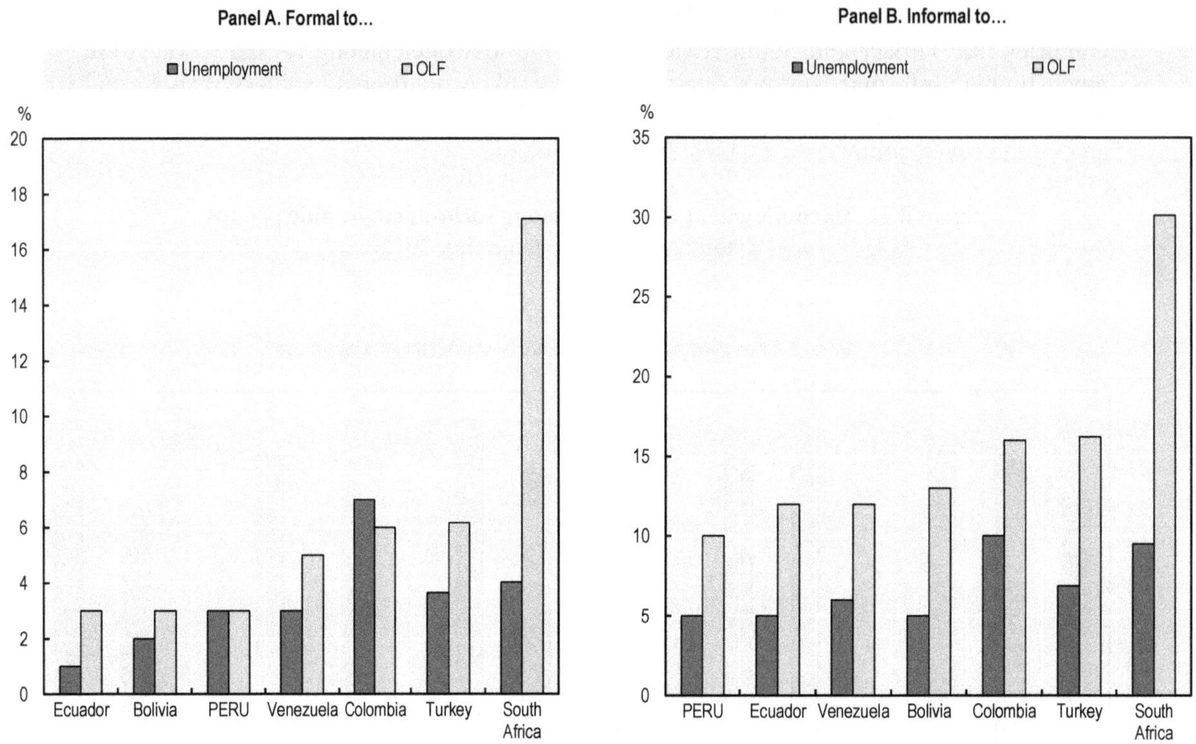

Note: For South Africa transition rates are between t and t-2. OLF (out of labour force) refers to working age population who are neither employed nor unemployed.

Source: OECD calculations based on Goñi Pacchioni, A. (2013), *Andemic Informality: Assessing Labor Informality, Employment and Income Risk in the Andes*, Inter-American Development Bank, IDB, Washington, D.C and OECD (2015c), "Enhancing job quality in emerging economies", in *OECD Employment Outlook 2015*, OECD Publishing, Paris.

StatLink http://dx.doi.org/10.1787/888933265351

Job-finding rates are high in Peru although individuals are more likely to enter the labour market through informal jobs than formal ones. For those outside the labour force it is not easy to get straight into the formal sector and many individuals find it easier to get an informal job first. As in many developing countries, social assistance to jobless individuals is limited so most people accept the first job offer, even if it is of poorer quality and in the informal sector. Figure 2.26 shows job-finding rates over two consecutive years for the unemployed and for those who are out of the labour market. In general, it is more common for the unemployed to find a job in the informal sector in all countries except for Venezuela. Ecuador, followed by Peru, has the highest rates of transition from unemployment to informal jobs, whereas Bolivia, followed by Peru, has the lowest transition rate from unemployment to formal jobs. Among individuals who are out of the labour force, Peru has by far the highest transition rates to the informal employment. The probability of entering into formal jobs is lower than the probability of entering informal jobs in all countries except South Africa and Venezuela.

Figure 2.26. **Job-finding rates in benchmark countries, 2009-10**

(*t-1* and *t*)

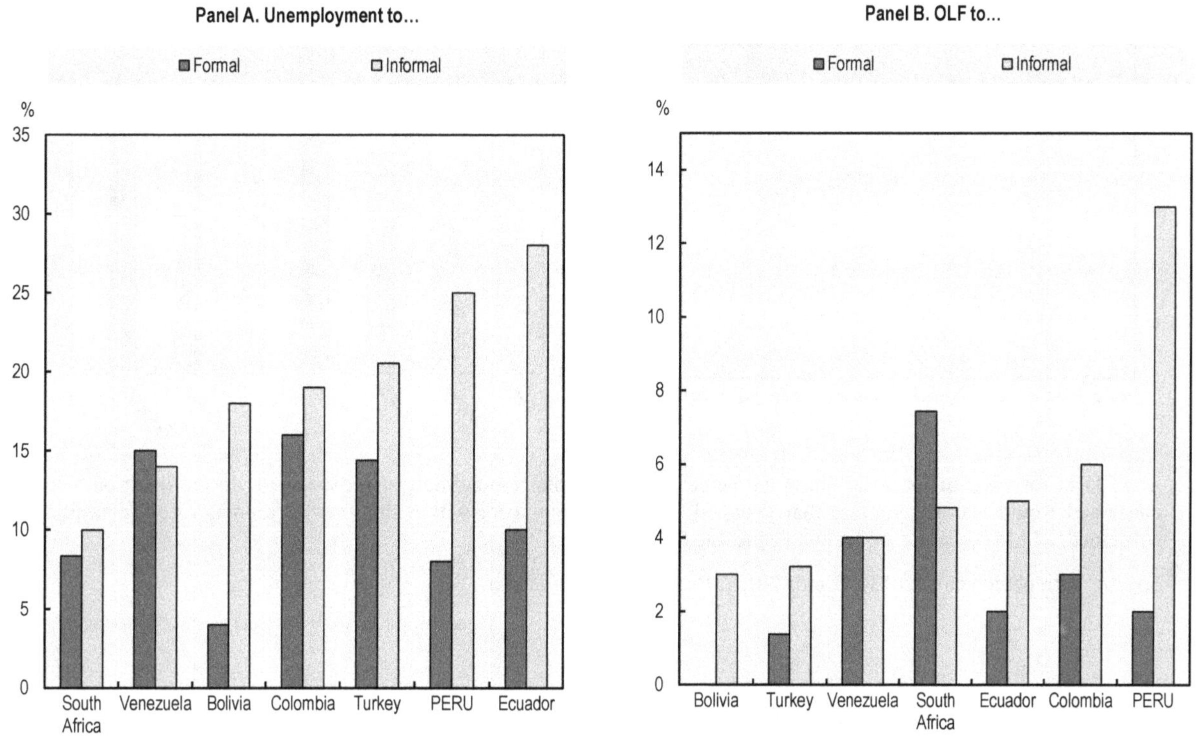

Note: For South Africa transition rates are between *t* and *t-2*. OLF (out of labour force) refers to working age population who are neither employed nor unemployed.

Source: OECD calculations based on Goñi Pacchioni, A. (2013), Andemic Informality: Assessing Labor Informality, Employment and Income Risk in the Andes, Inter-American Development Bank, IDB, Washington, D.C and OECD (2015c), "Enhancing job quality in emerging economies", in OECD *Employment Outlook 2015*, OECD Publishing, Paris.

StatLink http://dx.doi.org/10.1787/888933265361

Subjective job insecurity is also low in Peru. Figure 2.27 presents the percentage of workers who report being very concerned that they will be left without work in the next 12 months. Panel A shows that fear of job loss in Peru fell remarkably between 2004 – when it reached to the highest point in the last 10 years – and 2013. Only 23% of Peruvian workers in 2013 feared they could be left without work. This reflects the country's relatively low job-loss rate and high job-finding rates. In other Latin American countries the share of workers reporting subjective job insecurity in 2011 was 40% in Mexico, 37% in Colombia and 34% in Ecuador and Costa Rica – all levels much higher than Peru.[4]

Figure 2.27. **Subjective job insecurity in Peru and in the region**

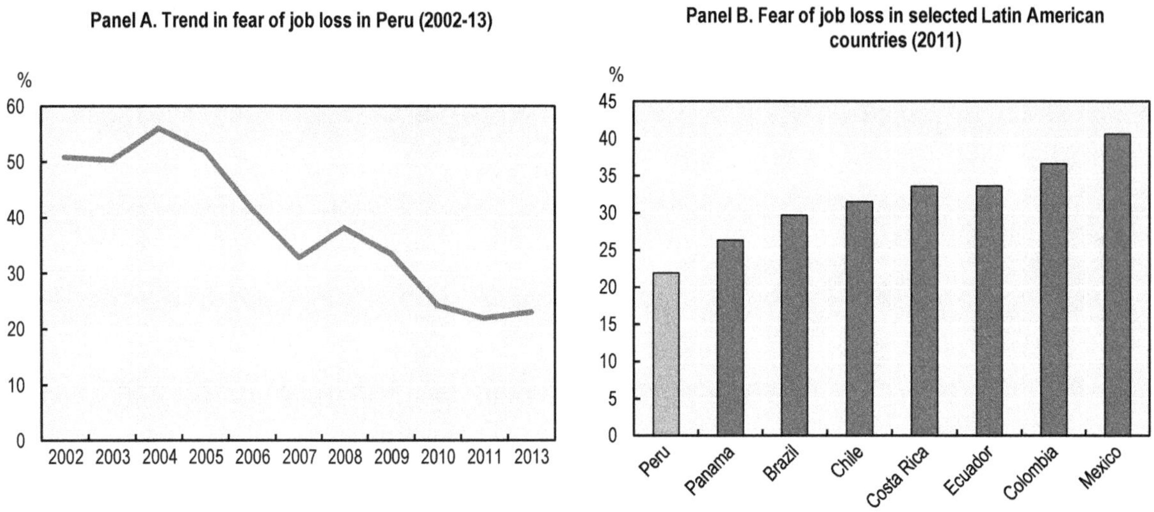

Note: Data for "fear of job loss" show the percentage of people responding "very concerned" to the question "How concerned would you say you are that you will be left without work within the next 12 months? Very concerned, concerned, a little concerned or not at all concerned? "

Source: Latinobarometro (2013), "Datos 2013", Banco de Datos (dataset), www.latinobarometro.org.

StatLink http://dx.doi.org/10.1787/888933265379

Informal employment in Peru remains high

The high employment rate outlined above is largely explained by the high proportion of people in informal work (Figure 2.28, Panel A). There is a large informal labour market in Peru, and access to formal employment is unequal. There are a number of international definitions for informality, and depending on the definition, between half and two-thirds of individuals are employed informally. According to the legal definition of CEDLAS and World Bank (i.e. informal worker is one who does not have the right to a pension when retired) 49.9% of workers in Peru were in informal work in 2011, the latest year for which we have comparable data for our benchmark countries. When using the "productive" definition (i.e. an employee in a firm with five or fewer employees, a non-professional self-employed, or a zero-income worker) 59.4% of workers fell into the informal category in 2012. International Labour Organization's (ILO) non-agricultural informal employment rate for Peru, 68.8% in 2012, was the highest share in all the benchmark countries. Using the legal definition, only Mexico has a greater share of informal employment, while Colombia has slightly higher informality rates according to the productive definition.

Figure 2.28. **Informal employment in benchmark countries and among socio-demographic groups in Peru**

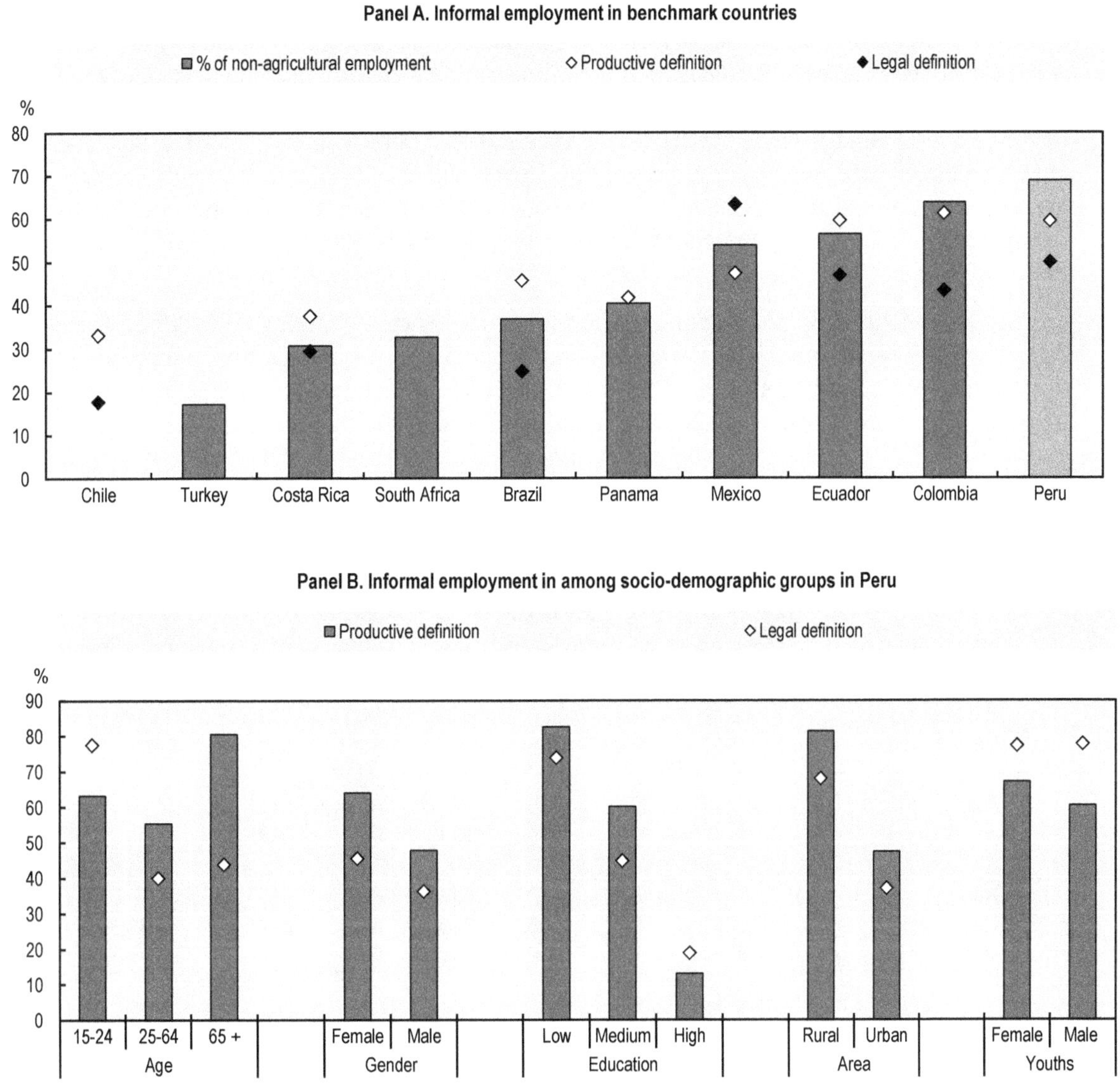

Note: Non-agricultural employment rate are based on 2013 data for Brazil, Colombia, Costa Rica, Mexico, Panama, Peru and Turkey; 2010 data for South Africa and Ecuador. No data available for Chile in that indicator. Productive and legal definitions are based on 2011-2012 data.

Source: CEDLAS and World Bank (2014), *Socio-Economic Database for Latin America and the Caribbean (SEDLAC)* (database) for legal and productive definitions, http://sedlac.econo.unlp.edu.ar/eng/index.php and ILO (2014), Key Indicators of the Labour Market, 8th Edition, International Labour Office, Geneva for non-agricultural definition.

StatLink http://dx.doi.org/10.1787/888933265385

There are also remarkable differences across socio-demographic groups with respect to access to formal employment. Taking the productive definition first, informality is higher among young and older workers, women, the less educated and those working in rural areas. Informality reaches 80% among workers over 65 years, the less educated and rural workers, whereas it is only 13% among highly educated workers. These inequalities also hold when using the legal definition of informality. The only difference in the pattern relates to the older workers. The shares of prime-age and older workers who do not have right to a pension when retired are similar, at 40% and 43.8% respectively. By this measure, 77% of Peru's young people are in informal work (Figure 2.28, Panel B).

There are also significant regional discrepancies in access to formal jobs. The sharpest contrast is between Metropolitan Lima and the rest of the country: 53.7% of employment was informal in Metropolitan Lima in 2013, compared with 84.1% for the rest of Peru (INEI, 2014a; Table 2.1).[5] A similar contrast persists between urban and rural employment, where informal jobs represent 66.5% and 95.4% of the total respectively. Similarly, the Costa regions have the lowest incidence of informal employment: 65.1% compared with 83.4% in the Sierra regions and 84.6% in the *Selva* regions. Similar regional disparities can be observed in levels of labour productivity (Chapter 5).

While there has been a remarkable reduction in informal employment in the Lima Metropolitan region, other urban areas and in the Costa regions, the decline in informality in the more disadvantaged, areas has been modest, increasing further the gap across regions. For example between 2008 and 2013 informality decreased by 7.8% in urban areas (from 72.1% to 66.5%), whereas in rural areas there was only a 1.2% decline (from 96.5% to 95.4%, Table 2.1).

Table 2.1. **Informal employment trends in Peru's regions, 2008-13**

Percentages

	2008	2009	2010	2011	2012	2013	% change
National	79.1	77.2	77.1	75.0	74.3	73.7	-6.84
Lima Metropolitan	60.4	56.8	58.0	54.3	54.6	53.7	-11.04
Rest of the country	88.6	87.4	86.8	85.7	84.6	84.1	-5.07
Urban	72.1	69.6	69.9	67.4	66.8	66.5	-7.82
Rural	96.5	96.3	96.1	96.1	95.9	95.4	-1.17
Costa	71.8	69.1	69.5	66.4	65.8	65.1	-9.31
Sierra	87.2	86.1	85.6	84.5	84.2	83.4	-4.33
Selva	87.6	87.2	86.6	86.2	84.7	84.6	-3.39

Source: INEI (2014a), *Producción y Empleo Informal en el Perú: Cuenta Satélite de la Economía Informal 2007 – 2012*, INEI, Lima, Peru.

To sum up, there are significant discrepancies in access to formal employment in Peru, especially for younger workers, women, those with low education and workers from rural areas. The next section discusses the structural barriers to formal employment and whether these discrepancies are permanent, analysing transitions between the formal and the informal employment.

Moving into formal employment is not easy for all groups

Looking at rates of informal employment is useful to assess differences in levels of formality and informality across countries and across socio-demographic groups. However, it is also important to consider the persistence of employment in the two types of employment as well as transitions between them in order to examine the inequalities in the labour market. High persistence in formal and informal employment signals a high degree of segmentation in the labour market. While those with formal jobs benefit from better pay and social protection, those in informal employment remain on the periphery with poorer quality jobs. On the other hand, frequent transitions between formal and informal jobs hamper skills development and the accumulation of rights and benefits, such as severance pay and retirement benefits. This section looks at year-to-year transition rates between the two forms of employment.

There is a relatively large degree of segmentation in the Peruvian labour market, with limited mobility between formal and informal employment. Looking at the employment status of individuals over two consecutive years, we see that a large degree of persistence in formal employment characterises all the selected benchmark countries (Figure 2.29). In all countries shown in Figure 2.29, between 65% and 86% of workers were in formal employment for both 2009 and 2010, with Peru placed in the middle at 79%. Persistence in informal employment, however, is less widespread, with more cross-country variation. In Turkey, only 10% of workers were informally employed two years in a row, while in Bolivia and Peru more than half of those with informal jobs were still in informal employment a year later. This comparison supports the view that the degree of segmentation in the Peruvian labour market is relatively large.

Figure 2.29. **Persistence in formal and informal employment in benchmark countries, 2009-10**

Transitions between year *t-1* and *t*

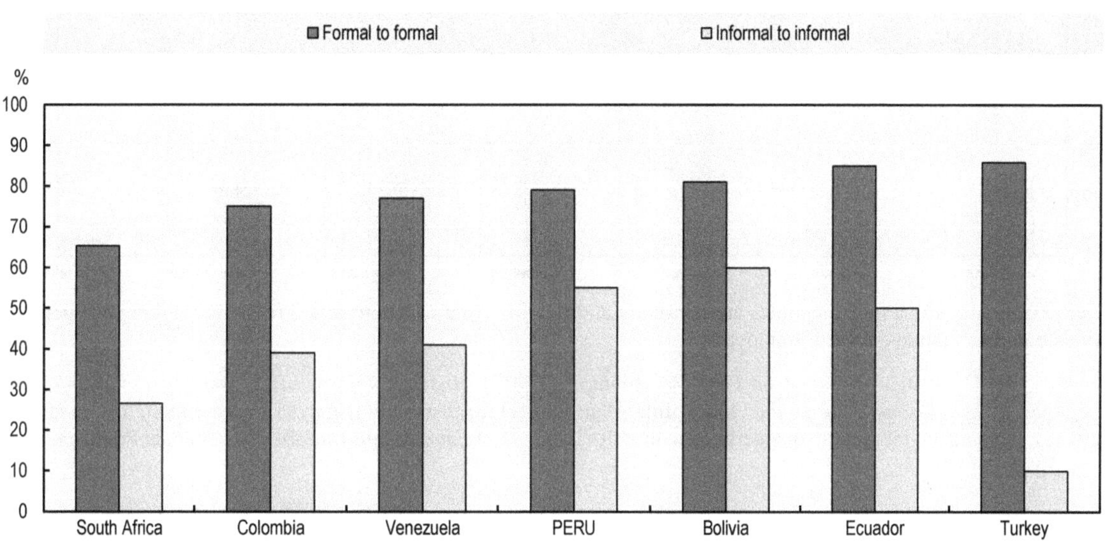

Note: For South Africa transition rates are between t and t-2. OLF (out of labour force) refers to working age population who are neither employed nor unemployed.

Source: OECD calculations based on Goñi Pacchioni, A. (2013), *Andemic Informality: Assessing Labor Informality, Employment and Income Risk in the Andes*, Inter-American Development Bank, IDB, Washington, D.C and OECD (2015c), "Enhancing job quality in emerging economies", in *OECD Employment Outlook 2015*, OECD Publishing, Paris, http://dx.doi.org/10.1787/empl_outlook-2015-en.

StatLink http://dx.doi.org/10.1787/888933265392

The other side of the coin is the flow of workers between the two types of employment: these also point to segmentation in the Peruvian labour market. Figure 2.30 shows that it is quite unlikely for people with formal jobs to move back to informal ones. With 8% of formal workers shifting to informal employment, Peru is placed right in the middle of the range among benchmark countries. The share of informal workers moving to formal jobs in one year is larger than the share of those moving from formal to informal employment in all countries except for Bolivia. The formalisation rate is particularly high in Turkey, with 62% of informal workers finding a formal job the following year. Conversely, the formalisation rate in Peru is 12%, the second lowest after Bolivia. This signals a duality in the Peruvian labour market. Low transition rates from formal to informal employment suggest that only a small proportion of workers are at risk of interrupting their skill development and accumulation of right to benefits when they have a formal job. However, high persistence in both formal and informal employment, low rates of transition from informal to formal employment, and high informality in absolute terms indicates a substantial level of segmentation in the labour market in Peru.

Figure 2.30. **Transition rates between formal and informal employment in benchmark countries, 2009-10**

Transitions between year *t-1* and *t*

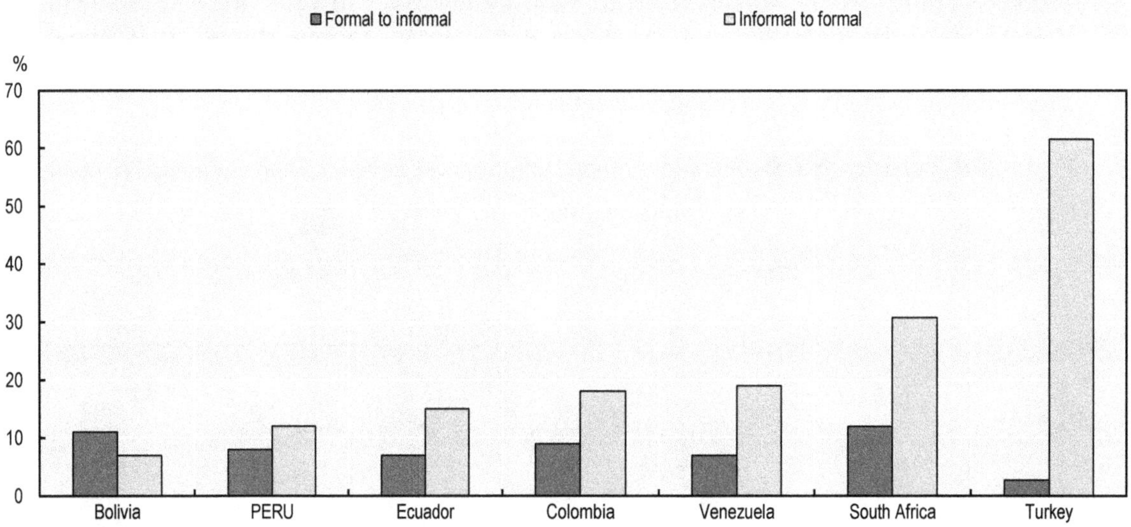

Note: For South Africa transition rates are between t and t-2. OLF (out of labour force) refers to working age population who are neither employed nor unemployed.

Source: OECD calculations based on Goñi Pacchioni, A. (2013), *Andemic Informality: Assessing Labor Informality, Employment and Income Risk in the Andes*, Inter-American Development Bank, IDB, Washington, D.C and OECD (2015c), "Enhancing job quality in emerging economies", in *OECD Employment Outlook 2015*, OECD Publishing, Paris, http://dx.doi.org/10.1787/empl_outlook-2015-en.

StatLink http://dx.doi.org/10.1787/888933265400

Labour flow analysis by socio-demographic groups reveals notable differences in labour market mobility in Peru. Figure 2.31 shows very small difference across socio-demographic groups in persistence in informal work over two consecutive years. However, there are remarkable differences across groups in terms of persistence in formal employment. Women, prime-age workers, high-school graduates, and workers in firms with ten or more employees are more likely to stay in formal employment than other groups.

Figure 2.31. **Persistence in formal and informal employment by socio-demographic group, 2009-10**

Transitions between year *t-1* and *t*

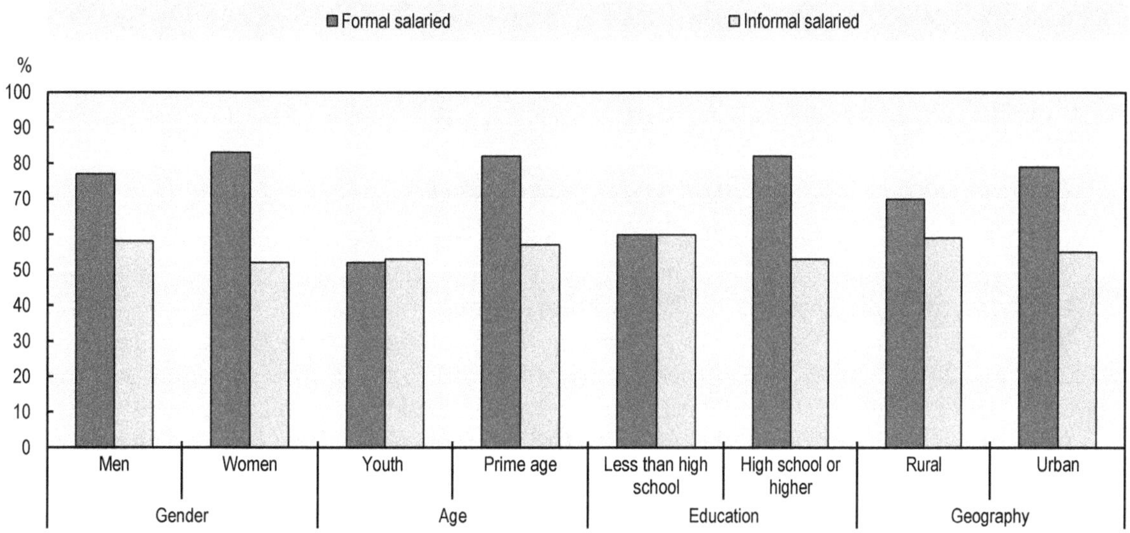

Source: OECD calculations based on Goñi Pacchioni, A. (2013), *Andemic Informality: Assessing Labor Informality, Employment and Income Risk in the Andes*, Inter-American Development Bank, IDB, Washington, D.C.

StatLink http://dx.doi.org/10.1787/888933265416

Figure 2.32. **Transition between formal and informal employment by socio-demographic group, 2009-10**

Transitions between year *t-1* and *t*

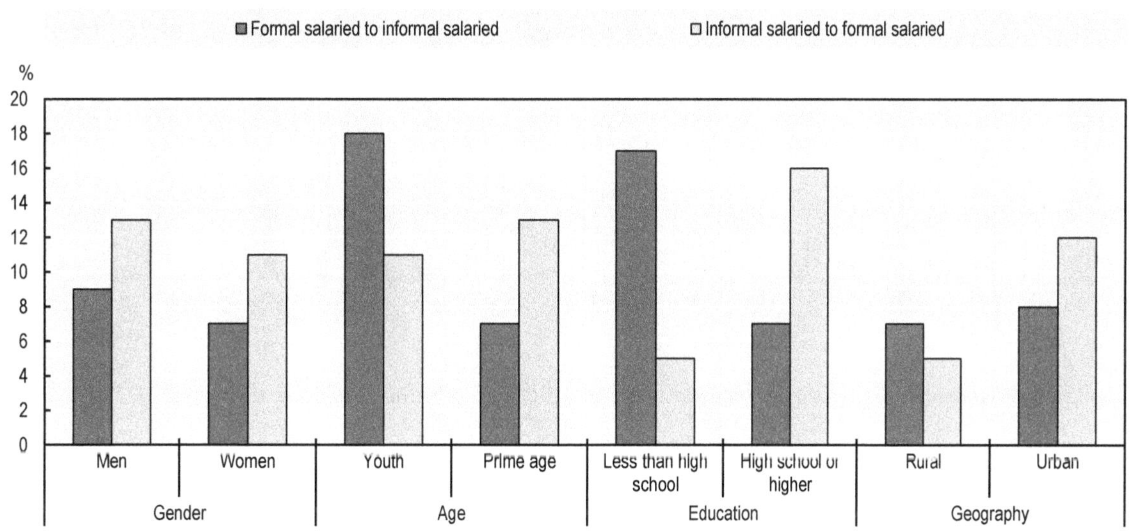

Source: OECD calculations based on Goñi Pacchioni, A. (2013), *Andemic Informality: Assessing Labor Informality, Employment and Income Risk in the Andes*, Inter-American Development Bank, IDB, Washington, DC.

StatLink http://dx.doi.org/10.1787/888933265424

The socio-demographic differences in transitions between formal and informal work are more concerning (Figure 2.32). Both men and women are more likely to move from informal to formal employment than from formal to informal employment, with little difference between their transition rates. However, for young workers between 16 and 25, for the low skilled and for rural workers, the probability of moving from formal to the informal jobs is greater than the probability of moving from informal to formal jobs. In contrast, prime-age workers, high-school graduates and urban workers are more likely to move into the formal sector than out of it. These figures reinforce the picture of higher incidence of informality among the same socio-demographic groups: young, low-skilled and urban workers face barriers to both accessing and remaining in formal employment.

Pay and work hours have improved in recent years

The material conditions of households in Peru depend heavily on workers' wages. The economic conditions of working individuals have improved substantially in the last ten years, with the share of workers who are extremely poor (i.e. those who live in households with less than USD 1.25 per day, PPP) falling from 13.1% to 5% between 2000 and 2010 (Figure 2.33). The share of workers in the middle class also grew over the same period. Nonetheless, one-third of employed individuals were still considered "poor" in 2010, with a daily income below USD 4 (PPP). This places Peru behind other Latin American countries such as Chile, Costa Rica, Brazil, Mexico, Panama, Ecuador and Turkey in terms of the share of workers who are 'poor' and only outperforming Colombia and South Africa.

Figure 2.33. **Employment and economic class**

Shares, in total employment

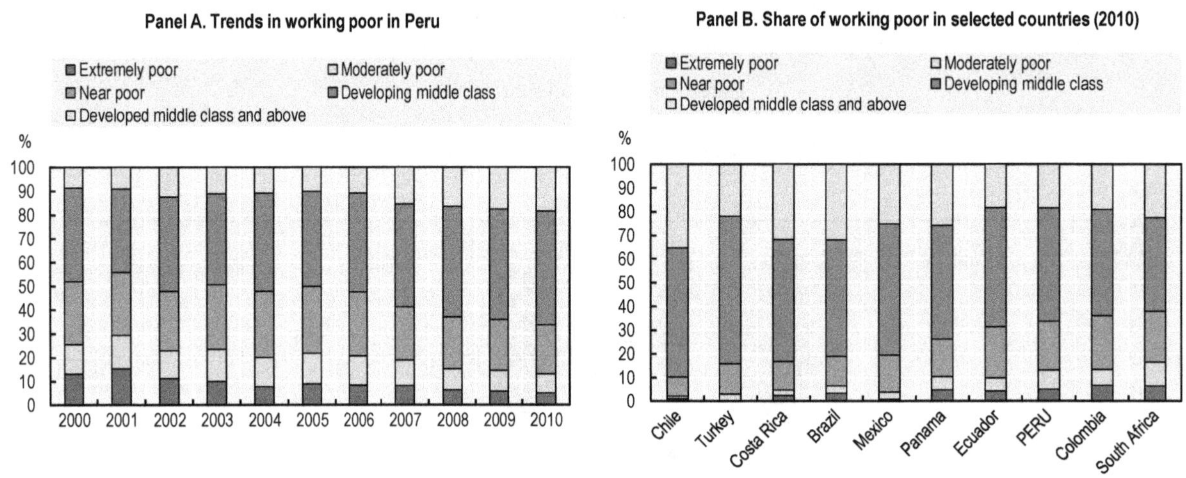

Note: Extremely poor: <USD 1.25, PPP; moderately poor: ≥USD 1.25 & <USD 2, PPP; near poor: ≥USD 2 and <USD 4, PPP; developing middle class: ≥USD 4 and <USD 13, PPP; developed middle class: ≥USD 13, PPP.

Source: ILO (2014), *Key Indicators of the Labour Market*, 8th Edition, International Labour Office, Geneva.

StatLink http://dx.doi.org/10.1787/888933265436

The minimum wage in Peru has risen in the last five years, placing Peru among those countries with a relatively high minimum-to-mean wage ratio. In absolute terms, the minimum wage increased from PEN 500 (Peruvian soles, equivalent to USD 153) to PEN 750 (USD 269) between 2007 and 2013. Panel B of Figure 2.34 shows the ratio of the minimum wage to mean wage in Peru, in the Lima Metropolitan area, and in the rest of the country. Two periods can be distinguished. Minimum wage relative to mean wage shrank steadily between 2007 and 2010, falling from 0.67 in 2007 to 0.57 in 2010. Following the recent rises in the minimum wage, this ratio increased to 0.63 by 2013. Similarly, the minimum wage was 41% of the mean wage in the Lima Metropolitan area in 2009 (the lowest level observed since 2007) but recovered to 48% in 2013. In 2007 the minimum wage was 85% of the mean wage in the regions outside the Lima area. This ratio steadily decreased until 2010 to a level of 68% and recovered partly in 2013 to 76%. Empirical evidence suggests that when the minimum wage exceeds remuneration based on productivity levels, job creation in the formal sector can be hampered (Jaramillo, 2012; Céspedes, 2006). In order to ensure that minimum wage does not increase informality, further increases in minimum wage should be linked to improvements in labour productivity.

Figure 2.34. **Minimum wages and the ratio of minimum wages to mean wages**

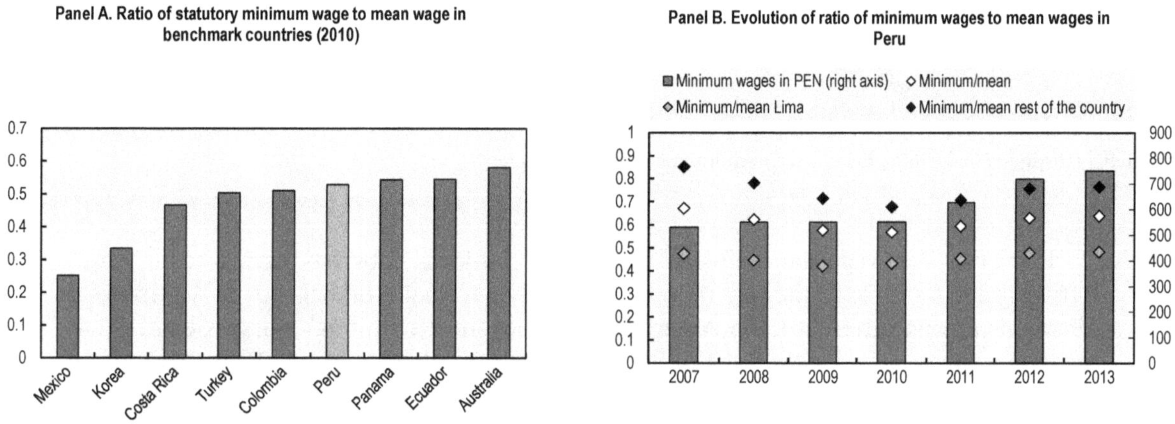

Source: ILO (2015), "Global Wage Report, Earnings and Employment Related Income" (database), International Labour Organisation, Geneva for benchmark countries, http://www.ilo.org/ilostat/GWR?_afrLoop=1879138947117377&_adf.ctrl-state=vonxe8gvc_4 and "Evolución de los Indicadores de Empleo e Ingresos por Departamento", 2004-2013, Instituto Nacional de Estadística e Información (INEI) for trends in Peru.

StatLink http://dx.doi.org/10.1787/888933265448

Peru exhibits large and persistent territorial inequalities in wage levels. Data from the INEI show that average wages were the lowest in Huancavelica, Ayacucho, Apurímac and Puno, and the highest in Tacna, Callao, Arequipa, Lima provincial, Moquegua and Madre de Dios in 2013 (Figure 2.35). Wages in the highest region, Madre de Dios, are 2.8 times higher than Huancavelica and 1.6 times higher than the mean wage in the country. These ratios were 2.9 and 1.4 in 2007. Even though minimum wages (and their ratio to mean wage) improved between 2010 and 2013, regional differences in mean wages seem to be persistent. Again, the main determinants of these disparities are differences in labour productivity across geographical regions (Chapter 5).

Informal employment is strongly associated with lower wages; thus regions with high rates of informality are likely to experience lower average wages. This is borne out for Peru's 25 administrative regions. The correlation between the share of informal employment and mean wages across regions is -0.75 (Figure 2.35). High informality depresses mean wages and thus decreases the mean-to-minimum-wage ratio.

Figure 2.35. **Regional variations in informal work and wages, 2013**

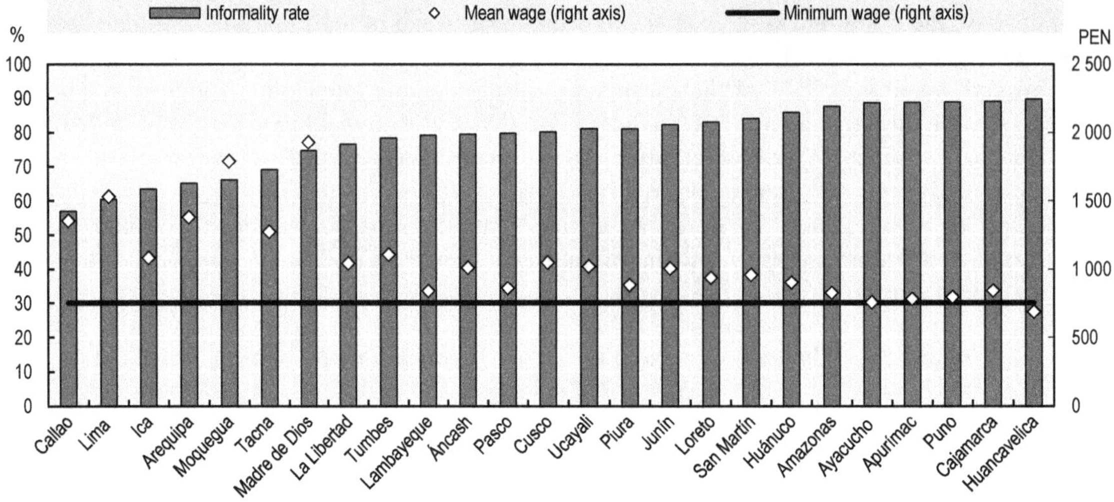

Source: INEI (2014b), *Perú: Evolución de los Indicadores de Empleo e Ingresos por Departamento, 2004-2013*, INEI (Instituto Nacional de Estadística e Informática), Lima, Peru.

StatLink http://dx.doi.org/10.1787/888933265455

However, the wage gap between formal and informal jobs has narrowed in Peru. Between 2003 and 2012 the pay ratio of informal to formal workers moved in different directions among different Latin American countries. In Peru formal workers earned 2.4 times more than informal workers in 2003, but the ratio decreased to 1.9 by 2012. This was one of the strongest declines, together with Panama, recorded in Latin America. In the case of Peru, the relative convergence in pay was mainly driven by an increase in the hourly pay for informal workers rather than by declines in the wages of formal workers.[6]

Working hours not only determine total earnings but also have important implications for worker well-being. While time-related underemployment is undesirable as it lowers productivity, working very long hours is typically associated with poor health. Long working hours generally reflect the degree of (or lack of) enforcement of regulations concerning working conditions. Actual weekly work hours in Peru are relatively high, especially compared to OECD countries (Chapter 3). Working hours are also significantly longer than in some Latin American countries such as Brazil, Panama and Ecuador. However, Peru has experienced a decline in weekly hours since 2008 for both men and women and for workers with different levels of education (Figure 2.36).

Figure 2.36. **Weekly working hours in benchmark countries and Peru**

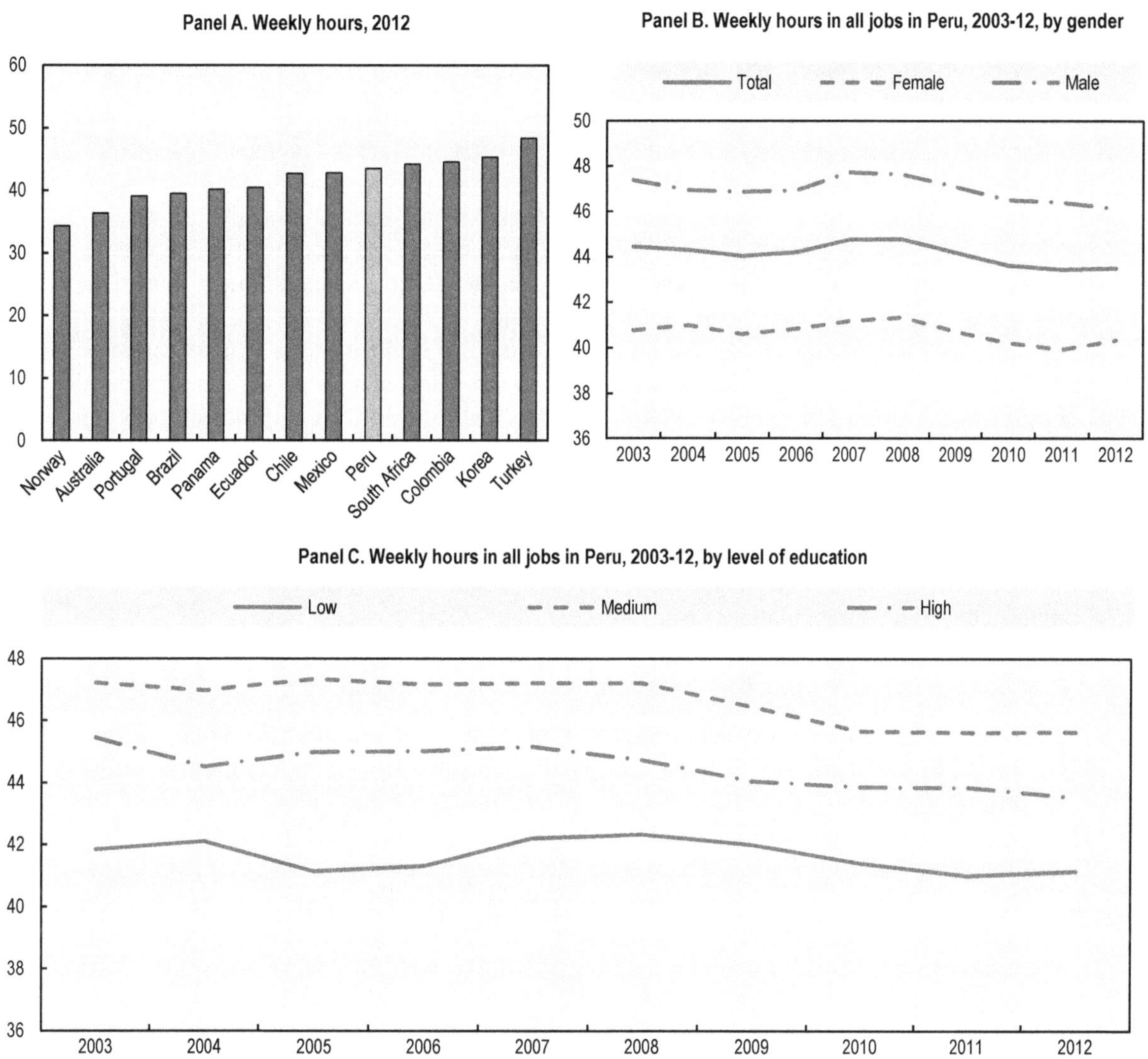

Source: OECD calculations based on CEDLAS and World Bank (2014), *Socio-Economic Database for Latin America and the Caribbean (SEDLAC)* (database) for Colombia, Ecuador, Panama and Peru, http://sedlac.econo.unlp.edu.ar/eng/index.php and OECD Labour Force Statistics (database), http://stats.oecd.org/Index.aspx?DataSetCode=AVE_HRS for Australia, Brazil, Chile, Korea, Mexico, Portugal and Turkey.

StatLink http://dx.doi.org/10.1787/888933265465

Labour regulation remains complex and its enforcement poor

Peru is one of the countries in the world with the lowest level of compliance with labour regulations but it remains one of the most regulated labour markets even after a series of deregulatory reforms. Peru went through two rounds of "flexibilisation", one in 1991/2 and the other in 1995/6, replacing its once highly regulated labour system. These reforms had, however, negative implications for working conditions and hiring procedures, as well as employment termination procedures. The rapid deregulation of the labour market shifted the balance heavily in favour of employers by eliminating many of the institutions responsible for granting collective bargaining power to workers (Chacaltana, 2003). This has had a negative impact on job quality for workers in small and medium-size enterprises. Furthermore, the 2008 Legislative Decree 1086 substantially weakened the terms and conditions of work in the majority of workplaces, lowering the amount of paid leave and wages for all workers in workplaces of 100 or fewer workers. Poor enforcement mechanisms by the Ministry of Labour and the Promotion of Employment, and little oversight by local authorities on SME's intensified the deterioration of worker rights and benefits.

Peru has an elaborate but fragmented labour legislation. All labour contracts, in principle, are open ended. With either a verbal or written contract, a job is assumed to be of indefinite duration until there is mutual agreement on its termination. After a probationary period, employees are protected against arbitrary dismissal. However, Peruvian law specifies a number of conditions that permit employees to be contracted on a fixed-term or part-time basis, either directly by employers or through temporary work agencies. Regulations for fixed-term contracts distinguish between nine forms falling into three main groups: contracts with a temporary nature (beginning new activity, market needs and corporate restructuring), contracts with an accidental nature (occasional, replacement and emergency) and contracts for a specific work or service (for certain work or specific services, intermittent services and seasonal activities). In addition, a special labour regime regulates working conditions of employees in SME's. On the whole, there are nearly 40 different labour regulations applying to different types of work in Peru (India stands out as another country where employment is regulated by 45 distinct legislations). This fragmentation contributes to Peru's low compliance with labour regulations.

Efforts to reduce informality have yet to have much impact

Peru has made efforts to reduce informality, but there is ample room for improvement. Over the last few decades, the Peruvian state has implemented various programmes to create jobs, provide vocational training and encourage formalisation. These include *Construyendo Peru, ProEmpleo, Programa de Capacitación Laboral Juvenil* (PROJOVEN) and Red de Centros de Intermediación Laboral Pro-empleo (RedCIL ProEmpleo) for the creation of jobs, as well as *Mi empresa,* aimed at promoting new ventures, competitiveness and the formalisation and development of micro and small enterprises. However, most of these programmes have not had a major impact on workers' conditions and access to social benefits, or on formal employment. Only PROJOVEN made substantive improvements in training provision and in the conditions of young people in Peru (Toyama et al., 2009).

The extent of recent formalisation in Peru was dependent on two factors: the supervision and oversight capacity of the Labour Inspectorate, and the actions of the courts and labour chambers in resolving disputes. Thanks to the favourable economic climate, Peru achieved significant reductions in informality between 2004 and 2012 through initiatives undertaken by the Ministry of Labour (Figure 2.37). Before the implementation of the e-payroll in August 2007, employers with three or more workers had to send a report to the Ministry of Labour regarding their workers, previous workers receiving old-age benefits from the firm, service providers, personnel in training courses, and outsourced workers. With the new electronic system, firms now send these reports directly to the National Tax Authority. This reform has increased the capacity of the Ministry of Labour to monitor compliance with labour obligations (FORLAC, 2014). Another initiative, *Plan Reto* (Mandatory Registration of Payroll Workers) was introduced between December 2008 and May 2011 to allow labour inspections of unregistered workers on enterprise payrolls. The plan is now complete but inspections of private enterprises continue. However, the judicial system is ineffective as it is overburdened and it cannot fully contribute to formalisation through resolving disputes, although the judiciary adopted some changes to reduce its workload.

Figure 2.37. **Formalisation outcomes in Latin America**

Panel A. Trends of informal employment in Peru

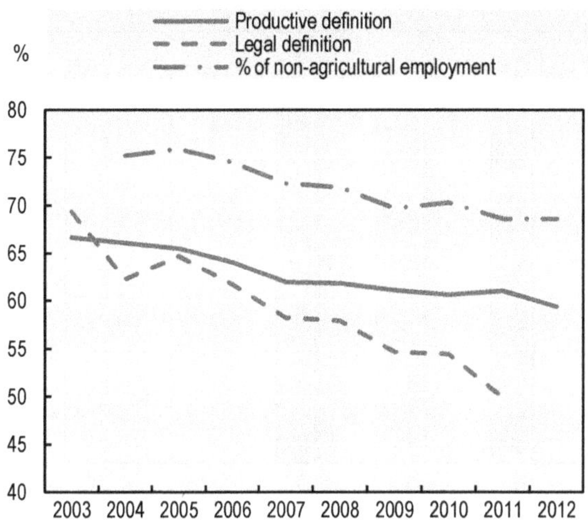

Panel B. Reduction in informal employment in selected Latin American countries

	Period	Decline in share
Mexico	2010-13	0.7
Colombia	2009-12	2.3
Peru	2004-12	6.6
Ecuador	2009-12	10.8
Brazil	2002-12	13.9

Source: CEDLAS and World Bank (2014), *Socio-Economic Database for Latin America and the Caribbean (SEDLAC)* (database) for legal and productive definitions, http://sedlac.econo.unlp.edu.ar/eng/index.php; ILO (2014), Key Indicators of the Labour Market, 8th Edition, International Labour Office, Geneva for non-agricultural definition, and FORLAC (2014), *Notes on Formalization: Trends in informal employment in Peru: 2004-2012*, International Labour Organisation, Regional Office for Latin America and the Caribbean, for reduction in informality.

StatLink http://dx.doi.org/10.1787/888933265477

Another recent initiative was the *Ley de Régimen Laboral Juvenil* (known as "Ley Pulpín") aimed at promoting youth access to labour markets and social protection. The law was passed in the congress in December 2014 and advocated as a key policy to solve the problem of high informality and low productivity among young people. The new law was controversial because it gave tax benefits to employers reducing their labour costs while cutting benefits (wages, holidays and severance payments) to young people. The law was scrapped in early 2015 by the congress as a result of strong opposition, particularly from the youth.

Incentives to formalise jobs have focused mainly on cost reduction, rather than creating market-based incentives for enterprises opting for formality. Non-wage labour costs are high in Peru. Despite deregulation of the labour market, the wedge created by compulsory payment increased drastically during the 1990s (Chong et al., 2007). In 2008, contributions and taxes, vacations, dismissal pay and other benefits were estimated to represent 59% of the total remuneration in Peru (Pagés, 2010). This value was the highest among Latin American and Caribbean countries for which comparable data were available, and well above levels observed in Jamaica (10.4%), Venezuela (22.9%), Chile (31.7%), Costa Rica (33%) and Mexico (36.4%). More recent data comparing Peru and Colombia with OECD countries show that the wedge created by compulsory payments in Peru was among the highest, at 46.7% of total labour cost (Figure 2.38). High non-wage labour costs provide incentive to firms to remain informal. However, labour reforms targeting cost cutting only at SMEs by reducing employee benefits will not have enough impact, let alone improve working conditions. The government should rather adopt active policies focusing on market incentives, for example by providing special treatment for investment in training programmes or frameworks for improving productivity and competitiveness.

Figure 2.38. **Average compulsory payment wedge as a percentage of augmented total labour costs in selected OECD benchmark countries and Peru**

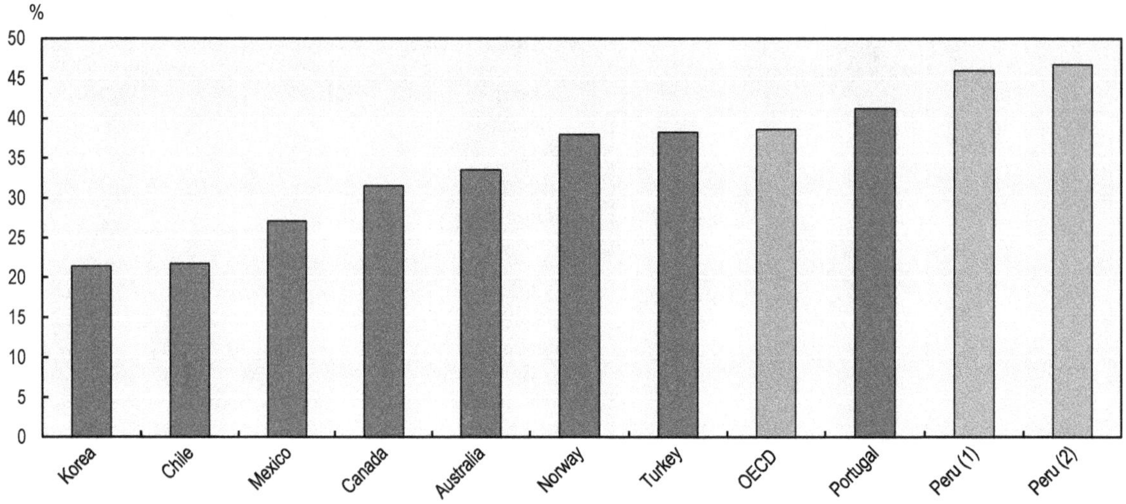

Note: 2014 data. (1) Basic. (2) Manufacturing workers with SENATI.

Source: OECD (2015d), *OECD Tax Database*, http://www.oecd.org/tax/tax-policy/tax-database.htm for OECD countries, and online tax calculator http://www.elempleo.com.pe/empresas/calculadora/calculadora_empresasPe.aspx for Peru.

StatLink http://dx.doi.org/10.1787/888933265488

Reforms to labour regulations have also reduced enterprises' firing costs but other obstacles remain, limiting firms' capacity to formalise their jobs. Individual dismissals are not allowed unless there is a legal basis or misconduct on the part of the worker; otherwise workers have a right to severance pay consisting of 1.5 times their monthly salary for each year of service up to a maximum of 12 monthly salaries in the case of an indefinite-term relationship. Neither the notice period for redundancy nor severance pay are very high in Peru (Figure 2.39). Furthermore, the firing cost (measured in weeks of wages) was reduced to 17 weeks in 2010 (from 52 weeks in 2005, Figure 2.40). However, regulations regarding dismissals in the case of bankruptcy or financial difficulty prevent firms from dismissing workers individually, unless they dismiss ten or more workers at the same time. Allowing enterprises to process individual lay-offs for economic reasons could lower overall firing costs, hence encouraging firms to hire more workers on a formal basis (Toyama et al., 2009).

Informality and low labour productivity are closely related. The improvements in the Peruvian economy have not so far translated into an adequate increase in labour productivity (Chapter 3). The drastic decline and slow recovery in labour productivity are caused by the economic instabilities experienced in the 1980s and 1990s and the change in the demographic structure of the country, as the young and unskilled population became more important (Chacaltana and Yamada, 2009). Declining productivity in the 1990s together with a remarkable increase in the non-wage labour cost, both to employers and to employees, lowered firms' incentives to formalise, and many small firms opted for operating informally (Chong et al., 2007). Workers in the lowest quintile of the earnings distribution had to opt for current compensation over future compensation by voluntarily taking informal jobs where they do not contribute for benefits (Yamada, 1996; Saavedra and Chong, 1999).

Figure 2.39. **Dismissal and severance pay regulations in benchmark countries**

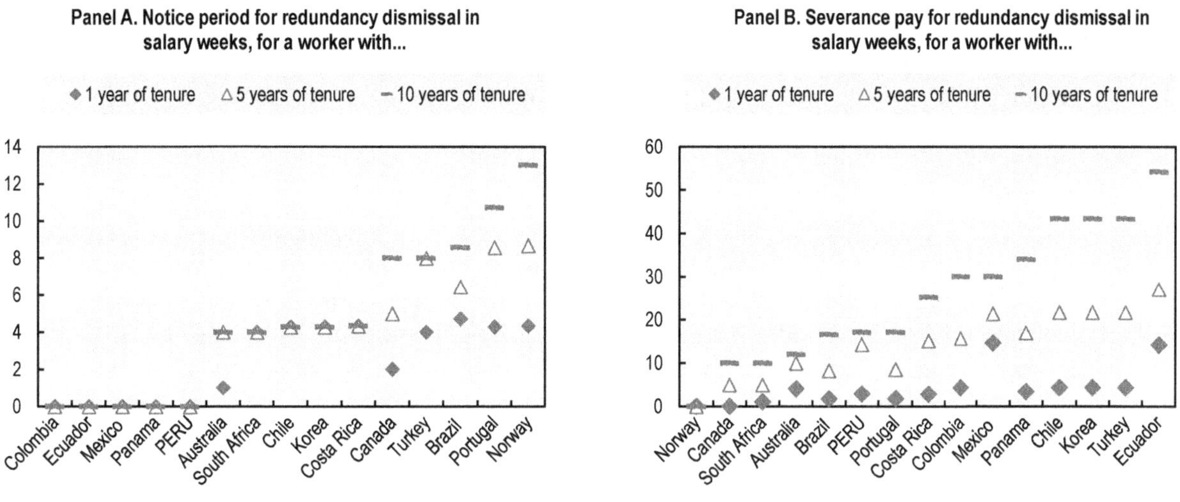

Source: World Bank (2015c) Doing Business, Labour Market Regulations (database), http://www.doingbusiness.org/data/exploretopics/labor-market-regulation.

StatLink http://dx.doi.org/10.1787/888933265500

Figure 2.40. **Firing cost measured in weeks of wages in benchmark countries, 2005 and 2010**

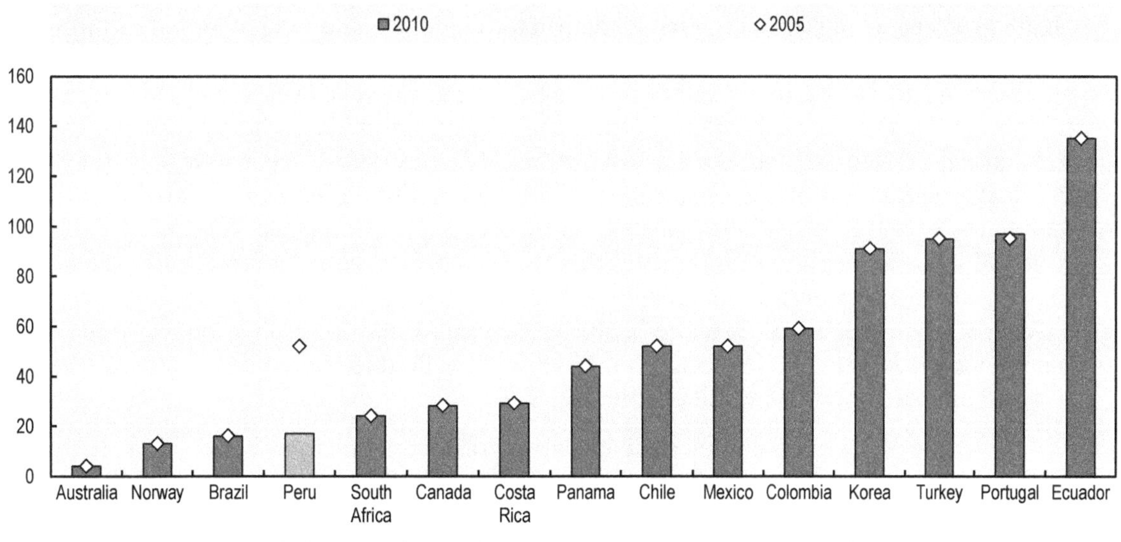

Note: Firing cost is the cost of advance notice requirements, severance payments and penalties due when terminating a redundant worker, expressed in weekly wages. One month is recorded as 4 and 1/3 weeks. Data are listed for 2010 are for June 2011.

Source: World Bank (2012), *The Little Data Book on Private Sector Development 2012*, World Development Indicators, World Bank, Washington, DC.

StatLink http://dx.doi.org/10.1787/888933265497

The productivity differences between the formal and the informal jobs are mainly due to high non-wage labour costs and skill differences between workers in formal and informal employment. Recent efforts to reduce the non-wage labour cost should be maintained, combined with a comprehensive skill strategy to increase the human capital of the Peruvian labour force. The PROJOVEN programme, mentioned above, offered training to disadvantaged youth and resulted in improvements in individuals' productivity and lower informality among the target population (Chong et al., 2007). There are also significant differences in productivity levels between different sectors of the Peruvian economy; this requires orienting the economy towards the more productive sectors but also developing sector-specific policies to promote productivity (Chacaltana and Yamada, 2009).

Conclusions

Peru has made great social and economic strides in recent years. Poverty levels have fallen, the size of the middle class has increased, and inequalities have been reduced. However, the gaps between different socio-economic groups are still very large, and many people are at risk of falling back into poverty. In this context, the three areas of health, education and skills, and work are key to inclusive and sustainable development and ultimately improving the well-being of all. There have been advances in all three areas within the last decade, in part due to the favourable economic climate and to policy reforms adopted by the administration. However, the analysis presented in this chapter reveals the existing challenges in these dimensions that are still holding the country back on its sustainable and inclusive development path.

Although life expectancy at birth, a general indicator of overall health, is close to the one expected for a country at Peru's level of economic development, many people live with disability and child mortality rates are high. The share of Peruvians who report health problems is higher than in most comparator countries, and the proportion of those who are satisfied with their personal health is also lower. Peru has made remarkable advances in terms of health insurance provision over the last seven years, particularly due to *Sistema Integral de Salud* (SIS), a non-contributory insurance scheme covering the most disadvantaged segments of the population. However, major inequalities remain in the quality and extent of the healthcare services between those who are covered by SIS and those covered by *EsSalud* and the army and police insurance scheme. This is reflected in lower levels of satisfaction, access to and confidence in the healthcare system. Despite increasing coverage, the quality of health system falls short of acceptable levels especially in remote areas. Training health professionals and increasing the capacity of human resources in the health sector will be critical for Peru to overcome the inequalities in healthcare and improve overall quality.

In terms of education, considerable expansion of access has been achieved in recent years, although gaps still remain when compared to OECD standards. The poor quality and relevance of education are still challenges, as are the low levels of financial resources devoted to it. Public investment in education in Peru is well below the OECD average, and there is room for more investment. Improving the quality of teaching and learning, as well as reducing overall inequalities should be the priority. School-specific policies such as extra classes taken by students, feedback from the school principals to teachers, and weekly classroom time can help improve students' performance (Avendano et al., 2015).

The education system is also not well-geared to the needs of the labour market, and there is a mismatch between the available pool of skills and what the economy demands. The role of vocational education and training, as well as a stronger emphasis on the skills most needed by the business sector (i.e. technical and soft skills) remain crucial to foster a better matching between the demand and supply of skills, as well as to favour employability and social inclusion. Effective mechanisms for skills matching between demand and supply are needed, such as providing information on career paths through qualification frameworks and setting up mechanisms to anticipate future demands, even at the sectorial level. Life-long learning is also key, including mechanisms to provide training at the workplace to update and renew workers' skills.

Peru stands out as a society with a remarkably high employment rate. However, informal work accounts for a large share of employment, the labour market is highly segmented, working conditions are poor and there are large inequalities in the workforce. High informality and poor working conditions are perpetuated by the high costs of formalising, strict regulation of the labour market, weak labour inspections and the lack of an overarching labour law which is obstructing the enforcement of labour laws. In recent years Peru adopted a number of programmes to reduce informality and improve job quality. Nonetheless, informality remains high, even compared to other Latin American economies. More needs to be done to increase formalisation and improve the working conditions for all segments of the population. To reduce informality, a combination of policies should be adopted, such as programmes facilitating companies' and workers' registration in the formal sector, reductions in non-wage labour costs, and improving labour productivity through training programmes.

Notes

1. The poverty gap is a measure of the "intensity of poverty". It measures how far the poor are from the poverty line. It is calculated as a proportion of the poverty line, and thus expressed as a percentage, so that the larger the percentage, the larger the distance.

2. According to INEI, total poverty includes individuals who belong to a household where either income or consumption per capita is less than the cost of a minimum basket and essential goods and services; extreme poverty includes those where either income or consumption per capita is below the value of a minimum basket of food.

3. Based on data provided by INEI.

4. The latest year with comparable data.

5. Note that there is a small discrepancy between the numbers from CEDLAS and World Bank, and those from INEI due to different definitions of informality. INEI defines informal employment as the set of jobs that do not have the benefits mandated by law.

6. Based on CEDLAS and World Bank (2014) data.

References

Alfageme, A. and J. Guabloche (2014), "Educación Técnica en el Perú: Lecciones aprendidas y retos en un país en crecimiento", *Revista Moneda 157*, March, Banco Central de Reserva del Perú.

ANR (2012), Asamblea Nacional de Rectores (Datos Estadísticos Universitario, Dirección de Estadística), http://censos.inei.gob.pe/cenaun/redatam_inei/doc/ESTADISTICA_UNIVERSITARIAS.pdf

Apoyo Consultoria, (2013), "Cuatro medidas para enfrentar la escasez de mano de obra calificada", *Propuesta de Política*, No. 1, Julio 2013.

Avendano R., F. Barrera, S. Nieto-Parra and F. Vever (2015), "Understanding student performance beyond traditional factors: Evidence from PISA 2012 in Latin America", Development Centre Working Paper, OECD Publishing, Paris.

Barro, R. and J-W Lee (2010), "A new Data Set of Educational Attainment in the World, 1950-2010", *Journal of Development Economics,* vol. 104, pp. 184-198.

CAF (2014), "Educación técnica y formación profesional en América Latina. El reto de la productividad", *Serie Políticas Públicas y Transformación Productiva,* No. 13/2014, CAF, http://publicaciones.caf.com/media/38365/educacion_tecnica_formacion_profesional.pdf.

Castro, J.F. and G. Yamada (2013), "Evolución reciente de la calidad de la educación superior en Perú: No son buenas noticias", in Calidad y Acreditación de la educación superior: retos urgentes para el Perú, Universidad del Pacífico and Consejo de Evaluación, Acreditación y Certificación de la Calidad de la Educación Superior Universitaria.

Castro, J.F. and G. Yamada (2011), "Brechas étnicas y de sexo en el acceso a la educación básica y superior en el Perú", *Working Papers,* No. 11-04, Departamento de Economía, Universidad del Pacífico.

CEDLAS and World Bank (2014), *Socio-Economic Database for Latin America and the Caribbean (SEDLAC)* (database), CEDLAS (Centre for Distributive and Labour Studies) and the World Bank, http://sedlac.econo.unlp.edu.ar/eng/index.php

CEPALSTAT (2015), *Databases and Statistical Publications, Economic Commission for Latin America and the Caribbean*, Accessed on April 2015.

Céspedes, N. (2006), "Efectos del salario mínimo en el mercado laboral peruano", *Estudios Económicos*, 13, Banco Central de Reserva del Peru, Lima.

Chacaltana, J. (2003), "Public policy and employment in micro and small enterprises in Peru", *SEED Working Paper*, No. 56, International Labour Office, Geneva.

Chacaltana, J. and G. Yamada (2009), "Calidad del empleo u productividad laboral en el Perú", *IDB Working papers*, No 691, IDB (Inter-American Development Bank), Washington, DC.

Chong, A., J. Galdo and J. Saaverda-Chanduvi (2007), "Informality and productivity in the labor market: Peru 1986-2001", *Economics Faculty Scholarship*, Paper 141, Syracuse University.

Cuenca, R. (2015), "Políticas en Educación superior en Perú", in J.J Brunner (ed.), *Políticas de Educación Superior en Iberoamérica.*

ECLAC (2014), *Panorama Social de América Latina 2014*, (LC/G.2635-P), Santiago de Chile, 2014.

ESCALE (2015), *Estadística de la calidad educativa* (database), Ministerio de Educación, http://escale.minedu.gob.pe/

Ferreira, F., J. Messina, J. Rigolini, L-F. Lopez-Calva, M.A. Lugo and R. Vakis (2013), *Economic Mobility and the Rise of the Latin American Middle Class*, World Bank Latin America and Caribbean Studies, Washington DC, World Bank.

FORLAC (2014), *Notes on Formalization: Trends in Informal Employment in Peru: 2004-2012*, FORLAC (Programme for the Promotion of Formalization in Latin America and the Caribbean) and ILO (International Labour Organization).

Gallup Organisation (2015), *Gallup World Monitor* (database).

Goñi Pacchioni, A. (2013), *Andemic Informality: Assessing Labor Informality, Employment and Income Risk in the Andes*, IDB, Washington, DC.

Hanushek, E. and L. Woessmann, (2007), "The role of education quality in economic growth", *World Bank Policy Research Working Paper*, No. 4122, World Bank, Washington DC, https://openknowledge.worldbank.org/bitstream/handle/10986/7154/wps4122.pdf.

ILO (2014), *Key Indicators of the Labour Market*, 8th Edition, International Labour Office, Geneva.

INEI (2015), *Estadísticas: índice temático sociales* (database), INEI (Instituto Nacional de Estadística e Informática), Lima, Peru, http://www.inei.gob.pe/estadisticas/indice-tematico/sociales/

INEI (2014a), *Producción y Empleo Informal en el Perú: Cuenta Satélite de la Economía Informal 2007-2012*, INEI (Instituto Nacional de Estadística e Informática), Lima, Peru.

INEI (2014b), *Perú: Evolución de los Indicadores de Empleo e Ingresos por Departamento, 2004-2013*, INEI (Instituto Nacional de Estadística e Informática), Lima, Peru.

Jaramillo, M. (2012), "Ajustes del mercado laboral peruano ante cambios en el salario mínimo: la experiencia de la década de 2000", *Documento de Investigación GRADE No. 63*, Lima.

Latinobarometro (2013), *Datos 2013*, Banco de Datos dataset, www.latinobarometro.org.

Lavado, O., J. Martinez, and G. Yamada (2014), "Una promesa incumplida? La calidad de la educación universitaria y el subempleo profesional en el Perú", *Working Paper* No. 23, Asociación Peruana de Economía.

Lavigne, M. (2013), *Social Protection Systems in Latin America and the Caribbean: Peru*, Santiago, Chile, ECLAC (Economic Commission for Latin America and the Caribbean), Santiago, Chile (ECLAC).

Manpower (2014), *Talent Shortage Survey 2014, Research Results*, Manpower Group, Milwaukee, WI.

Manpower (2013), *Talent Shortage Survey 2013, Research Results*, Manpower Group, Milwaukee, WI.

Martinez-Restrepo, S. and G. Gray-Molina (2013), "Los frutos más difíciles de alcanzar en el desarrollo de América Latina", Nota de Investigación Sobre Desarrollo Humano para América Latina y el Caribe 1/2013, UNDP, Nueva York.

Mesa-Lago, C. (2005), *Las Reformas de Salud en América Latina y el Caribe: Su Impacto en los Principios de la Seguridad Social*, Project document LC/W.63, ECLAC, Santiago, Chile.

Meza-Cornejo, E. (2007), *Medicine Prices, Availability, Affordability and Price Components in Peru*, Health Action International, Latin American Coordination Office.

Ministerio de Educación (2015), Unidad de Estadística Educativa (UEE), Ministerio de Educación, Lima, Peru.

Ministerio de Educación (2014), "Ministro Saavedra sustenta presupuesto del sector educación", Ministerio de Educación, http://www.minedu.gob.pe/noticias/index.php?id=29699

Mora-Bernasconi, C. (2006), Peru - Parasalud Segunda Fase: Plan Para los Pueblos Indígenas, World Bank, Lima, Peru, http://documents.worldbank.org/curated/en/2006/06/10117710/peru-second-adaptable-program-loan-health-reform-program-project-indigenous-peoples-plan-peru-parasalud-segunda-fase-plan-para-los-pueblos-indigenas.

MTPE (2015), Principales resultados de la encuesta de demanda ocupacional en los principales departamentos del Perú, Ministerio del Trabajo y Promoción del Empleo, Lima.

OECD (2015a), *All on Board: Making Inclusive Growth Happen*, OECD Publishing, Paris, http://dx.doi.org/10.1787/9789264218512-en.

OECD (2015b), *E-Learning in Higher Education in Latin America*, Development Centre Studies, OECD Publishing, Paris, http://dx.doi.org/10.1787/9789264209992-en.

OECD (2015c), "Enhancing job quality in emerging economies", in OECD *Employment Outlook 2015*, OECD Publishing, Paris, http://dx.doi.org/10.1787/empl_outlook-2015-en

OECD (2015d), *OECD Tax Database*, OECD, www.oecd.org/tax/tax-policy/tax-database.htm.

OECD (2013), *PISA 2012 Results: Excellence through Equity (Volume II): Giving Every Student the Chance to Succeed*, PISA, OECD Publishing, Paris, http://dx.doi.org/10.1787/9789264201132-en.

OECD (2012a), "Does money buy strong performance in PISA?", PISA in Focus 13/02, OECD, Paris.

OECD (2012b), *Better Skills, Better Jobs, Better Lives: A Strategic Approach to Skills Policies*, OECD Publishing, Paris, http://dx.doi.org/10.1787/9789264177338-en.

OECD (2011), *Starting Strong III: A Quality Toolbox for Early Childhood Education and Care,* OECD Publishing, Paris, http://dx.doi.org/10.1787/9789264123564-en.

OECD/CAF/ECLAC (2014), *Latin American Economic Outlook 2015: Education, Skills and Innovation for Development*, OECD Publishing, Paris, http://dx.doi.org/10.1787/leo-2015-en.

Pagés, C. (Ed) (2010), *La era de la productividad: Como transformar las economías desde sus cimentos*, Banco Interamericano de Desarrollo, Washington, D.C.

QS University Rankings (2015), "QS World University Rankings(R) 2014/15", QS Top Universities website, www.topuniversities.com/university-rankings/world-university-rankings/2014.

Rivero, J. (2010), "Teacher performance and its impact on the quality of education in Peru", *Policy Paper*, October 2010, FOCAL (Canadian Foundation for the Americas), Ottawa, Canada.

Saavedra, J. and A. Chong (1999), "Structural reforms, institutions and earnings: Evidence from the formal and informal sectors in urban Peru", *Journal of Development Studies* Vol. 35(4), pp. 95-116.

Schady, N. (2012), "El desarrollo infantil temprano en América Latina y el Caribe: acceso, resultados y evidencia longitudinal de Ecuador", in M. Cabrol and M. Székely (eds.), *Educación para la Transformación*, BID Educación, pp. 77-92.

Seinfeld, J. and K. La Serna (2007), "Análisis económico de las compras públicas de medicamentos", *Discussion Document*, DD/07/10, Centro de Investigación, Universidad del Pacífico.

Tornarolli, L. (2014), "The evolution of the Middle Class in Latin America", *Working Paper* No. 128, International Policy Centre for Inclusive Growth, Brasilia.

Toyama Miyagusuku, J., V. Rosas Chávez, and M. Tostes Vieria (2009), "Challenges involved in the introduction of flexicurity in Peru" in Jürgen Weller (ed.), *Regulation, Worker Protection and Active Labour-Market Policies in Latin America*, UN Economic Commission for Latin America and the Caribbean, Santiago, Chile.

UNESCO/UIS (2015), UNESCO Institute for Statistics database, http://www.uis.unesco.org/Pages/default.aspx.

UNESCO (2014), *Tercer Estudio Regional Comparativo y Explicativo (TERCE),* Primera Entrega de Resultados, Oficina Regional de Educación para América Latina y el Caribe, UNESCO, Santiago, Chile.

UNESCO (2013), *Situación Educativa de América Latina y el Caribe: Hacia la Educación de Calidad para Todos al 2015*, Oficina Regional de Educación para América Latina y el Caribe, UNESCO, Santiago, Chile.

Vegas, E. and C. Coffin (2015), "Cuando el gasto en educación importa: Un análisis empírico de información internacional reciente", Documento de Trabajo del BID No.574, Banco Interamericano de Desarrollo.

Verdisco, A and H. Ñopo (2012), "Intervenciones tempranas y el reto de los recursos humanos", in M. Cabrol and M.Székely (eds.), *Educación para la Transformación*, BID Educación, pp. 93-126.

Woodhead, M., P. Ames, U. Vennam, W. Abebe, and N. Streuli (2010), "¿Equidad y Calidad? Retos para la educación inicial y la primaria en Etiopía, India y Perú", Cuadernos sobre desarrollo infantil temprano No.55, Bernard Van Leer Fondation.

World Bank (2015a), *World Development Indicators* (database), Washington, DC, http://data.worldbank.org.

World Bank (2015b), *Enterprise Surveys*, World Bank Group, www.enterprisesurveys.org/data.

World Bank (2015c), *Doing Business 2015: Going beyond Efficiency*, World Bank, Washington, DC.

World Bank (2012), *The Little Data Book on Private Sector Development 2012*, World Development Indicators, World Bank, Washington, DC.

World Bank (2011), Strengthening Skills and Employability in Peru: Final Report, Washington DC.

Yamada, G. et al. (2013), "Mayor acceso con menor calidad en la educación superior algunas evidencias desde las habilidades de los estudiantes" Universidad del Pacífico, Vol. XL N 72, 2013, pp. 7-32.

Yamada, G. (1996), "Urban informal employment and self-employment in developing countries: Theory and evidence", *Economic Development and Cultural Change*, Vol. 44(2), pp. 289-314.

Chapter 3
Competitiveness and economic diversification in Peru

Most of the gap in GDP per capita between Peru and the OECD economies can be explained by Peru's low labour productivity. The few economic sectors in Peru with high labour productivity, such as mining, create only a small number of jobs. Improving total factor productivity will be key for promoting inclusive growth. A national strategy needs to be implemented to take advantage of Peru's natural resources to capture further value-added. Upping the levels and quality of investment in research and development, innovation, transport infrastructure and logistics will boost competitiveness and increase efficiency. Continuing to improve the business environment, including contract and competition enforcement and support to small businesses will all help boost confidence and promote sustainable development.

Peru's productivity and competitiveness remain poor despite recent efforts to diversify and increase value-added across the economy. Several ambitious reforms to boost productivity and competitiveness are being rolled out – their successful implementation, together with a sound macroeconomic framework, should lead to further inclusive growth.

Peru's low level of labour productivity is explained by a variety of structural factors which are holding back the performance of human capital and total factor productivity. This chapter analyses the Peru's productivity and competitiveness gaps. In addition to education and skills, and the mismatches between labour and demand in the labour market (Chapter 2), other aspects can affect productivity. This chapter identifies the structural factors which need strengthening and outlines broad-based policies to improve its productive capacity, such as the quality of its infrastructure and logistics, innovation, and product market regulation as well as competition.

Improving productivity is fundamental to sustainable growth

Recent growth has not been enough for Peru to catch up with its peers

Over the last 50 years, Peru's GDP per capita growth has been modest (Figure 3.1). In the 1960s, Peru's GDP per capita was close to Hong Kong, China and Portugal and higher than Brazil, Korea, Malaysia, Singapore and Turkey. Between 1960 and 2014, Peru's GDP per capita annual growth was only 1.6% on average. This was well below the average growth rates in upper middle-income (3.7%) and middle-income (3.2%) countries, and also was lower than the GDP per capita growth in OECD (2.2%), high-income (2.3%) and Latin American (1.9%) countries in the same period.

Despite an impressive surge in GDP per capita performance over the last decade, Peru has not been able to close the gap with other emerging markets. GDP per capita growth in the past ten years has been close to 5.0% annually, much higher than in previous decades, but below the aggregate growth of 5.4% a year for upper middle-income countries in the same period.

Figure 3.1. **GDP per capita in Peru, 1960-2014**

Constant prices, base 100 = 1960

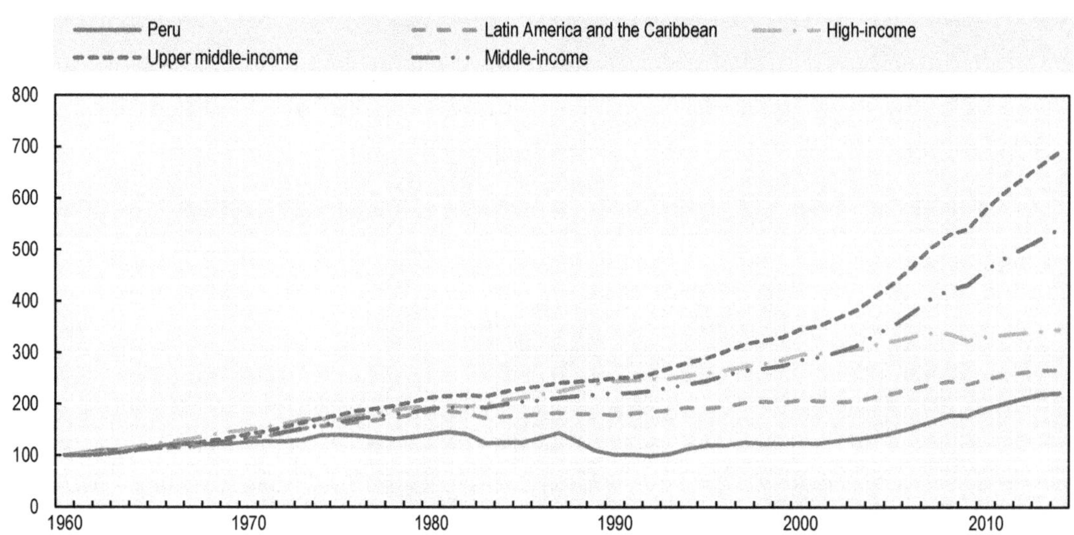

Source: World Bank (2015), *World Development Indicators* (database), Washington, DC, http://data.worldbank.org.

StatLink http://dx.doi.org/10.1787/888933265519

Productivity performance has been poor in Peru

Low labour productivity largely explains the significant GDP per capita gap between Peru and the most advanced OECD countries (Figure 3.2). Despite growing more than seven times the OECD rate over the past decade, the GDP per capita gap remains around 75% compared to the 17 OECD countries with the highest GDP per capita – a bigger difference than for other Latin American countries such as Brazil, Chile, Colombia, and Mexico (Figure 3.2, Panel A). This difference in income per capita can be broken down into gaps in labour productivity and gaps in labour utilisation. Peru, like Brazil, People's Republic of China (China) and Korea, features relatively high labour utilisation, which means that the key culprit stifling GDP per capita is labour productivity (Figure 3.2, Panel B). In fact, Peru's labour productivity shortfall compared to the average of the richest 17 OECD countries was close to 80 percentage points in 2013 (Figure 3.2, Panel B).

Figure 3.2. **Sources of GDP per capita differences**

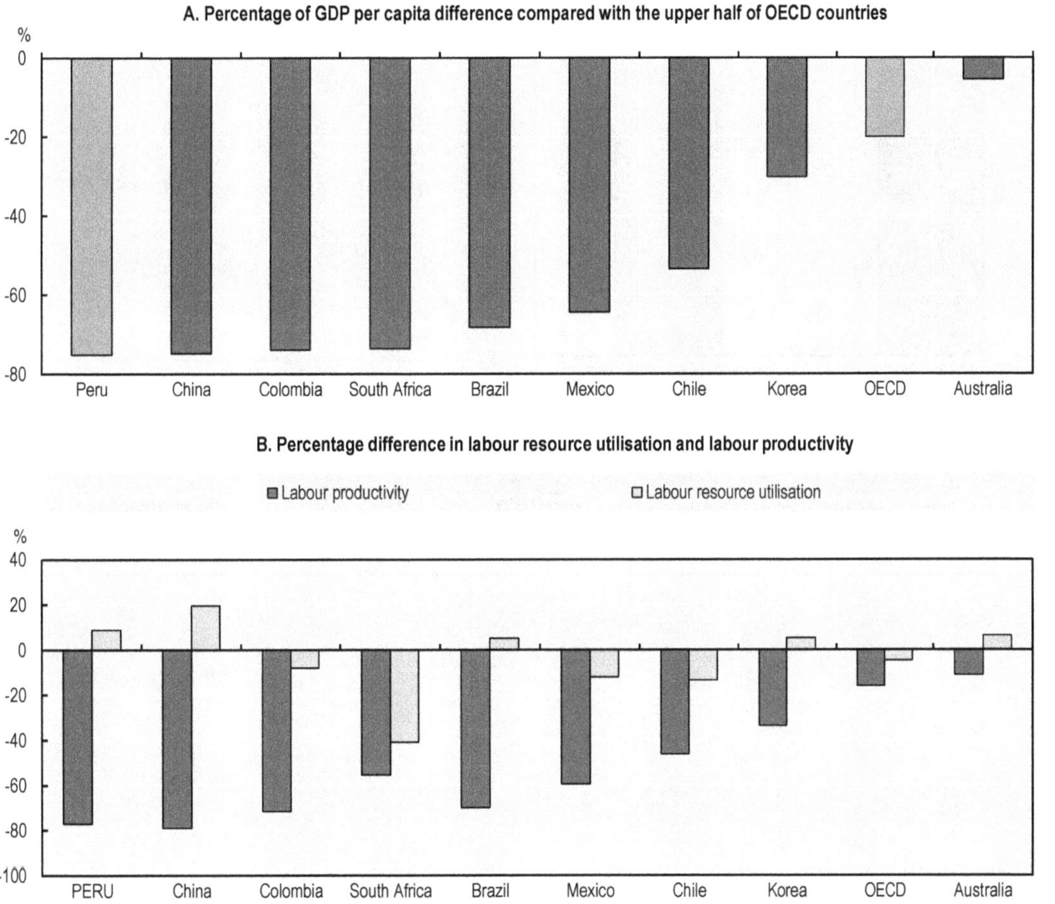

Notes: Compared to the simple average of the 17 OECD countries with the highest GDP per capita in 2013 based on 2013 purchasing power parities (PPPs). The sum of the percentage difference in labour resource utilisation and labour productivity does not add up exactly to the GDP per capita difference since the decomposition is multiplicative. Labour productivity is measured as GDP per employee. Labour resource utilisation is measured as employment as a share of population.

Source: OECD National Accounts Database, http://www.oecd-ilibrary.org/fr/economics/data/oecd-national-accounts-statistics_na-data-en; World Bank (2015), World Development Indicators (database), Washington, DC, http://data.worldbank.org; ILO (International Labour Organization), Key Indicators of the Labour Market (KILM) Database for employment data on Peru http://www.ilo.org/empelm/what/WCMS_114240/lang--en/index.htm.

StatLink http://dx.doi.org/10.1787/888933265526

Labour productivity, calculated as the output per worker, can be broken down into human capital, physical capital, and total factor productivity (TFP).[1] The differences in output per worker between Peru and the United States can be accounted for mainly by human capital and TFP (Figure 3.3, Panel A). TFP alone explains 49% of the labour productivity gap, while years of schooling and quality of education account for 27% and 22% of the labour productivity gap, respectively (Figure 3.3, Panel A). Peru's TFP has grown at an annual rate of less than 2% over the last two decades, not enough to close the gap with OECD economies and most of the benchmark countries (see Annex 1.A1 of Chapter 1 for a description of benchmark countries). This performance is also disappointing when compared to some of the benchmark countries (Figure 3.3, Panel B; Céspedes and Ramirez-Rondán, 2014).

Figure 3.3. **Decomposition of the labour productivity gap in Peru**

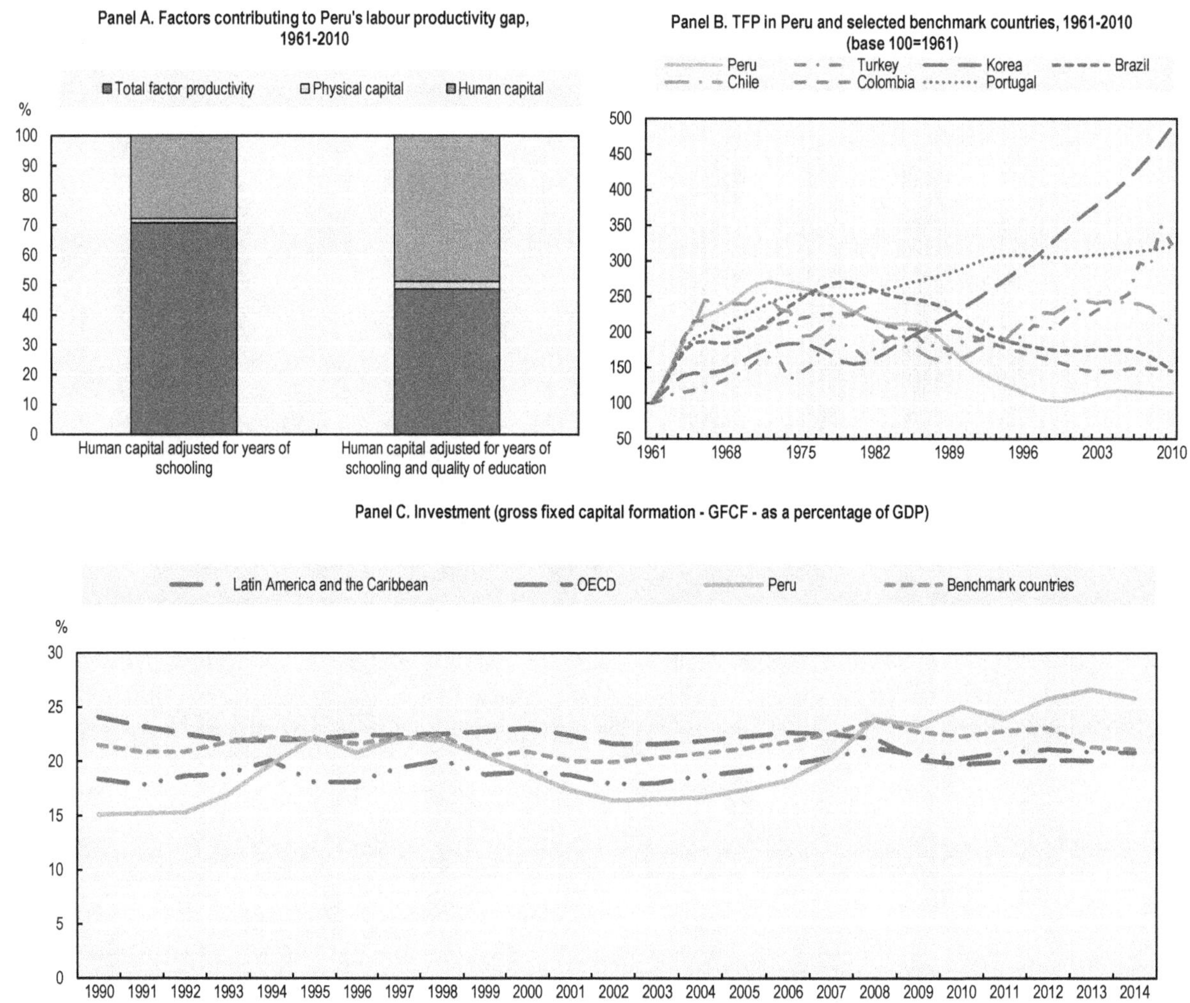

Note: Total factor productivity and the sources of GDP per worker are estimated by using a Cobb-Douglas function. Human capital is adjusted first for the years of schooling, and second for both years of schooling and quality of education. The capital-share production function parameter is set equal to one-third, as is standard in the literature. The gap refers to the difference in PPP-adjusted GDP per worker with respect to the United States.

Sources: Panels A and B: OECD calculations based on Penn World Table (http://datacentre.chass.utoronto.ca/pwt/alphacountries.html), Barro and Lee database (http://www.barrolee.com/), Hanushek and Woessmann (2012) and OECD PISA 2012 database (http://www.oecd.org/pisa/keyfindings/pisa-2012-results.htm). Panel C: World Bank (2015), World Development Indicators (database), Washington, DC, http://data.worldbank.org.

StatLink http://dx.doi.org/10.1787/888933265533

These results suggest that in addition to education and skills (covered in Chapter 2), broad-based policies affecting TFP should be considered to improve Peru's poor GDP per capita performance. These include factors associated with transport costs, such as quality of the investment in infrastructure and logistics, and better business environment, such as the rule of law, and innovation.

On the positive side, investment has been buoyant in recent years. Improvements in the security situation, a better macroeconomic framework and modest gains in TFP have provided the impetus for increasing investment. In recent years, Peru's level of investment as a share of GDP has been higher than the average of Latin American, OECD and benchmark countries (Figure 3.3, Panel C).[2]

Employment is highly concentrated in the least productive sectors

Labour productivity varies widely across economic sectors in Peru. The recent expansion of labour productivity is a result of both increases in labour productivity within sectors, and the reallocation of labour from less productive sectors into more productive ones (Kaldewei and Weller, 2013). Mining, finance, energy and water, and telecommunications have high labour productivity, while retail and restaurants, and agriculture are particularly low (Figure 3.4). This trend is consistent with the average productivity observed over the past decade. Mining is the most productive sector, with a level of labour productivity of more than 7 times the average for Peru, and more than 40 times the level for agriculture. Similarly, at the sub-national level, departments with high labour productivity are characterised as being dependent on commodities (Chapter 5).

In common with other Latin American countries, labour productivity varies widely depending on the size of the firm (Céspedes et al., 2014a). Large and medium-sized firms have a labour productivity of 8 and 3.5 times the productivity of small firms, respectively (Távara et al., 2014). Small and medium-sized firms are concentrated in sectors with low productivity, such as agriculture and retail, while only large firms are involved in the mining sector and in other high productivity service sectors, such as finance, electricity and water supply.[3]

Most of Peru's jobs are concentrated in the most unproductive sectors. More than half of all workers were in Peru's two most unproductive sectors: retail and restaurants, and agriculture (Figure 3.4). In contrast, the manufacturing sector accounts for more than twice the average labour productivity in Peru, yet provides only 10.6% of total employment – a share that has decreased from 12% since the start of the century. This picture is even more striking for the most productive sectors. Together, mining, finance, energy and water, and telecommunications represent less than 4% of total employment. The mining sector alone accounts for less than 1.5% of total employment. While these findings seem to imply a misallocation of labour, they also present enormous potential for growth-enhancing structural transformation.

High labour productivity in a few sectors also translates into high wages for only a few workers, creating income inequalities (Chapter 2). However, the size of this disparity is not as significant as the difference in labour productivity. The average wage is more than six times higher in the four sectors with the highest labour productivity than in the two sectors with the lowest. The average wage in the mining sector is 12.5 times higher than the average wage in agriculture (Távara et al., 2014), which is less than the 40-fold difference in productivity between those sectors.

Figure 3.4. **Labour productivity in Peru's economic sectors, 2013**

Relative value-added as a percentage of workers and employment by economic sectors
(y axis: 100 = total labour productivity and x-axis: % of employment)

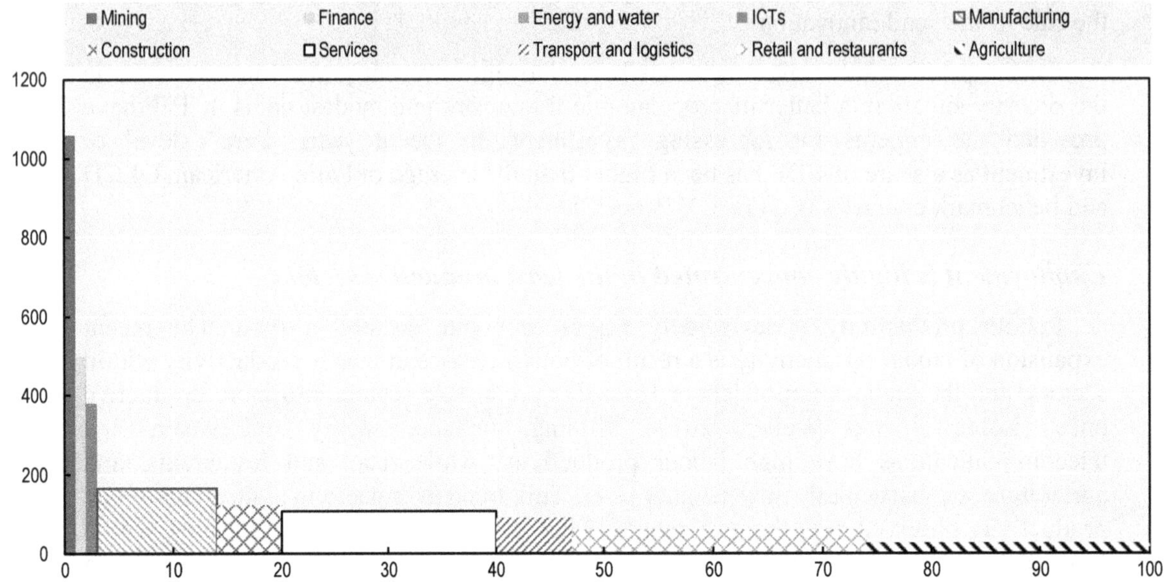

Note: Number of workers is based on Peru's National Households Survey (INEI). "Energy and water" is the item with the lowest employment contribution, representing less than 0.5% of total employment.

Source: OECD calculations based on data provided by INEI (National Institute of Statistics).

StatLink http://dx.doi.org/10.1787/888933265549

Peru has a challenging agenda of broad-based policies to boost productivity and competitiveness, to be implemented during the period 2014-18. The overall objective of the Agenda de Competitividad 2014-2018 is to increase competitiveness, and to foster formal employment and the well-being of the population. Its targets are to increase labour productivity by 15%, to formalise 5% of current informal workers and to reduce logistics costs from 32% to 23% of product value. To achieve these targets, specific policies will need to be implemented in a number of areas. Chapter 2 considers the area of education and human capital and Chapter 5 aspects of governance. The rest of this chapter will cover the current situation and policies in the areas of international trade, sustainable management of natural resources, Peru's position in global value chains, innovation and use of technology, infrastructure and logistics, and the overall business environment.

Commodities dominate Peru's international trade and foreign investment profile

The mining sector, characterised by high labour productivity yet little job creation (see above), plays a crucial role in Peru's balance of payments. First, commodities are a key component of Peru's export trade balance. Second, the contribution of raw materials to the capital account has been increasing in recent years through foreign direct investment. This section studies these two aspects of the Peruvian economy and compares it with OECD and benchmark countries.

Peru remains reliant on its diverse natural resources

Despite a recent decline in their significance, commodities accounted for close to 50% of total export revenues in 2014, notably higher than their share of GDP (close to

12%). The trade balance has benefitted from rising commodity prices, increased production of key mineral resources and widespread promotion of trade openness and bilateral trade agreements. Although Peru exports a diverse range of commodities, copper and gold accounted for more than 60% of its natural resources exports in 2014. Copper and gold represented 17% and 14% of total exports, respectively.[4] In contrast, the manufacturing and agriculture sectors represented 24% and 26% of the total exports in the same year, respectively (Figure 3.5; BCRP, 2015). Over the past decade, the mining industry has grown faster than other industries, at 21% annual growth at nominal prices versus 19% for other industries combined. While Peru's share of commodities is higher than the OECD and Latin American averages, other countries remain more reliant on natural resources (Figure 3.5). These include OECD countries such as Australia and Norway; and Latin American countries, such as Colombia and Ecuador.

Figure 3.5. **Composition of exports in Peru and benchmark countries, 2014**

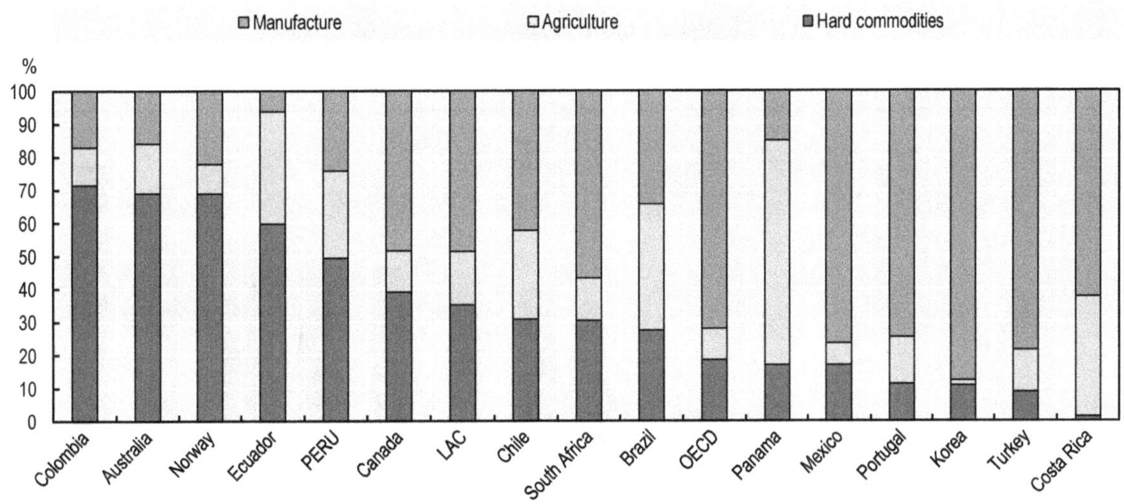

Note: 2013 data for Australia, Colombia, Ecuador, Korea, and Mexico.

Source: WITS / UN Comtrade, Trade Indicators (database) and Central Bank of Peru (Banco de la Reserva del Perú), http://www.bcrp.gob.pe/estadisticas.html

StatLink http://dx.doi.org/10.1787/888933265554

With its abundant and diverse supplies of natural resources, Peru stands among the top global producers of minerals such as copper, lead, silver, tin and zinc (Table 3.1). Furthermore, Peru contains a significant share of the world's reserves for certain commodities, such as silver, tellurium, cadmium, selenium and copper (Figure 3.6). Peru's primary mineral production is competitive due to the quality of its resources (e.g. good mineral grades and its wealth of multiple metals) and the low cost of production inputs. Labour and energy costs account for 15-25% of the total costs of production (McKinsey, 2013).

International experience shows that countries which have managed their raw material resources appropriately have seen positive benefits. The experience of OECD countries in particular shows that commodities can be a crucial source of resources for increasing the productivity and competitiveness of their economies (OECD, 2009). Proper management of the extraction process and the revenues raised from commodities can add value for the country's productivity and total revenues. In particular, to take advantage of abundant natural resources, it is fundamental to address social and environmental challenges in Peru's mining industry (Box 3.1).

Table 3.1. **Peru's position in mineral production, 2013-14**

Mineral	2013		2014	
	World	Latin America	World	Latin America
Tin	3	1	3	1
Zinc	3	1	3	1
Copper	3	2	3	2
Silver	3	2	3	2
Lead	4	1	4	1
Molybdenum	4	2	4	2
Gold	5	1	7	1

Source: Ministry of Energy and Mining (*Ministerio de Energía y Minas*), Dirección General de Minería.

Figure 3.6. **Peru's natural resource reserves, 2013**

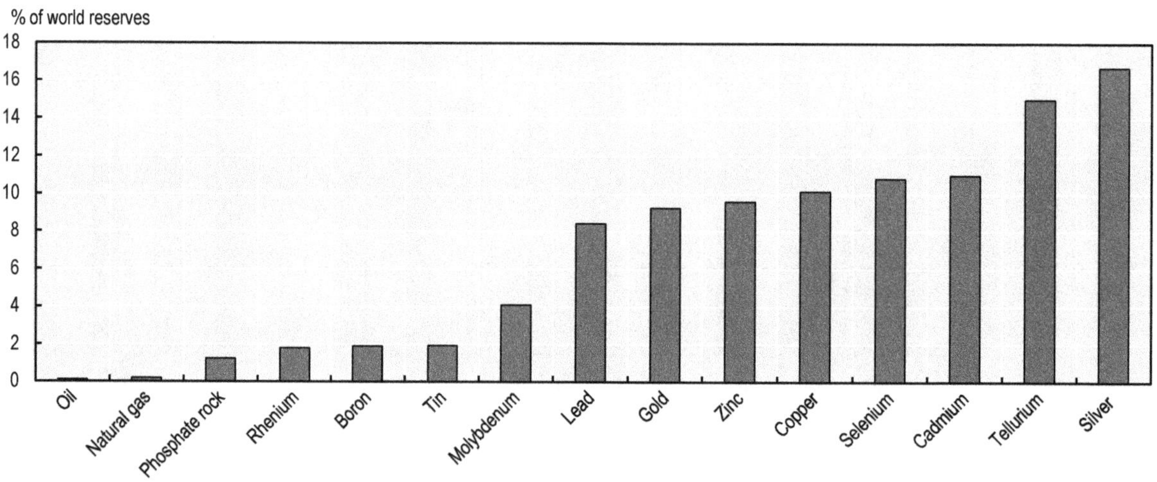

Source: USGS (2014), *Mineral Commodity Summaries 2014*, USGS (U.S. Geological Survey), http://minerals.usgs.gov/minerals/pubs/mcs/2014/mcs2014.pdf; BP (2014), *BP Statistical Review of World Energy June 2014*, 63rd Edition, BP, www.bp.com/content/dam/bp/pdf/Energy-economics/statistical-review-2014/BP-statistical-review-of-world-energy-2014-full-report.pdf

StatLink http://dx.doi.org/10.1787/888933265564

In recent years the share of commodities in Peru's total exports has declined. On average, commodities made up close to 55% of all exports over the past decade, while agriculture made up close to 20%, lower than the 26% share registered in 2014. While agriculture exports have increased in real terms by more than 60% in the past decade, commodities and manufacturing exports have increased by only 25% and 12%, respectively. In particular, the shift towards the agriculture sector has increased in the past five years.

Peru's dependence on exports is relatively low and declining. In 2014, total exports accounted for close to 25% of GDP, down from 30.5% in 2007. This is below the OECD average (53.7%) as well as benchmark countries with similar export compositions, such as Norway (38.9%) and Ecuador (29.2%).

Box 3.1. **Social and environmental challenges in Peru's mining industry**

Peru is the world's seventh largest mining producer, and the mining industry has become one of the primary generators of national wealth (PwC, 2013). As discussed in Chapter 5, aside from its greater vulnerability to fluctuating commodity prices, concentrated production in this sector also presents severe challenges to sustainability. These include long-term environmental impacts, lack of job creation capacity, weak links to local economic sectors and rising social conflicts (SECO, 2013). Overcoming growing opposition to mining will require a continuous relationship between communities and mining, with the industry making greater contributions at local, regional and national levels. This may be achieved by establishing and advancing environmental standards as well as adopting technological improvements to production to monitor and reduce adverse effects while offering the greatest opportunity for development progress. The Operational Framework on Public-Private Collaboration for Resource-based Value Creation being developed as part of the OECD Policy Dialogue on Natural Resource-Based Development (included in the OECD Country Programme with Peru) is a reference to help Peru address these challenges.

Furthermore, social conflicts and escalating opposition to mining in the region threaten to delay Peru's announced investment portfolio (see Chapter 5). Among the most widely publicised and controversial of these projects are Conga (a USD 4.8 billion investment), halted in 2011 following widespread protest; Tia Maria (USD 930 million investment), stalled after protests in 2011 turned violent over fears of pollution in nearby agricultural valleys; and the Santa Ana Project (USD 71 million investment), delayed by communities fighting to protect local water supplies from pollution. Depending on the outcome, project suspensions and cancellations could delay close to 40% of the mining investment announced over the coming years (McKinsey, 2013). Long delays could undermine Peru's potential to benefit from its abundant natural resources.

The change in the structure of Peruvian exports and the increasing role of China in the global economy has changed Peru's export destinations dramatically (Figure 3.7). In 2014, more than 18% of Peru's total exports went to China (about 4% of GDP), of which 81% were metals. China takes more than one-third of Peru's copper exports, 64% of its gold exports and 22% of its other mineral commodities. However, China's increasing role in Peruvian exports poses challenges and opportunities for economic diversification. In the future, a commodity-based model will not necessarily be beneficial or sustainable given the changes of China's import composition induced by its rebalancing process. Peru will need to anticipate these changes and adapt its commodity-concentrated export profile (OECD/CAF/ECLAC, 2015). The picture has also changed for imports. In 2004 the United States accounted for more than 50% of Peruvian imports and China less than 6%. A decade later both countries provide nearly 30% of Peru's total imports.[5]

Mineral exports have also been one of the key sources of recent growth in total Foreign Direct Investment (FDI) inflows to Peru. FDI averaged more than 5% of GDP over the period 2010 13, and averaged close to 3.5% of GDP over the last decade (Figure 3.8, Panel A). From 2000 to 2013, the share of total FDI to the mining and petroleum industry combined increased by more than 12 percentage points, reaching 27% in 2013, the largest share of FDI for any sector (Figure 3.8, Panel B). Peru's efforts to boost production and its continual announcements of large-scale mining projects have fuelled expectations and lead to greater levels of investment in recent years. Many of Peru's largest investors, such as the United Kingdom and the United States, invest primarily in mining and petroleum. However Spain, Peru's primary investor, concentrates its investment in communications, while the Netherlands and Chile invest more in Peru's financial industry.

Figure 3.7. **Peru's main export destination, 2014 vs. 1970**

% share in Peru's exports

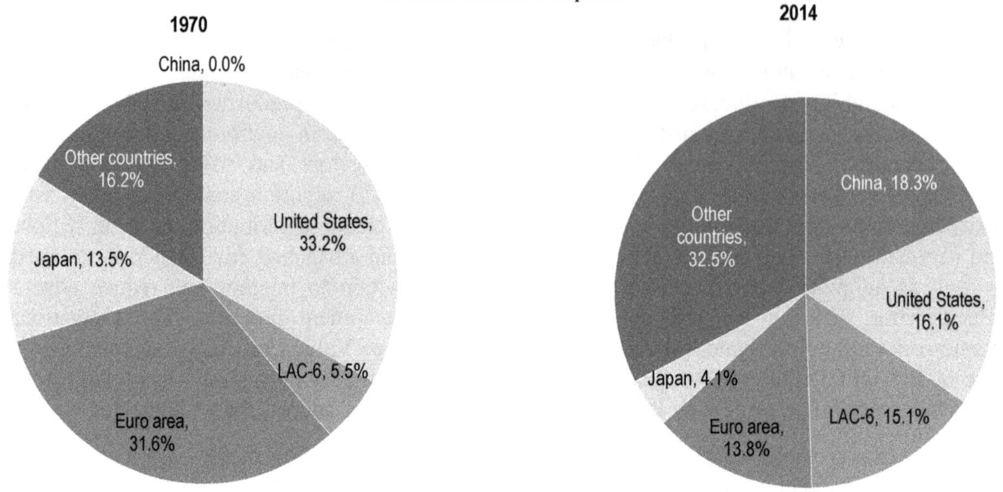

Note: LAC-6 comprises Argentina, Brazil, Chile, Colombia, Mexico and Venezuela.

Source: Direction of Trade Statistics (International Monetary Fund – IMF), accessed on 15 June 2015. http://data.imf.org/?sk=9D6028D4-F14A-464C-A2F2-59B2CD424B85

StatLink *http://dx.doi.org/10.1787/888933265572*

Figure 3.8. **Foreign direct investment in Peru**

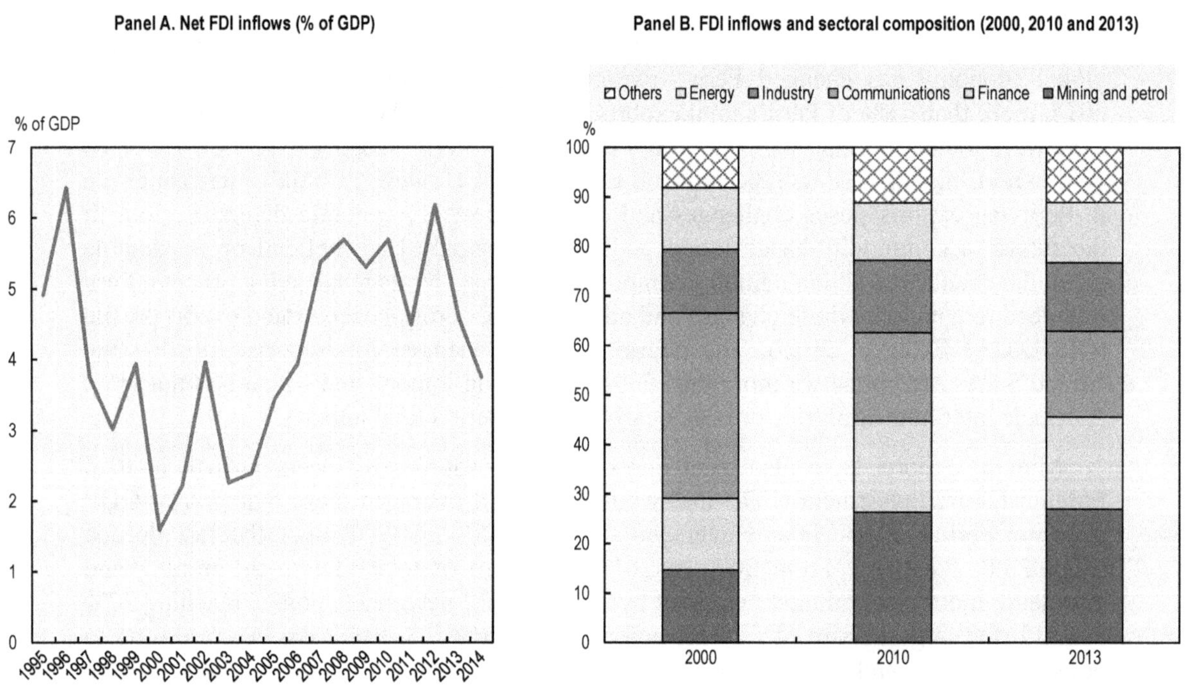

Note: The classification "Others" in Panel B includes retail, services, tourism, construction, agriculture, transport, and housing sectors.

Source: ProInversión (2015), *Estadísticas Generales (database),* ProInversion (Agencia de Promoción Privada – Perú), Accessed on 1 August 2015, www.proinversion.gob.pe.

StatLink *http://dx.doi.org/10.1787/888933265580*

Dependence on primary exports leaves Peru vulnerable to external shocks

The economic cycle has long been closely linked to the export sector. Its narrow export base means earnings are prone to fluctuate with international price fluctuations and demand. Such fluctuations, especially in the case of commodities, can be very large. In the case of metals, the difference between the maximum and minimum annual average prices was more than 300% in the period 2000-14. Macroeconomic instability and negative exogenous shocks from international prices in Peru's primary export sectors triggered an economic collapse from the beginning of the 1980s to the mid-1990s. This left Peru in a period of stagnation until the macroeconomic framework improved and international prices in mining and fuels increased in the early 1990s (Hausmann and Klinger, 2008). However, Peru underwent very little structural transformation in response to this export collapse.

Figure 3.9. **Trade prices and revealed comparative advantages in Peru**

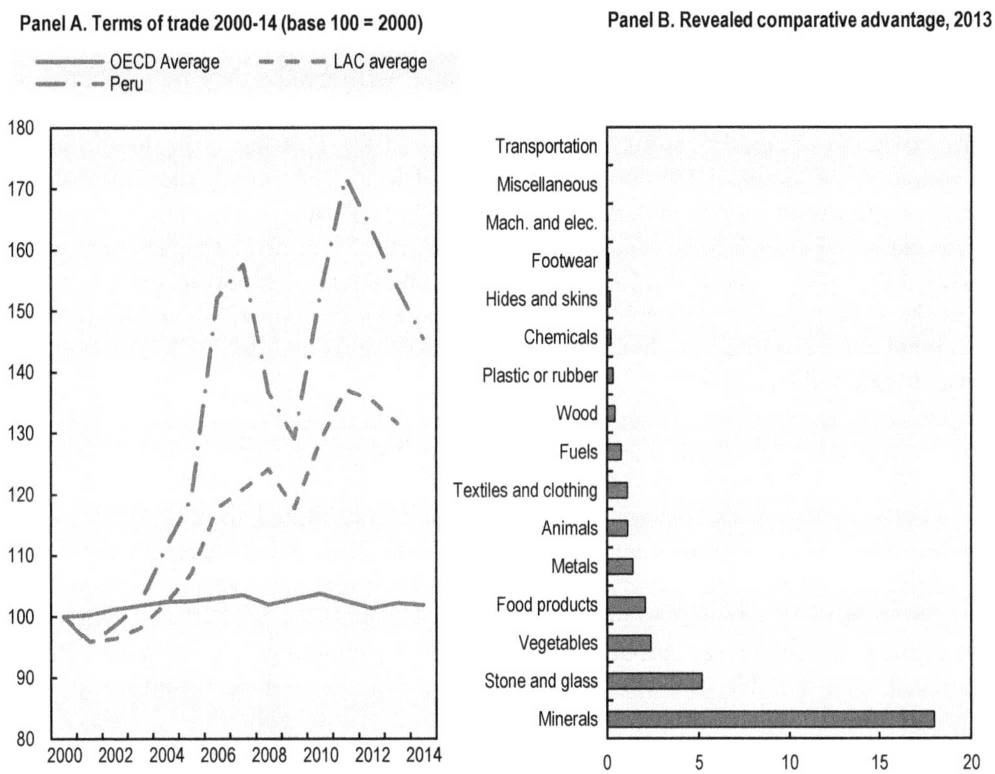

Notes: Panel B: Revealed comparative advantage (RCA) is an index based on Balassa (1977) that measures the ratio between the contribution a product makes to the exports of a country and the same product's contribution to world trade. See OECD/CAF/ECLAC (2013), *Latin American Economic Outlook 2014, Logistics and Competitiveness for Development*, OECD Publishing, Paris, http://dx.doi.org/10.1787/leo-2014-en for more details of this indicator.

Source: Panel A: OECD Terms of Trade Indicators (database) https://data.oecd.org/trade/terms-of-trade.htm; BCRP (2015), *Annual Series* database, BCRP (Banco Central de Reserva del Peru), https://estadisticas.bcrp.gob.pe/estadisticas/series/anuales; and UNCTAD (database). Panel B: OECD calculations based on export data from WITS / UN Comtrade.

StatLink http://dx.doi.org/10.1787/888933265596

With favourable terms of trade, complemented by increases in mineral production, Peru achieved persistent trade surpluses from 2002 to 2012. In particular, Peru's favourable terms of trade in recent years can be largely attributed to the boom in commodity prices. Peru's terms of trade are above the average for OECD economies and Latin America and Caribbean (LAC) countries (Figure 3.9, Panel A). However, benchmark countries such as Australia, Chile and Norway enjoy more favourable terms of trade.

Peru continues to specialise in commodity production because of its comparative advantage in these sectors. A country is considered to have a "revealed comparative advantage" in exporting a product if that product's share in the country's exports is higher than the product's overall share in world trade. During a period of favourable commodity prices, growing trade relations and robust international demand, Peru experienced gains from increased production and concentration in sectors where its comparative advantage persisted. In particular, Peru increased its share of world trade in high-growth sectors such as minerals, stone and glass, food, animal and vegetable products, metals, and textiles and clothing (Figure 3.9, Panel B).

The recent downturn in Peru's terms of trade performance may be attributed to the latest decline in commodity prices (Figure 3.9, Panel A). Peru has experienced declining terms of trade since 2012 and trade deficits since 2013. This has been due, in part, to a decrease in the demand for commodities from China, reinforcing the vulnerability of Peru's dependence on raw materials. In 2014, 95% of Peru's products exported to China were classified as minerals, metals or food products. From 2011 to 2014, the prices of metals fell by more than 25%. Copper, Peru's main source of export income, fell by 22% over the same period (see Chapter 4). Chinese demand for copper, which constitutes 40% of global consumption, has plummeted in the recent years and, in 2014, Chinese demand for gold also fell by 25%.

Peru's exports can be diversified by moving up global value chains

Peru's concentration on commodities has not contributed to a shift toward more sophisticated products involving manufacturing and other knowledge-intensive sectors. Over the past decade, Peru's technology exports have remained very low in comparison with most of the benchmark countries. In particular, in 2013, only 3% of Peru's exports were medium-technology products and 9% low-technology ones. While Peru has achieved considerable growth in production volumes of non-traditional exports (agriculture, fishing, chemical, manufacturing and textile goods[6]) – 2.6 times greater today than ten years ago – the majority of this increase is accounted for by products with low levels of sophistication (Ministerio de la Producción, 2015). On the other hand, Peru's imports include industrial machinery and equipment, crude and refined oil, and transportation and construction vehicles. This suggests that Peru is dependent on imports for manufactured goods and high-technology products.

The sophistication of a country's exports and the complexity of its production structure are both important determinants of long-term growth (Hausmann, Hwang and Rodrik, 2007; Hidalgo et al., 2007; Rodrik, 2008; Felipe et al., 2012). Yet the complexity of Peru's production structure is lower than most benchmark countries. The economic complexity indicator (ECI) ranks how diversified and complex a country's export basket is. It combines measures of a country's diversity (how many products a country produces) and the ubiquity of those products (the number of countries able to produce those products). In 2012, Peru ranked 80th out of 144 countries for economic complexity and, in contrast to most of the Latin American economies, its ECI has worsened over the past two decades (Figure 3.10).

Figure 3.10. **Economic complexity indicator (ECI), 1990-2012**

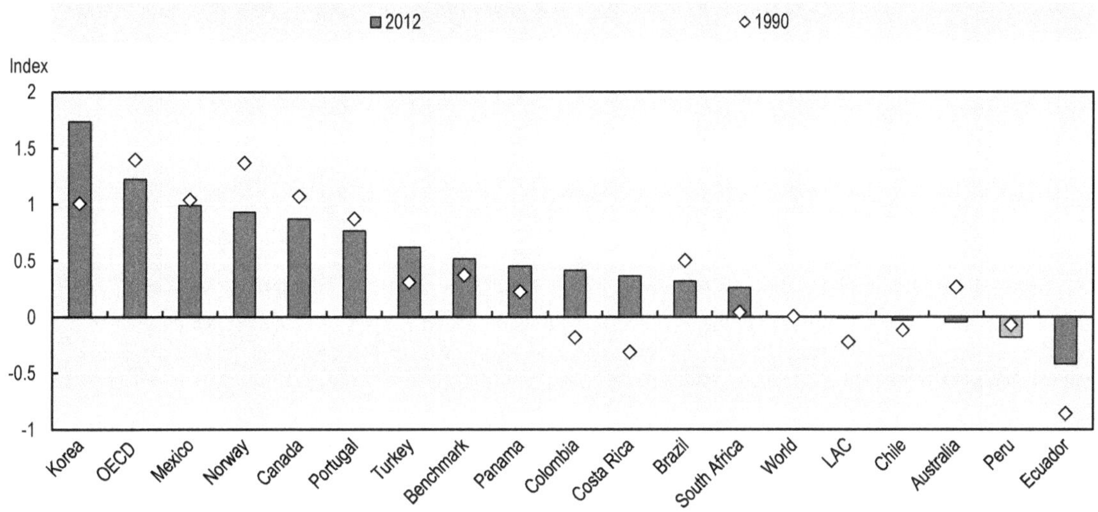

Note: ECI ranks how diversified and complex a country's export basket is. The most complex products are sophisticated chemicals and machinery, whereas the world's least complex products are raw materials or simple agricultural products.

Source: Hausmann, R. et al. (2012), *The Atlas of Economic Complexity*, Puritan Press, Cambridge, MA; Simoes, A.J.G. and C.A. Hidalgo (2012), "The Economic Complexity Observatory: An analytical tool for understanding the dynamics of economic development", Workshop at the Twenty-Fifth AAAI Conference on Artificial Intelligence, August, 2011, Cambridge, MA.

StatLink http://dx.doi.org/10.1787/888933265608

A key challenge to enhance value-added production in a country's existing comparative advantage is to identify segments that have not yet been exploited within these industries. Because Peru specialises in primary products, it largely participates in the lower end of supply chains, providing inputs to other countries' production processes (forward linkages), rather than receiving production inputs from abroad (backward linkages). Consequently, Peru participates more in global supply chains as a provider of value-added than as a recipient, and is among the top providers of domestic value-added used in foreign exports among LAC countries (Figure 3.11; Blyde, 2014).

In the context of the OECD Country Programme with Peru, the inclusion of Peru in the OECD–WTO Trade in Value-Added (TiVA) is fundamental to providing further analysis and insights into Peru's commercial relations. The OECD Initiative on Global Value Chains, Production Transformation and Development is another OECD platform that could help Peru to promote development through greater participation in and upgrading of global value chains.

Figure 3.11. **Share of foreign value-added and forward linkages in total exports, 1995-2011**

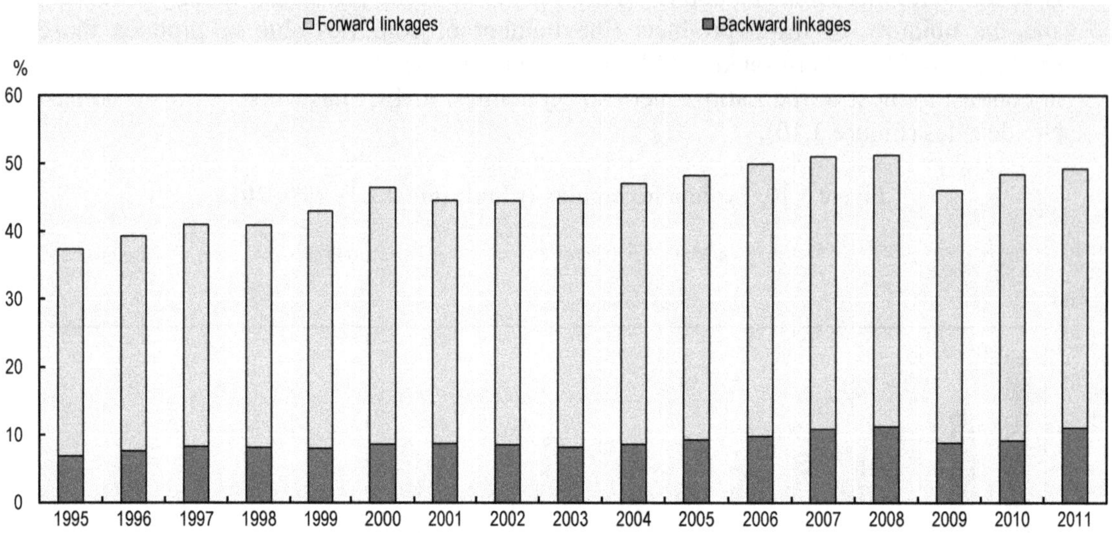

Notes: Computed shares of forward linkages (i.e. domestic value-added exports of a country which goes into exports of other countries) and backward linkages (foreign value added to gross exports of a country) by dividing over total value of real exports.

Source: EORA (database), http://worldmrio.com/.

StatLink http://dx.doi.org/10.1787/888933265616

Peru's growing market openness offers an opportunity to diversify the economy. Over the last decade, Peru has expanded the use of policy instruments in the areas of unilateral tariff liberalisation, international trade negotiations, and internal competitiveness and development policies related to foreign trade. This openness of the economy, bolstered by a number of free trade agreements (FTAs), has contributed to increasing both labour productivity and total factor productivity among firms involved in international trade (Céspedes et al., 2014b). Peru holds free trade agreements with nearly all major trading partners including the United States, China, European Union and European Free Trade Association (EFTA), MERCOSUR (the Southern Common Market) and, more recently, the Pacific Alliance. Today, nearly 95% of Peru's exports are covered by free trade agreements. These agreements and improved market openness allow Peru to increase the number of exported products and exporting companies, especially of non-traditional products (agriculture, fishing, chemical, manufacturing, and textile goods). Though traditional products still account for 78% of total exports, Peru benefits from the ability to diversify its range of non-traditional goods. For instance, within the first three years of establishing an FTA with the United States, Peru produced and shipped an additional 488 non-traditional products to the United States, and within two years of the established FTA with China, Peru exported 204 new non-traditional products to China (EY, 2015). As highlighted below, however, high transport costs and low investment in innovation are key barriers to taking greater advantage of these FTAs.

Peru has long-term strategies to diversify exports and promote value-added through the National Strategic Export Plan (PENX). The plan was first implemented from 2003-13 as an instrument to co-ordinate public and private-sector efforts to ensure the expansion and sustainability of Peru's exports. It focused on advancing and diversifying non-traditional sectors that generate greater added value and employment. Ten priority productive sectors were identified: agriculture, crafts, leathers, forestry-timber, jewellery, metalwork, fisheries and aquaculture, chemicals, textiles, and services (MINCETUR, 2015). During this time Peru increased non-traditional exports by 18% annually, above the national average.

Peru recently announced a revised ten-year export plan to diversify exports, promote private and public sector co-ordination, and develop its position as a regional exporter of products and services. The renewed plan, PENX 2025, was announced by the Ministry of Foreign Trade and Tourism in March 2015. It proposes actions towards sustainable medium and long-term progress through enhancing productive capacity in the coming years. This will need to address concerns over aggregate productivity by moving to specialise in sectors that produce more value-added and reduce productivity gaps across regions, sectors and companies within the same industry (Ministerio de la Producción, 2015). The plan focuses on the development of technology-driven service sectors such as software, electronics, engineering consultancy and franchises to enhance sophistication and productivity. It also emphasises the need to promote greater internationalisation of Peruvian companies to better integrate with the global economy and adapt to changing market dynamics. Successful implementation over the next decade may see Peru's export industries become a sustainable driver for greater inclusive growth. This revised plan places further emphasis on aligning Peruvian companies and production goals with medium and long-term government objectives necessary for Peru's social and economic progress. To do so, key agenda items, such as the advancement of skills and education (Chapter 2), innovation, and infrastructure (see below), must be complemented by promoting knowledge-intensive sectors and diversifying production across all regions in Peru.

Limited innovation outcomes are holding Peru back

Government and businesses are investing little in research and development

Investment in human capital and knowledge lags well behind most Latin American countries. While Peru's total budget for science and technology was USD 17.4 million in 2013, Colombia's was USD 210 million and Chile's was USD 546 million (World Bank, 2014b). In 2014, Peru ranked 117th out of 144 countries for the quality of its scientific research institutions, 109th for university-industry collaboration in research and development, 119th for company spending on research and development, and 100th for total capacity for innovation. These rankings mark Peru as one of the countries with the greatest challenges for innovation in Latin America (World Economic Forum, 2014). Peru's business expenditure on research and development remains significantly below the average for OECD countries and many other countries in Latin America (Figure 3.12). Greenfield foreign investment in research and development, engineering and design in Peru makes up less than 0.5% of total greenfield foreign investment. By comparison, in OECD and Latin America these ratios are, on average, close to 4% and 2%, respectively (OECD/CAF/ECLAC, 2014). Attracting further investment in activities linked to innovation remains a significant challenge for Peru.

Low levels of investment in research and development are hindering innovation in Peru. A key measure of the output of innovation is the number of patents. Peru's patent applications per million inhabitants are below all of the benchmark countries, as well as the Latin America and Caribbean (LAC) average (Figure 3.13). While the patent applications have increased in recent years, from 0.23 per million inhabitants in 2008-09 to 0.28 per million inhabitants in 2010-11, this number remains well below OECD average. OECD countries receive, on average, more than 100 patent applications per million members of the population.

Figure 3.12. **Business expenditure on research and development**

2002 and 2013 (or latest available year)

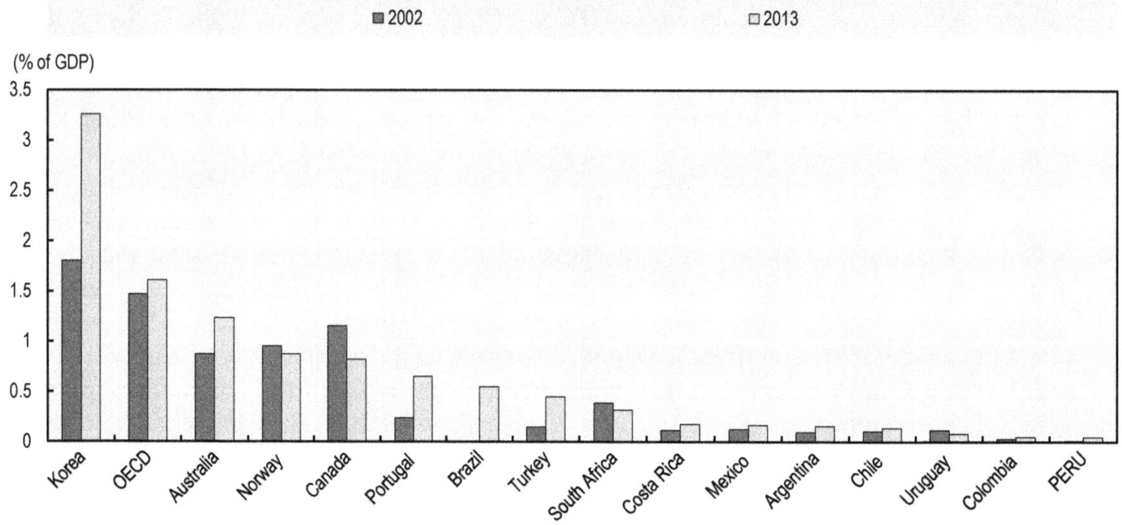

Note: Latin American economies (excluding Argentina, Brazil, Chile, and Mexico): 2012. Argentina and Chile: 2013. South Africa: 2012. Australia and Mexico: 2011. Brazil: 2010.

Source: OECD (2015), *Main Science and Technology Indicators*, (Database), www.oecd.org/sti/msti; and OECD calculations based on Red de Indicadores de Ciencia y Tecnología -Iberoamericana e Interamericana- (RICYT), accessed on 1 August 2015.

StatLink http://dx.doi.org/10.1787/888933265624

Figure 3.13. **Patent applications per million people**

Patent Cooperation Treaty, 2010-11 average

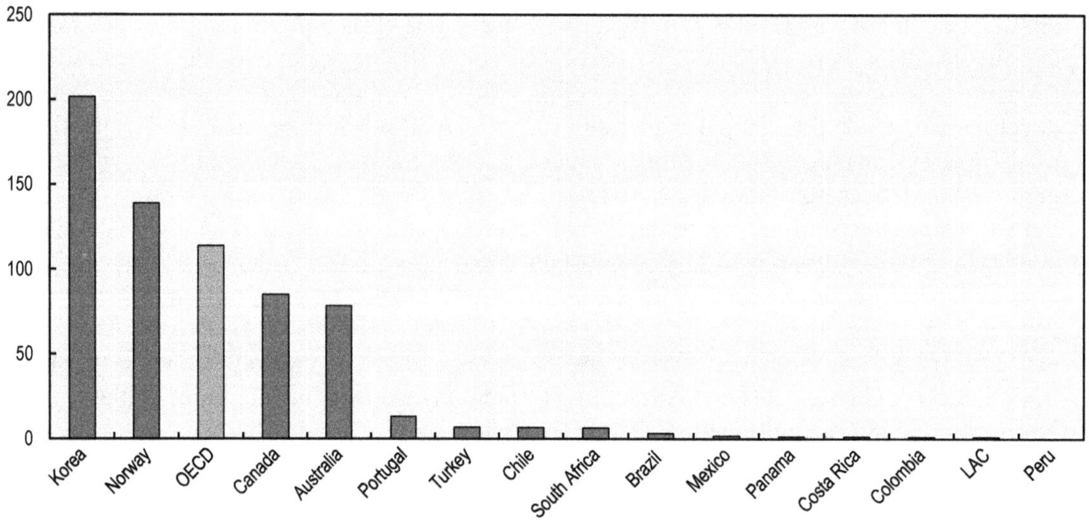

Note: Data based on 2010-11 averages. No values available for Ecuador from given source thus excluded from LAC and benchmark countries.

Source: OECD Indicators on Patents (database), OECD, www.oecd.org/sti/inno/oecdpatentdatabases.htm.

StatLink http://dx.doi.org/10.1787/888933265630

Furthermore, in comparison with benchmark and OECD countries, Peru remains well below average for intellectual property imports and exports, revealing low levels of use of and contribution to global activity in research and development. Intellectual property exports measure the amount paid by foreigners to use intellectual property owned by domestic residents. Peru's exports of intellectual property have increased in recent years, most notably from USD 1.5 million in 2009 to USD 11.5 million in 2012. However, exports of intellectual property are much higher from other LAC countries – such as Chile (USD 75.4 million), Colombia (USD 89.8 million), and Mexico (USD 95.6 million) – suggesting more advanced activity in research and development (IMF, 2012). Peru is also a relatively small importer of intellectual property. Though these imports have increased, from USD 152 million in 2009 to USD 229 million in 2012, other Latin American countries are again much more active users of intellectual property. Low levels of intellectual property imports are a likely result of both Peru's export composition (see above) and limited returns on usage within the country's current productive capacities and business climate.

Similar to other Latin American countries, this significant innovation gap is largely explained by the country's framework conditions, which do not make innovation a profitable form of business investment. There are persistent deterrents to innovation, including the market structure to which firms are exposed, firms' position in the value chain, the scarcity of qualified human resources, and the long-term inability of firms to accumulate in-house innovation capabilities (OECD/CAF/ECLAC, 2014).

Peru has established institutions for the purpose of attracting private investment in research and development and innovation and to develop science, technology and innovation policies. For instance, the National Science and Technology Council (CONCYTEC) has introduced a series of instruments to reduce bottlenecks in the innovation system and increase business research and development. These include a 30% tax deduction on activities and projects related to science, technology and innovation since 2013, and a fund to finance credit guarantees or risk-sharing mechanisms for businesses through the financial system. CONCYTEC has increased its budget from USD 5 million in 2012 to approximately USD 43 million in 2014. In addition, the Ministry of Production (PRODUCE) promotes industrial development and business innovation. PRODUCE manages two key policy instruments: the Research and Development Fund for Competitiveness (FIDECOM/*Innóvate Perú*), a competitive fund to co-finance projects aimed at promoting research and development for innovation; and Technological Innovation Centres. Furthermore, the Ministry of Education is responsible for generating resources to develop the advanced human capital necessary for research and development and innovation activities. Finally, the Presidency of the Council of Ministers is in charge of some innovation projects and instruments, including the National Institute for the Defence of Competition and Protection of Intellectual Property (INDECOPI), and the Fund for Innovation, Science and Technology (FINCyT) (OECD, 2013a).

Policy institutes provide a means to prioritise start-ups and adapt national and regional business environments to foster innovation projects. As with many other countries in the region, start-ups are gaining momentum in Peru and provide fresh opportunity for the country to exploit newly productive sectors. As part of a renewed interest in innovation, the Peruvian government is seeking to develop greater support for start-ups, cultivate a more competitive economy, diversify production and unlock future growth potential. Both PRODUCE and the Ministry of Labour and Employment Promotion have revised their policy mix to promote start-ups (OECD, 2013a).

A number of programmes supporting start-ups have been launched in recent years. Startup Peru, introduced by PRODUCE in late 2012, seeks to offer integrated support to new entrepreneurs, issuing calls for technology start-ups to apply for seed capital and business training. In addition, the Ministry of Labour and Employment Promotion promotes the programme *Vamos Perú*, which provides resources to cover the training costs of high-school graduates who are either temporarily employed or at risk of unemployment. These programmes are often partnered with private initiatives such as capacity building through universities and training institutes. Firms that have already been in business for at least one year can obtain support from two programmes: FINCyT's Innovative Projects in Individual Enterprises (*Proyectos de Innovación en Empresas Individuales*); and Small Productive Innovation Projects (*Proyectos Menores de Innovación Productiva*) run by FIDECOM/Innóvate Perú.

In order to consolidate these different programmes and policies, the government increased in recent years its funds for investing in research and development and new, innovative firms. The *Fondo Marco para la Innovación, Ciencia y Tecnología* (FOMITEC) was created in 2013 to bring fresh resources to Startup Peru and CONCYTEC. In particular, FOMITEC contributes to the creation of new technological and innovative firms (in co-ordination with FINCyT), and innovation mechanisms in the areas of health, agriculture and environment. In addition, this fund promotes the financing of new researchers in information and communication technology (ICT), and the creation of new research centres helping to boost productivity in Peru.

Consolidating existing initiatives and expanding these programmes are direct methods to provide integrated support for start-ups and innovation systems. One of the main objectives of FOMITEC is precisely to facilitate capital for new firms. Furthermore, the government recognises the need to target policy tools further to improve financing, business services, and entrepreneurial training to encourage start-ups.

A crucial challenge for Peru will be to adopt a more proactive role in fostering innovation to develop new comparative advantages. In addition to expanding scientific and technological capacity, government intervention must bolster demand for innovation, particularly among the business sector, to enhance productive dynamism in Peru (Rodrik, 2004; OECD, 2011). Developed countries such as Australia, Canada and Norway and emerging economies such as Brazil and Chile possess natural resource endowments comparable to Peru and have higher levels of public and private investment in science, technology and innovation to boost competitiveness through diversification. Peru has made progress to increase non-traditional exports in recent years thanks to the PENX. However, future plans must continue to promote institutional and policy reforms to make better use of new sources of growth.

Peru recognises the need to promote knowledge and innovation as a tool for future productivity gains, resource management, and inclusive growth. One of the primary objectives of Peru's 2002 National Accord (*Acuerdo Nacional*) is the development of science and technology as a means to use advanced knowledge, develop human resources, improve the management of natural resources and increase the competitiveness of Peruvian companies.[7] The current government has established a number of national strategies aligned with the National Accord, which Peru will target until 2016. These priorities include improving the quality and accessibility of higher education, the greater use of value and production chains to exploit comparative advantages, and more persistent development of technical assistance, market information, and production infrastructure. A number of wide-reaching national programmes have been recently introduced to complement this effort, including the National Plan for Productive Diversification, developed by the Ministry of Production.

Peru has shown notable ambition to promote science, technology and innovation in recent years. The effectiveness of any plan to increase science, technology and innovation will depend on the development of political, scientific, technological and financial subsystems, and their capacity to collaborate so as to create, distribute and use scientific and technical knowledge (UNCTAD, 2013). Innovation and greater productive competitiveness can be promoted both through developing human capacity within individual companies and creating and maintaining favourable environments for innovation. Peru's ability to advance innovation within the business sector will be a key determinant of its level of productivity and competitiveness in the coming years.

Infrastructure gaps are a barrier to inclusive growth

Greater and more strategic investment in infrastructure is another key priority for the Peruvian authorities. The development of infrastructure is one of the six strategic axes in Peru's development plan "*Plan Bicentenario: El Perú Hacia el 2021*". This plan, defined by the central planning agency, CEPLAN, sets out the roadmap and goals for 2021, when Peru will celebrate the bicentenary of its independence. Improved infrastructure is identified as a key element in reducing inequality in resources and capabilities between Lima and the regions and among the regions themselves. Such inequality leads to structural difficulties in reducing poverty, achieving adequate living standards, attracting investment and developing high-tech driven productive activities (CEPLAN, 2011).

Bringing Peru's infrastructure up to international levels requires more investment

As with most countries in the region, Peru's public service infrastructure is poor compared to other emerging and developed economies. The investment required between 2012 and 2021 to close Peru's infrastructure gap has been assessed at USD 87 975 million, 33% of the country's projected GDP over the same period (AFIN, 2012). The energy sector has the highest investment needs, accounting for 37.5% of the total infrastructure gap. This is explained by a higher-than-expected increase in the demand for electricity. The second biggest investment need is for transport infrastructure (23.8% of the gap) with the main deficit being in roads and railways, requiring investment of about 6% and 3% of current GDP, respectively. Growing transport investment needs are hindering the country's structural development by increasing transport costs and reducing the environmental competitiveness of Peru's firms.

Current investment in infrastructure falls short of the levels needed to ensure Peru's prosperity. Total investment in energy, transport, telecoms and water, including private investment, reached approximately USD 3.7 billion in 2012, almost 2% of GDP. At least half of this was in energy infrastructure. Estimates show that public-private partnership projects accounted for nearly USD 11 billion of investment (around 5% of current GDP) between in 2011 and 2014.[8]

Although improving, the quality of Peru's infrastructure remains well below OECD standards. Between 2006 and 2014, Peru improved its score for infrastructure overall by 36% in the Global Competitiveness Rankings (WEF, 2014). While this was better than the 22% average improvement among Latin American countries, it is similar to the average improvement for upper middle-income economies overall. Despite this progress,

Peru remains low in the Global Competitiveness rankings for infrastructure, moving from 93rd out of 125 countries in 2006 to 105th out of 144 in 2014. The perceived quality of Peru's overall infrastructure in 2014 was similar to other Latin American countries, but considerably below OECD economies (Figure 3.14).

Figure 3.14. **Perceived quality of overall infrastructure, 2014**

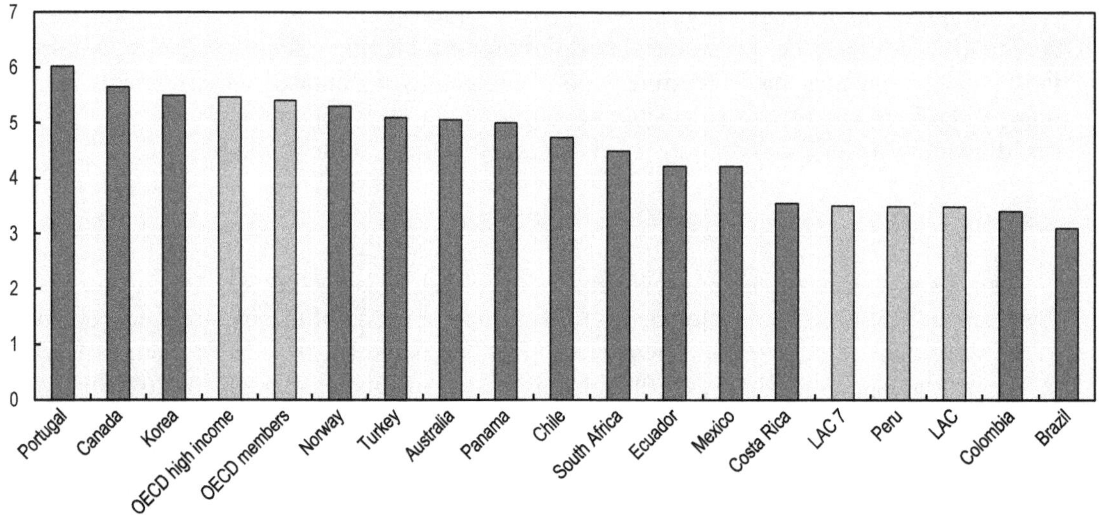

Note: This indicator uses a scale from 1 to 7 where a higher score means a better quality of infrastructure. Latest available data for Ecuador is for 2013

Source: WEF (2014), *The Global Competitiveness Report 2014-2015*, WEF (World Economic Forum), Geneva, http://www3.weforum.org/docs/WEF_GlobalCompetitivenessReport_2014-15.pdf.

StatLink http://dx.doi.org/10.1787/888933265644

Examining Peru's infrastructure needs in more detail reveals a range of challenges and opportunities. Peru is below OECD and regional standards for access to improved water sources and electricity. Approximately 88% of the population has access to improved water sources, and 91% to electricity (Figure 3.15, Panel A). In terms of quality, Peru lags far behind OECD economies in the quality of its transport, telephony and electrical infrastructure. Apart from the quality of its electricity supply, the country remains inferior to its Latin American peers in all other indicators. Although advances have been made, its capital stock of infrastructure and access to basic services remain deficient (Figure 3.15, Panel B). While greater investment in infrastructure is essential, equal priority should be given to designing policies and mechanisms to remove obstacles to private investment, and to improve the quality of public investment (OECD, 2014). Improving the quantity and quality of investment in infrastructure would have a large range of benefits for the country, including enhancing well-being (Box 3.2).

Figure 3.15. **Access to public services and infrastructure quality**

Panel A. Percentage of the population with access to water and electric services

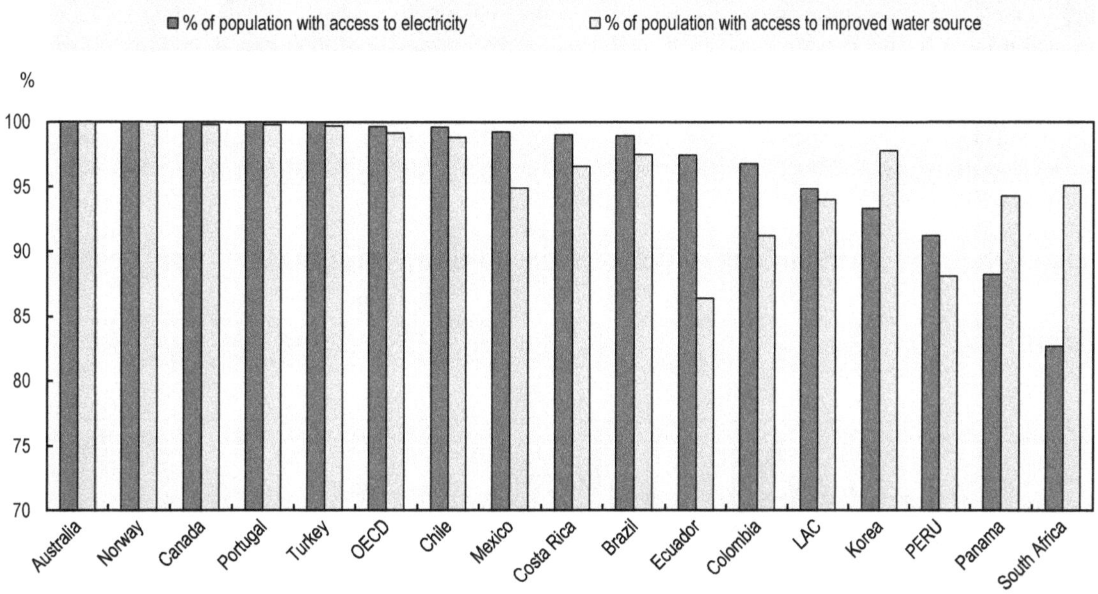

Panel B. Quality of public service infrastructure 1-7 (best), 2014

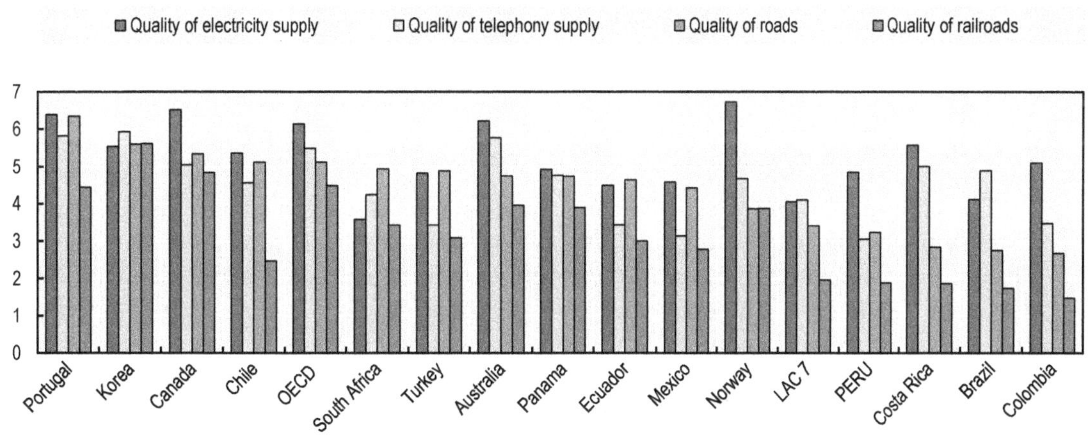

Note: In Panel A the data correspond to the latest information available, 2012 for access to electricity and 2010 for access to water. Peru's data are for 2012 in both indicators. In Panel B the indicator for quality of telephony supply corresponds to the weight on the *Electricity and Telephony Infrastructure* component corresponding to mobile telephone subscriptions and fixed telephone lines. This indicator uses a scale from 1 to 7 where a higher score means a better quality. LAC7 refers to the seven largest economies as measured by GDP: Argentina, Brazil, Chile, Colombia, Mexico, Peru and Venezuela. Both panels contain selected benchmark countries and Peru.

Source: Panel A –World Bank, *World Development Indicators* Database and *Instituto Nacional de Estadística e Informática* (INEI) for Peru's data. Panel B – WEF (2014), *The Global Competitiveness Report 2014-2015*, WEF (World Economic Forum), Geneva, http://www3.weforum.org/docs/WEF_GlobalCompetitivenessReport_2014-15.pdf.

StatLink http://dx.doi.org/10.1787/888933265655

Box 3.2. The links between infrastructure, well-being and the environment

A key pillar in the OECD well-being framework is satisfaction with the environment (Chapter 1). Poor infrastructure can leave people feeling dissatisfied with the state of their environment. This is particularly evident in Peru, where only 62% of individuals report that they are satisfied with the quality of the air, and 61% with the quality of the water (Figure 3.16). This places Peru at the bottom of the 15 benchmark countries (along with Chile in terms of air quality). Poor infrastructure and water quality contribute to environmental degradation, becoming a negative externality for Peruvians and a threat to future access to other non-renewable natural resources in the coming years.

Figure 3.16. Satisfaction with the environment, 2014

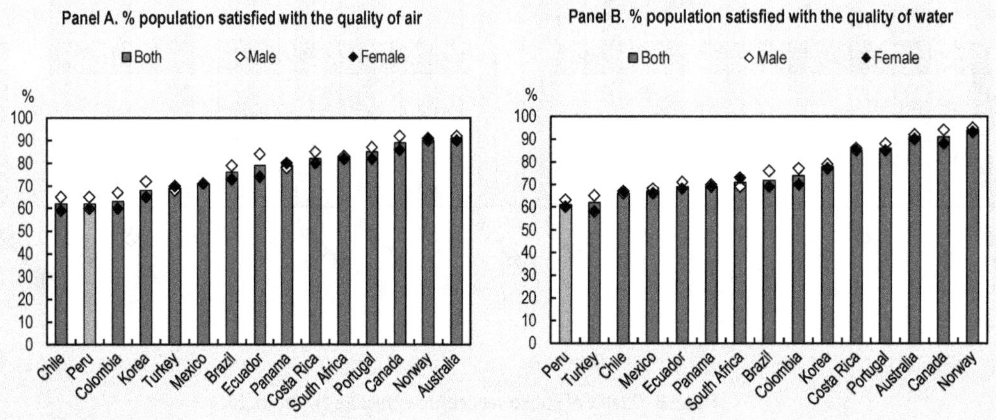

Source: Gallup Organisation (2015), *Gallup World Monitor* (database).

StatLink http://dx.doi.org/10.1787/888933265668

Reducing transport costs is key to Peru's competitiveness

The poor quality of transport infrastructure is a key factor in Peru's high transport costs; bringing down transport costs is key to boosting Peru's competitiveness. Good transport infrastructure can make the economy more efficient and ensure sustainable and high economic growth. The quality of Peru's roads and railroads are low in comparison with OECD economies and even Latin American ones (Figure 3.15, Panel B). In 2014, fewer than 15% of Peru's roads were paved.[9] In addition, the quality of Peru's port and air transport infrastructure is well below OECD standards (WEF, 2014). Peru does not just need to invest in new transport infrastructure – it must also improve its existing infrastructure. Getting the balance right between investing in new construction and in maintaining existing infrastructure is fundamental, since the overall cost of preservation for a road that is poorly maintained is three to seven times more than for a road that is perfectly maintained (OECD/ECLAC, 2012). In that sense, the national public investment system in Peru contributes to a better assessment of how infrastructure projects are chosen (Carranza et al., 2011).

Peru has traditionally concentrated on road transportation, and the use of other transport modes is low. While the country's rail network stagnated at around 2 000 km between 1999 and 2012, the roads networks increased by nearly 80% over the same period, from 78 127 km to 140 672 km.[10] Despite recent growth, shipping in Peru is largely concentrated in a just a few ports, meaning that high port costs keep the country's container traffic below its closest competitors, Colombia and Chile (AFIN, 2013). Greater use of rail and water transport could reduce transport costs and environmental degradation while promoting greater international integration.

The progress Peru has made in advancing trade agreements has not been accompanied by a reduction in transportation costs. The ratio of freight costs to tariffs for trade is higher than OECD and benchmark countries, based on costs of trade with the United States (Figure 3.17). In 2014, the ratio for Peru was about 25 times the OECD average. The cost of exporting a standard container of goods from Peru is approximately USD 890, much higher than in Singapore (USD 460) or China (USD 620) (World Bank, 2014a). Reducing transport costs would allow Peru to diversify its economy, as it would significantly lower prices and thus promote the competitiveness of many of its tradable goods.

Figure 3.17. **Ratio of freight costs to tariffs, 2012 and 2014**

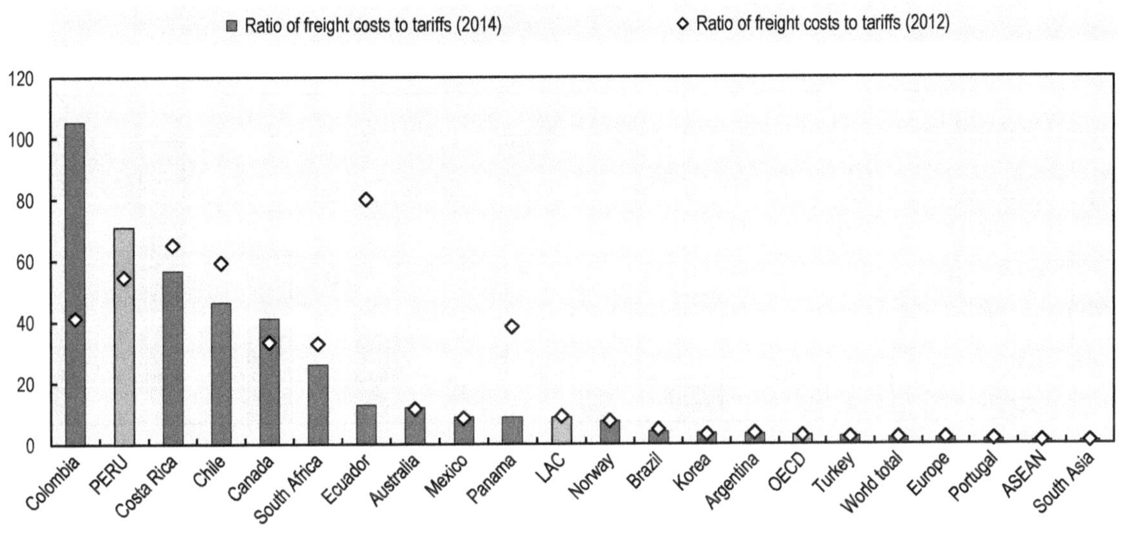

Note: Calculations based on imports from the US market. This figure shows the ratio of freight cost to tariffs on imports to the United States (Units). ASEAN is the Association of Southeast Asian Nations. Latin America and the Caribbean (LAC) consists of 20 countries.

Source: Based on data from the US Census Bureau. FT920: U.S. Merchandise Trade.

StatLink http://dx.doi.org/10.1787/888933265673

High transport costs also in Peru remains remain an obstacle to promoting regional integration with other countries in the region. Regional trade integration in Latin America is weaker than in other regions. For instance, in 2014, 61% of Europe's exports remained in its region, while only 17% of Latin America's total exports do the same (OECD/CAF/ECLAC, 2015). A 10% reduction in freight costs and tariffs would increase the LAC countries' bilateral imports by 45% and would increase regional imports by 60% (Rodrigue, 2012). The Pacific Alliance offers an excellent opportunity to boost intra-regional trade among LAC countries, but only if accompanied by strategies to significantly reduce transport and logistics costs.

Increasing the efficiency of logistics will boost productivity and trade

Along with hard components such as transport infrastructure, the "soft" components of a country's customs and logistics performance can also create a bottleneck. After controlling for other variables affecting economic growth, there is a significant link between improved logistics performance on the one hand, and productivity gains and sophistication of exports on the other (OECD/CAF/ECLAC, 2014).

Due to the composition of Peruvian exports, high transport costs have a negative impact on its competitiveness in regional and global markets. "Logistics intensity" refers to the dependence of an economic sector on its logistics performance. Based on logistics costs or time, one can measure the impact of logistics performance on each sector (OECD/CAF/ECLAC, 2013). Peru has a relative high share of logistics-intensive and time-sensitive exports, which account for 17% of all exports, 1.38 times higher than the OECD median (Figure 3.18). If transport costs were reduced, these economic sectors (being highly affected by the efficiency and quality of goods processing) could make a much greater contribution to the economy.

Figure 3.18. **Time-sensitive and logistics-intensive exports, 2012**

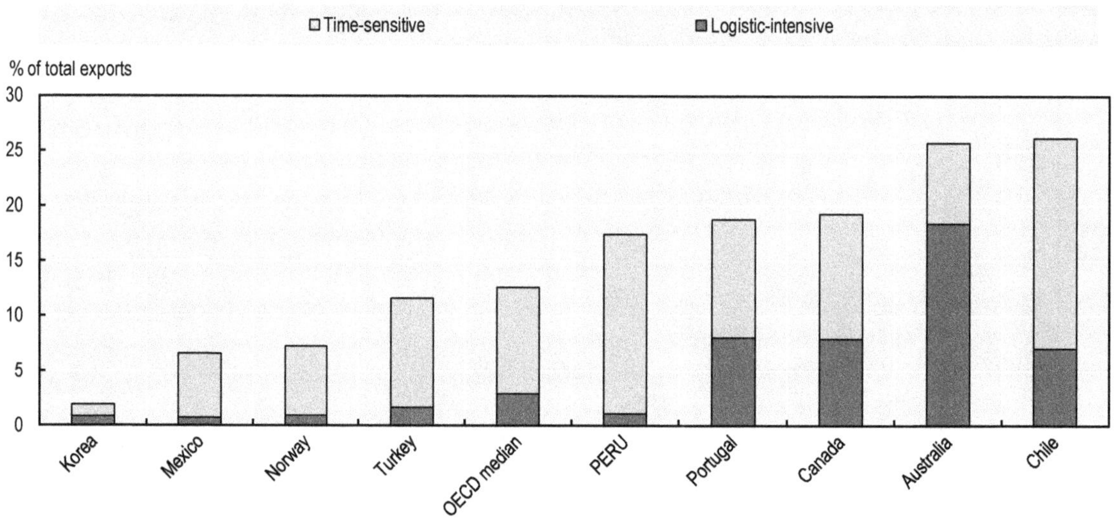

Note: Logistic-intensive sectors include mining, forestry and logging, wood manufacturing, paper publishing and printing. Time-sensitive sectors include agriculture, fisheries, food and drink manufacturing and horticulture.

Source: UN COMTRADE Database (accessed on 15 July 2015), http://comtrade.un.org/db/default.aspx.

StatLink http://dx.doi.org/10.1787/888933265680

Logistics costs in Peru account for 29% of GDP, while the average in Latin America is 24% and close to 9% in OECD countries (AFIN, 2013). More efficient logistics performance could therefore considerably improve Peru's competitiveness. The World Bank's Logistics Performance Index (LPI) measures logistics across six components, divided into two groups (Arvis et al., 2014). First, the regulatory and institutional components on which public policy has a direct effect: customs, infrastructure and logistics services. Second, the components that measure the performance of the logistics chain: timeliness of shipments, cost of shipments and traceability of consignments. Countries which improve their score by 1 in the LPI (which scores countries between 1 and 5) improve their labour productivity by about 35% on average. This would be the productivity gain Peru would enjoy if it were to achieve the same level of logistics performance as Canada.

Poor logistics performance remains a key challenge in Peru. Figure 3.19, Panel A shows the differences for each of the six LPI categories between the best-performing

OECD country and Peru, Latin America and OECD average. In the case of Peru, the largest gap is in customs, infrastructure and logistics services (Figure 19, Panel A). These are the components in which public policy plays a vital role. Peru performs worse than the OECD average and the seven biggest Latin American economies for all three of these indicators, and in customs its gap is worse than Latin American countries overall. Furthermore, Peru's overall logistics performance is worse than most of the benchmark countries (Figure 3.19, Panel B). In particular, Peru's gap is 48% larger than Chile's, the region's leading country. The Peruvian gap is also equivalent to three times the gap for OECD countries.

Figure 3.19. **Logistics performance gap to the best-performing OECD country, 2014**

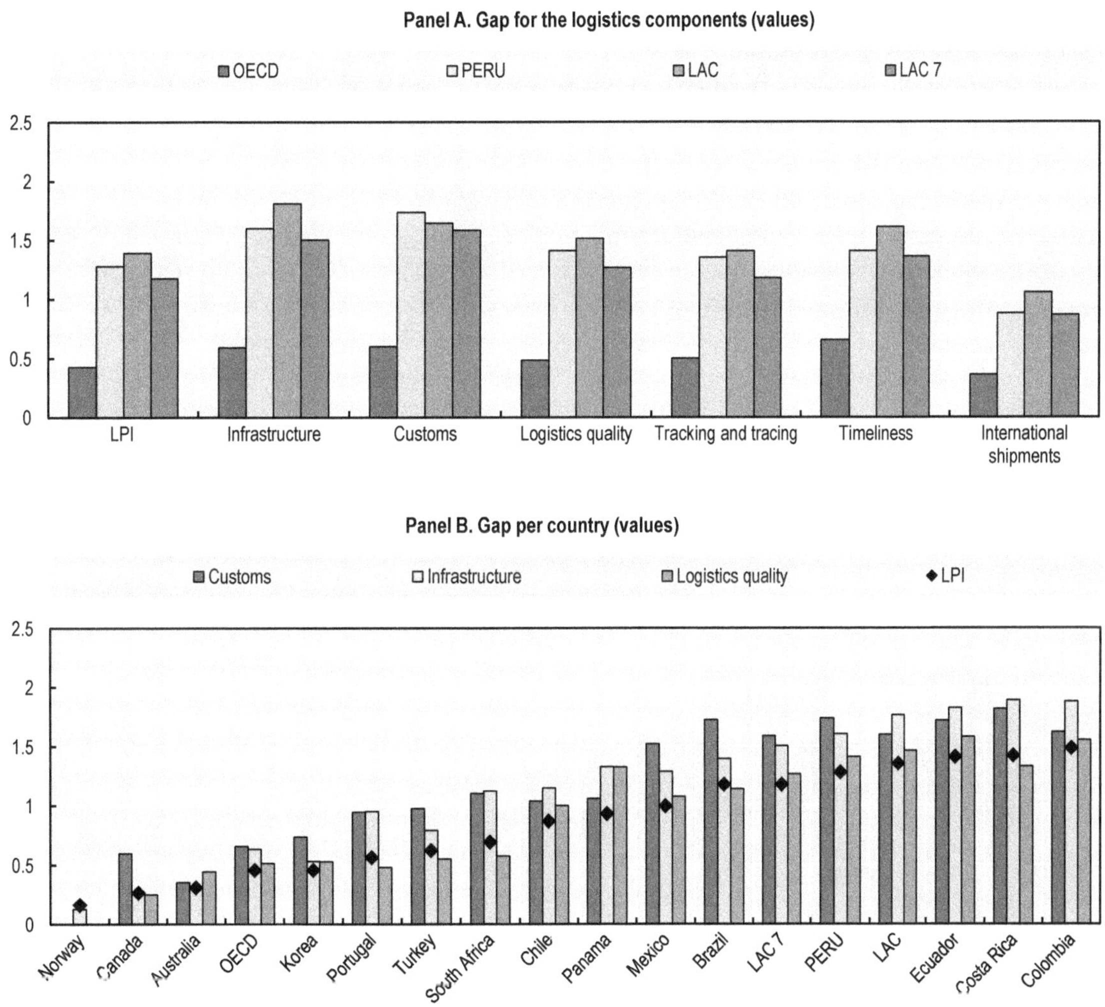

Note: The Logistics Performance Index (LPI) has a scale of 1 to 5, where 5 represents the best logistics performance. The gap refers to the difference for each logistics component with the best-performing OECD country, which is Germany for the overall LPI, infrastructure and tracking and tracing; Norway for customs and logistics quality; and Luxembourg for international shipments and timeliness. LAC7 refers to the seven largest economies in Latin America and the Caribbean as measured by GDP: Argentina, Brazil, Chile, Colombia, Mexico, Peru and Venezuela.

Source: Based on World Bank data (Logistics Performance Index) 2014, http://lpi.worldbank.org/.

StatLink http://dx.doi.org/10.1787/888933265691

Trade facilitation – measured as port efficiency, the customs and regulatory environment, and electronic business usage – has a significant impact on trade flows. Evidence suggests that customs clearance delays in Latin America increase transport costs by 4-12% (Guasch and Schwartz, 2008). Peru operates single-window facilities for foreign trade (*Ventanillas Únicas de Comercio Exterior*) as a policy tool to boost trade. In recent years it has streamlined border procedures and improved co-operation with neighbouring and third countries, according to the 2015 OECD Trade Facilitation Indicators which cover the full spectrum of border procedures (Elorza, 2012; OECD, 2015a).

Further efforts to address the bottlenecks in border processes would reduce trade costs and help Peru capitalise on its existing transport infrastructure. Areas where Peru lags behind other Latin American economies include external and internal co-operation among the country's various border agencies, and the simplification and harmonisation of documents (OECD, 2015a). Improving these would boost both trade and productivity in Peru and the country should take advantage of the Trade Facilitation Indicators to guide policy making.

Effective and available ICT can reduce transaction and logistics costs by lowering the cost of accessing information and encouraging efficient use of existing infrastructure. For instance, port gate management using ICT systems to schedule pick-up and delivery could reduce congestion at port terminals. There is a positive correlation between access to ICT and logistics performance after controlling for GDP per capita (OECD/CAF/ECLAC, 2013). As with other Latin American economies, in Peru the availability of the latest technologies and technology absorption by companies are lower than in OECD countries. The use of ICT remains well below the benchmark countries too (Figure 3.20).

Figure 3.20. **Use of information and communication technology, 2014**

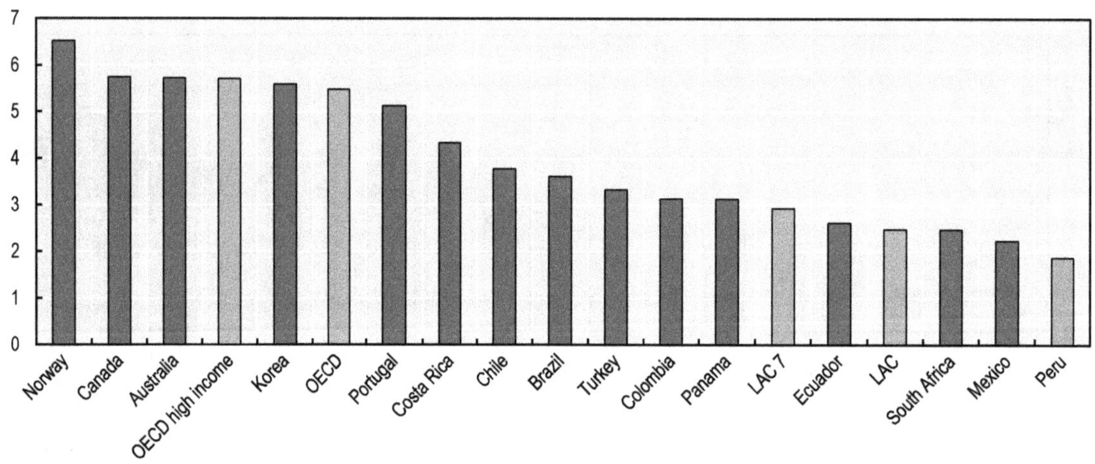

Note: The ICT use component is calculated based on Internet users, fixed broadband Internet subscription, Internet bandwidth and active mobile broadband subscriptions. This indicator uses a scale from 1 to 7 where a higher average score supposes a higher degree of usage. Latest available data for Ecuador is for 2013.

Source: WEF (2014), *The Global Competitiveness Report 2014-2015*, WEF (World Economic Forum), Geneva, http://www3.weforum.org/docs/WEF_GlobalCompetitivenessReport_2014-15.pdf.

StatLink http://dx.doi.org/10.1787/888933265705

Peru's business environment is improving but challenges remain

Peru has taken action to simplify its business regulations and strengthen legal institutions over the last decade in order to promote formal and transparent business practices, and boost entry and competition in domestic markets. In 2014, Peru ranked 35th out of 189 countries globally for overall ease of doing business, making it the second most highly ranked among all LAC economies (just after Colombia). Peru outperforms Mexico and Chile, as well as OECD countries such as Belgium and Turkey (Figure 3.21, Panel A). Furthermore, since 2004, Peru has reduced the number of procedures required to start a business from 10 to 6, the number of days required from 98 to 26, the overall cost from 39.4% to 9.2% of income per capita, while continuing to require zero minimum capital. All these indicate a better performance than the LAC average (Figure 3.21). Peru still has a way to go to reach OECD standards, however, where the average figures for setting up a business are 4.8 procedures lasting 9.2 days, and costing only 3.4% of income per capita. In recent years, Peru has improved public access to credit (ranked 12th out of 189 countries), with strong legal rights, accessible credit information and high credit bureau coverage. The country also offers simple procedures for registering property (26th out of 189 countries) and protecting minority business investors (40th out of 189 countries).

Figure 3.21. **Peru's business environment compared to OECD, Latin America and benchmark countries**

Panel A. Ease of doing business, 2014

Economy	Ease of Doing Business Rank
Korea	5
Norway	6
Australia	10
Canada	16
Portugal	25
OECD	25
Colombia	34
PERU	35
Mexico	39
Chile	41
South Africa	43
Panama	52
Turkey	55
Costa Rica	83
LAC	96
Ecuador	115
Brazil	120

Panel B. Number of procedures required to start a business, 2014

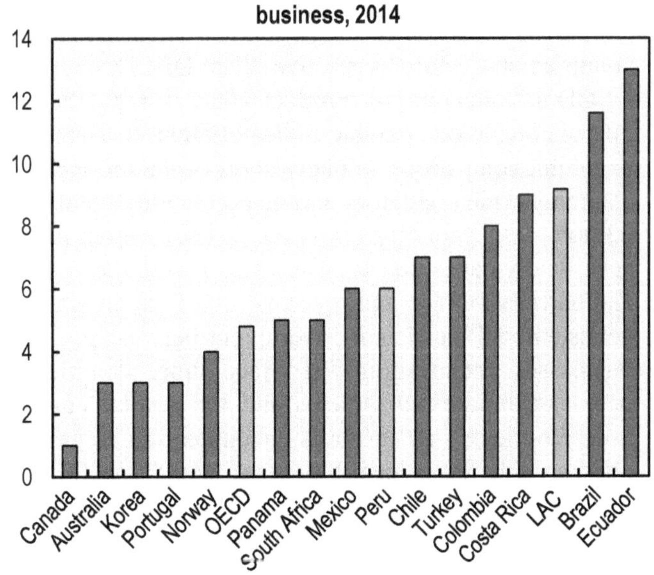

Figure 3.21. **Peru's business environment compared to OECD, Latin America and benchmark countries** (*cont.*)

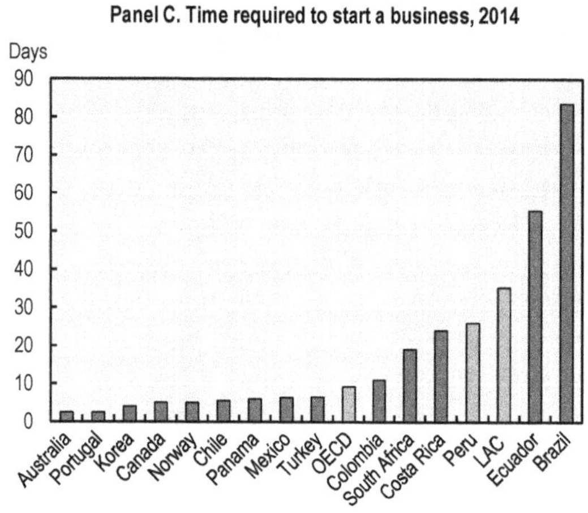

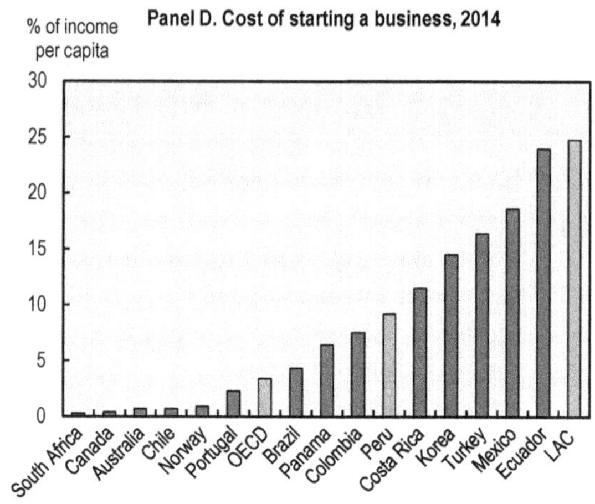

Note: OECD and LAC averages, and selected benchmark economies included. Panel A: Economies are ranked on their ease of doing business, from 1-189. A high ease of doing business ranking means the regulatory environment is more conducive to the starting and operation of a local firm.

Source: World Bank (2015), "Peru", *Doing Business – Measuring Business Regulations* (database), http://www.doingbusiness.org/data/exploreeconomies/peru.

StatLink http://dx.doi.org/10.1787/888933265713

Some procedural bottlenecks remain

Peru's Product Market Regulation is less restrictive than most non-OECD and LAC countries, but more restrictive than OECD countries on average (Figure 3.22). The OECD's indicators of product market regulation are a set of comprehensive and internationally comparable indicators that measure the degree to which policies promote or inhibit competition in many areas of the product market. These indicators measure the economy-wide regulatory and market environments in 34 OECD countries and in another 22 non-OECD countries (OECD, 2013b). Peru's product market regulation indicator was specifically developed in collaboration with the World Bank. Barriers to entrepreneurship and barriers to trade and investment in Peru are above OECD averages, driven largely by persistent and inefficient government bureaucracy. In comparison with OECD countries, businesses operating in Peru face more complex regulatory procedures – both for licensing and permit systems and for general communication of rules and procedures. Sole proprietor start-up firms encounter significantly larger administrative burdens. Peru does provide fewer legal barriers to entry than OECD countries on average, yet antitrust exemptions and barriers in network sectors still exceed many high-income and other economies with a comparable GDP (OECD, 2013b). Although Peru is considered a relatively open economy for trade and investment compared with its LAC counterparts, barriers to FDI, remaining trade facilitation barriers and differential treatment of foreign suppliers still exceed OECD averages – leaving ample opportunity for Peru to improve its investment climate and trade prospects.

Figure 3.22. **Components of product market regulation, 2013**

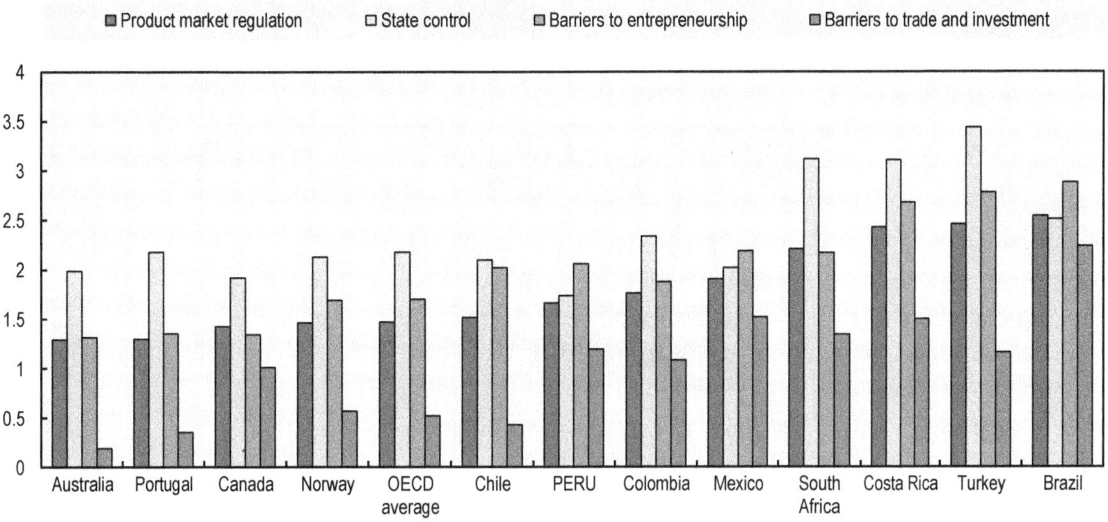

Note: The scale of the indicator is from least to most restrictive (from 0 to 6). The chart includes OECD countries and selected benchmark economies. Barriers to trade and investment, state control, and barriers to entrepreneurship are the three components of the Product Market Regulation indicator. The Product Market Regulation indicator for Peru was developed in collaboration with the World Bank.

Source: OECD, (2013b), *OECD Product Market Regulation 2013* (database), https://stats.oecd.org/index.aspx?DataSetCode=PMR.

StatLink http://dx.doi.org/10.1787/888933265725

Specific procedural requirements perpetuate bottlenecks for entrepreneurship in Peru. Though Peru has improved the business licensing process through federal and municipal regulatory reforms, there are still a number of costly and complicated compulsory procedures involved in establishing and operating a fully licensed business in Peru. The amount of time and number of procedures required for obtaining a construction permit and fulfilling tax obligations are above OECD averages, while those required for establishing an electricity supply are above both OECD and LAC averages (World Bank, 2014a).

Businesses in Peru also face a lack of transparency and functionality in the legal system, which hinders their ability to resolve business-related disputes. In order to address commercial sales disputes, Peru's judicial system must review and enforce contracts, a process which on average requires more than 40 procedures, 426 days, and costs up to 35% of the original claim (World Bank, 2015). Failure to provide timely trials and legal rulings significantly reduces the value of courts as a source of legal protection for small enterprises with limited resources to stay in operation. In addition, Peru's current bankruptcy law possesses a number of procedural and administrative bottlenecks. For instance, Peru's current solvency regime takes more than three years to process. In that context, improvements in institutions are essential for providing effective legal and financial protection to entrepreneurs, keeping viable businesses in operation, and providing greater incentives to participate in the formal business sector.

Stronger competition authorities are needed to promote market access

Competition between firms leads to increased productivity and economic growth. Policies promoting competition, access to markets and entry of new firms are linked particularly to improving total factor productivity. Experiences across different industries in emerging and developed markets show this positive relationship (Lewis, 2004; Cole et al., 2004). Furthermore, policies that lead to markets operating more competitively, such as enforcing competition law and removing regulations that hinder competition, result in faster economic growth (OECD, 2013c).

Peru has two competition authorities: the Instituto Nacional de Defensa de la Competencia y de la Protección de la Propiedad Intelectual (INDECOPI) and the Organismo Supervisor de Inversión Privada en Telecomunicaciones (OSIPTEL). INDECOPI enforces competition law and intellectual property law and protects consumers across the economy. It plays an important advocacy role by recommending the implementation of pro-competition measures to the legislative, political and administrative authorities (OECD/IDB, 2012). OISPTEL enforces competition law only in the telecommunications sector.

OSIPTEL, created in 1991, is a decentralised public body attached to the Presidency of the Council of Ministers. OSIPTEL had 261 employees and a budget of USD 27.2 million at the end of 2014. 32 employees work on competition issues, with a budget of USD 1.81 million. OSIPTEL carries out market studies and adopts and enforces regulatory measures involving competitive business practice in the telecommunications sector, acting both as a competition authority and a sector regulator (OECD, 2015b).

INDECOPI, created in 1992, is a specialised public body attached to the Presidency of the Council of Ministers. It promotes the free and efficient development of markets, protects consumer rights, safeguards intellectual property rights, and fosters a culture of free and fair competition in the Peruvian economy (OECD, 2015b). INDECOPI had 1 315 employees and a budget of USD 53.54 million in 2014. Human resources and budget constraints limit the number both of preliminary investigations that can be conducted and of cases that are resolved. Furthermore, improvements to the funding system are under consideration to make it independent of the amount of fines imposed, given the perverse incentives that this involves (OECD/IDB, 2012).

INDECOPI should improve the regulatory framework of cartels and other horizontal agreements as well as mergers. Peru's legislature is already discussing these two aspects as ways to improve the efficiency and effectiveness of investigations. First, clarifying the legal standards applicable to cartels and other horizontal agreements is needed. This is particularly relevant in Peru given that from 2008 to 2013 more than 90% of the cases initiated by INDECOPI were linked to cartel –lie agreements and 70% of the fines levied corresponded to those cases.[11] Second, merger control should be improved through the introduction of a compulsory pre-merger notification, with special emphasis placed on thresholds to be used for merger operations. The growing number of mergers and acquisitions in recent years calls for a better institutional framework for these operations. In the period 1995-2000, only 3 mergers and acquisitions were present in Peru, while the amount increased to 62 cases in the period 2010-14.[12]

INDECOPI's economic investigations department has developed a methodology to identify sectors most susceptible to anti-competitive practices (OECD/IDB, 2012). Any sector authority or business association can ask INDECOPI to prepare a market study, but these are prioritised according to the size and importance of the market, as well as the level of potential harm. While such market studies generally lead to recommendations to the government for legal and policy reform, there is no commitment on the part of the government to respond to these recommendations to explain if they will be implemented.

This change would give more strength to INDECOPI's role as competition advocate and would allow a more transparent debate on public policies can help or hinder competition.

Peru's competition authorities have used market studies as a tool for promoting competition. INDECOPI has conducted several market studies in the past five years (OECD, 2015b), including on competition in public procurement at the regional level, the domestic market for commercial airlines, the health system, the notary service market, the mobile market and the distribution of natural gas. In these last two sectors, Peru moved to reduce unnecessary regulatory constraints in both markets following these studies to promote greater competition. Similarly, OSIPTEL has increased the competition in the mobile market by forcing mobile operators to sell "unlocked" cell phones (i.e. cell phones that accept SIM cards from any operator).

The future challenge will be to further improve the effectiveness of INDECOPI and OSIPTEL in fostering competition in Peru. First, investing in more financial and human resources would allow them to undertake more investigations. Second, more independence from the political cycle and government ministries, particularly from the Ministry of Economy and Finance in INDECOPI's case, would increase credibility of competition agencies. Third, implementing a clearer legal framework for cartels, as well as introducing a compulsory notification procedure for mergers and acquisitions is needed to make competition enforcement stronger (OECD, 2015b; OECD/IDB, 2012). Third, developing stronger and more transparent relationships with stakeholders by publishing guidelines and greater information on the launch, results and outcomes of the market studies conducted would render market studies a more powerful tool.

A complete set of recommendations on how to foster competition in Peru could be achieved through a Peer Review of Competition Law and Policy. The OECD country reviews of national competition laws and policies assess how each country handles competition and regulatory issues, from the soundness of its competition law to the structure and effectiveness of its competition institutions. A competition law and policy peer review in Peru was carried out in 2004; in 2012, the OECD and the Inter-American Development Bank conducted a follow-up to it along with eight other Latin American countries (OECD/IDB, 2012). In addition, in 2014 the OECD published a report focusing on market studies (OECD, 2015b). A comprehensive and updated review on competition in Peru would be useful to improve the competition policy regime, thus helping to boost productivity and economic growth.

Greater attention is needed to encourage small businesses

Further reducing administrative barriers and formally targeting predatory business practices may provide opportunities to minimise Peru's informal business sector and increase total productivity. In 2010, small and micro enterprises made up approximately 95% of all enterprises in Peru, and employed more than 9.5 million people (Torres, 2010). As they are a primary source of employment, the government must continue to promote their proper growth and aid them in resolving factors that may hinder expansion. Poor regulatory practices tend to have the greatest negative impact on small businesses, where opting for informality may save significant opportunity costs in the face of complicated administrative procedures. Informal businesses are most often associated with low productivity as they offer limited opportunity for growth and lack protective social and labour regulations such as social security and working conditions (Haggarty et al., 2004). With the informal sector accounting for more than half of all labour activity (Chapter 2), a key challenge for Peru is to prioritise business ease and accessibility as a tool to incentivise formalisation, combat corruption and offer businesses opportunities to grow. Peru has improved the business environment for small and micro enterprises by expanding access to financing and reducing the costs and time required to start a business. Yet the country may foster superior economic gains by promoting and enforcing greater regulatory reforms at the national and subnational levels in order to ensure consistent standards, promote equal opportunities and reduce gaps in productivity.

Conclusions

One of the main obstacles to inclusive growth in Peru is its poor levels of productivity and competitiveness. Most of the gap in GDP per capita between Peru and OECD economies is explained by low labour productivity. In addition to skills, education and the match between labour supply and demand (covered in Chapter 2), total factor productivity is a driver of labour productivity. In Peru, the few economic sectors with high labour productivity account for only a small number of jobs. This is particularly evident in the mining sector, which provides less than 1.5% of Peru's jobs despite making up almost 50% of its exports and attracting more than 25% of its foreign direct investment. Peru's revealed comparative advantage is primarily concentrated in raw materials and in exports with low value-added. In addition, the sophistication and complexity of Peru's exports are well below that of OECD and most of the benchmark countries. Finally, the country largely participates in the lower end of global supply chains, providing inputs to other countries' processing activities rather than receiving inputs from abroad. These aspects reinforce the low level of competitiveness in Peru.

A key challenge for Peru is to take advantage of its income from its abundant and diverse natural resources to boost competitiveness. Peru could add value in natural-resource related supply chains in addition to its primary production. The experience of OECD countries such as Australia and Norway highlights the importance of the sustainable management of commodity resources to increase the competitiveness and productivity of their economies by exploiting methods to capture a relatively high value-added. Peru should pursue greater participation in global value chains, and identify segments of production that could contribute to higher value-added exports. This would enhance Peru's opportunities to diversify trade, promote industrialisation, and boost technology and knowledge concentration to advance the competitiveness of its export industry.

Inefficiencies in investment in research and development, and in ICTs, are holding back Peru's pursuit of value-added: innovation remains well below OECD levels. More and better investment in research and development is required to close the innovation gap.

The poor quality of Peru's transport infrastructure and logistics increases transport costs, which are a key source of inefficiencies for Peruvian firms. To reduce transport costs, Peru should increase the diversification of transport modes and improve "soft" components of logistics, such as customs and the use of ICTs in the transport sector.

Finally, despite recent improvements to reduce red tape and increase competition, certain inefficiencies in doing business remain in Peru. While the number and timing of bureaucratic procedures needed to set up a business have eased, there is still room for improvement in some areas such as contract enforcement and the administrative burdens for new businesses. This is in particular relevant for the sustainable development of small and micro enterprises, which represent approximately 95% of all enterprises in Peru. In addition, as with other Latin American economies, competition agencies need more financial and human resources to allow them to regularly undertake market studies and to take decisions on competition in product markets.

Notes

1. See Daude (2013) for a description of this methodology and an analysis of productivity in Latin America.

2. However, in order to close the GDP per capita gap with OECD economies, Peru needs to achieve investment rates close to 30% of GDP, as well as a change in the economic structure of Peru (Infante et al., 2014).

3. Furthermore, small and micro enterprises represent close to 99.5% of total private firms in Peru, accounting for more than 85% of total employment but generating less than 45% of private production (Díaz, 2014).

4. In 2014, the participation of oil, zinc, and lead ore in total exports was 9%, 3%, and 3%, respectively.

5. Based on data from the Direction of Trade Statistics (International Monetary Fund – IMF).

6. See Banco Central de Reserva del Perú, "Cuadros estadísticos", www.bcrp.gob.pe/estadisticas/cuadros-de-la-nota-semanal.html for a more specific definition of Peruvian non-traditional export goods.

7. For further information on the National Accord (*Acuerdo Nacional*), see http://acuerdonacional.pe/.

8. Based on data from the World Development Indicators and Infrascope for total investment and public-private partnerships in infrastructure, respectively.

9. Based on the statistics in transport provided by the Ministry of Transport and Telecommunications, http://www.mtc.gob.pe/estadisticas/transportes.html.

10. Based on INEI (National Institute of Statistics), transportation statistics, accessed on 15 June 2015. http://www.inei.gob.pe/estadisticas/indice-tematico/transport-and-communications/

11. Information provided by INDECOPI.

12. Based on Compemedia (2014).

References

AFIN (2013), *¿Obra Pública Tradicional o Asociación Público Privada? - Viabilidad del Comparador Público Privado en el Perú*, AFIN (Asociación para el Fomento de la Infraestructura Nacional), Lima, Peru.

AFIN (2012), *Por un Perú Integrado: Plan Nacional de Infraestructura 2012-2021*, AFIN, Lima, Peru.

Arvis, J.F. et al. (2014), *Connecting to Compete 2014: Trade Logistics in the Global Economy: The Logistics Performance Index and its Indicators*, International Trade Department, World Bank, Washington, DC.

Balassa, B. (1977), "'Revealed' comparative advantage revisited: An analysis of relative export shares of the industrial countries, 1953-1971", *The Manchester School*, Vol. 45/4, pp. 327-344.

BCRP (2015), *Annual Series* database, BCRP (Banco Central de Reserva del Peru), Peru, https://estadisticas.bcrp.gob.pe/estadisticas/series/anuales.

BP (2014), *BP Statistical Review of World Energy June 2014*, 63rd Edition, BP, www.bp.com/content/dam/bp/pdf/Energy-economics/statistical-review-2014/BP-statistical-review-of-world-energy-2014-full-report.pdf.

Bitran, E., S. Nieto-Parra and J.S. Robledo (2013), "Opening the black box of contract renegotiations: An analysis of road concessions in Chile, Colombia and Peru", *OECD Development Working Papers*, No. 317, OECD Publishing, Paris, http://dx.doi.org/10.1787/5k46n3wwxxq3-en.

Blyde, J.S. (ed.) (2014), *Synchronized Factories: Latin America and the Caribbean in the Era of Global Value Chains*, Springer-IDB, New York.

Carranza, L., C. Daude and Á. Melguizo (2011), "Public infrastructure investment and fiscal sustainability in Latin America: Incompatible goals?", *OECD Development Centre Working Papers*, No. 301, OECD Publishing, Paris, http://dx.doi.org/10.1787/5kg9xf1ncvzw-en.

CEPLAN (2011), *Plan Bicentenario: El Perú Hacia el 2021*, CEPLAN (Centro Nacional de Planeamiento Estratégico), Lima, Peru.

Céspedes, N. M. Aquile, A. Sanchez, and R. Tudela (2014a), "Productividad sectorial en el Perú: Un análisis a nivel de firmas", *Revista Estudios Económicos*, issue 28, pp. 9-26.

Céspedes, N., M. Aquile, A. Sanchez, and R. Tudela (2014b), "Productividad y tratados de libre comercio a nivel de empresas en Perú", *Working Papers*, 2014-014, Banco Central de Reserva del Perú.

Céspedes, N. and N. Ramirez-Rondán (2014), "Total factor productivity estimation in Peru: Primal and dual approaches", *Revista Economía*, Vol. 37(73), pp. 9-39.

CNC (2014), *La Agenda de Competitividad 2014-2018, Rumbo al Bicentenario*, CNC (Consejo Nacional de la Competitividad), Ministerio de Economía y Finanzas, Lima, Perú.

Cole, H. L. and L. E. Ohanian (2004), "New Deal policies and the persistence of the Great Depression: A general equilibrium analysis", *Journal of Political Economy*, 112(4), pp. 779-816, http://www.jstor.org/stable/10.1086/421169

Compemedia (2014), "Fusiones y Adquisiciones en el Perú 2012-2014: Análisis práctico de seis grandes operaciones desde la óptica de libre competencia", Lima, November, available at http://compemedia.org/wp-content/uploads/2014/11/COMPEMEDIA-INVESTIGA-FUSIONES-Y-ADQUISICIONES-EN-EL-PER%C3%9A-2012-2014.pdf

Daude, C. (2013), "Understanding Solow residuals in Latin America", *Economía*, Vol. 13(2), pp. 109-138.

Díaz, J.J. (2014), "Formalización empresarial y laboral", in R. Infante and J. Chacaltana (eds.) *Hacia un Desarrollo Inclusivo: El Caso del Perú*, ILO/United Nations/CEPAL, Santiago de Chile, pp. 173-260.

EIU (2014), *The 2014 Infrascope: Evaluating the Environment for Public-Private Partnerships in Latin America,* EIU (Economist Intelligence Unit), New York.

Elorza, J.C. (2012), "Ventanilla única de comercio exterior: Requisitos para una implementación exitosa en América Latina", *Serie Políticas Públicas y Transformación Productiva*, No. 8/2012, Corporación Andina de Fomento.

EY (2015), *Peru's Business and Investment Guide 2014/2015*, EY Peru, Lima, Peru, www.ey.com/Publication/vwLUAssets/Peru-Business-and-Investment-guide-2014-15/$FILE/Peru%C2%B4s%20Business%20and%20investment%20guide%202014-2015-2.pdf.

Felipe, J. et al. (2012), "Product complexity and economic development", *Structural Change and Economic Dynamics*, Vol. 23(1), pp. 36-68, Elsevier, Amsterdam.

Flor, L. and O. Rojas (2007), "¿Existe regulación por incentivos en las concesiones viales?: el caso peruano", *Revista de la Competencia y la Propiedad Intelectual,* Vol. 3(5), pp. 141-172.

Guasch J.L. (2004), *Granting and Renegotiating Infrastructure Concessions: Doing it Right,* World Bank, Washington, DC.

Guasch, J.L. and J. Schwartz (2008), "Reducing logistics costs in Latin America and the Caribbean: A logistics development agenda", manuscript, World Bank, Washington, DC.

Haggarty, L., K. Rada and E. Dohm (2004), *Cutting Red Tape: Simplifying Regulation at the Municipal Level in Latin America – Lessons From IFC's Experience in Peru and Nicaragua*, International Finance Corporation, www.businessenvironment.org/dyn/be/docs/81/Session4.2HaggartyDoc.pdf.

Hanushek E.A. and L. Woessmann (2012), "Do better schools lead to more growth? Cognitive skills, economic outcomes, and causation", *Journal of Economic Growth*, Vol. 17(4), pp. 267-321.

Hausmann, R. et al. (2012), *The Atlas of Economic Complexity*, Puritan Press, Cambridge, MA.

Hausmann, R., J. Hwang and D. Rodrik (2007), "What you export matters", *Journal of Economic Growth,*Vol. 12(1), pp. 1-25.

Hausmann R. and B. Klinger (2008), "Growth diagnostics in Peru", *CID Working Paper*, No. 181, Center for International Development, Harvard Kennedy School, Cambridge, MA, https://research.hks.harvard.edu/publications/getFile.aspx?Id=435.

Hidalgo, C.A. et al. (2007), "The product space conditions the development of nations", *Science*, Vol. 317(5837), pp. 482-487.

IMF (2012), *IMF eLibrary Data* (database), IMF (International Monetary Fund), http://elibrary-data.imf.org/DataExplorer.aspx.

Infante R., J. Chacaltana and M. Higa (2014), "Aspectos estructurales del desempeño macroeconómico del Perú. Situación actual, perspectivas y políticas", in R. Infante and J. Chacaltana (eds.) *Hacia un Desarrollo Inclusivo: El Caso del Perú*, ILO/United Nations/CEPAL, Santiago de Chile, pp. 97-172.

Kaldewei, C. and J. Weller (2013), "Empleo, crecimiento sostenible e igualdad" [Employment, sustainable growth and equity], *Macroeconomía del Desarrollo*, No. 145, ECLAC, Santiago, Chile.

Lewis, W. (2004). The Power of Productivity. University of Chicago Press. http://www.press.uchicago.edu/ucp/books/book/chicago/P/bo3623392.html

McKinsey (2013*), An Assessment of the Competitiveness and Health of Peru's Mining Industry*, McKinsey & Company, available from www.mckinsey.com/client_service/metals_and_mining/latest_thinking

MINCETUR (2015), *Plan Estrategíco Nacional Exportador: PENX 2025* [National Strategic Export Plan: PENX 2025], MINCETUR (Ministerio de Comercio Exterior y Turismo), Lima, Peru, www.mincetur.gob.pe/newweb/Portals/0/transparencia/proyectos%20resoluciones/RM_051_2015_PLAN.pdf.

Ministerio de la Producción (2015), *Plan Nacional de Diversificación Productiva* [National Plan of Productive Diversification], Ministerio de la Producción, Lima, Peru, 2015, www.produce.gob.pe/index.php/plan-nacional-de-la-diversificacion-productiva.

OECD (2015a) *Trade Facilitation Indicators* (database), OECD, www.oecd.org/tad/facilitation/indicators.htm.

OECD (2015b), *Competition and Market Studies in Latin America: The Case of Chile, Colombia, Costa Rica, Mexico, Panama and Peru*, OECD Publishing, Paris, www.oecd.org/daf/competition/competition-and-market-studies-in-latin-america2015.pdf.

OECD (2014), Latin America and Caribbean-OECD Investment Initiative, Conference on bridging infrastructure gaps through smart investment, Summary report, Lima, Peru, 7-8 July 2014, www.oecd.org/daf/inv/investment-policy/Summary-Report-LAC-Peru2014.pdf.

OECD (2013a), *Start-up Latin America: Promoting Innovation in the Region*, Development Centre Studies, OECD Publishing, Paris, http://dx.doi.org/10.1787/9789264202306-en.

OECD (2013b), *OECD Product Market Regulation 2013* (database), https://stats.oecd.org/index.aspx?DataSetCode=PMR.

OECD (2013c), "Evaluation of competition enforcement and advocacy activities: The results of an OECD survey", Working Party No. 2 on Competition and Regulation, Directorate for Financial and Enterprise Affairs, OECD. Available at: http://www.oecd.org/officialdocuments/publicdisplaydocumentpdf/?cote=DAF/COMP/WP2(2012)7/FINAL&docLanguage=En.

OECD (2011), *OECD Reviews of Innovation Policy: Peru 2011*, OECD Publishing, Paris, http://dx.doi.org/10.1787/9789264128392-en.

OECD (2009), *Natural Resources and Pro-Poor Growth: The Economics and Politics,* DAC Guidelines and Reference Series, OECD Publishing, Paris, http://www.oecd.org/bookshop?lang=en&pub=9789264041820

OECD/CAF/ECLAC (2015), *Latin American Economic Outlook 2016, China-Latin America: Development Partners in Transition*, OECD Publishing, Paris (forthcoming).

OECD/CAF/ECLAC (2014), *Latin American Economic Outlook 2015: Education, Skills and Innovation for Development*, OECD Publishing, Paris, http://dx.doi.org/10.1787/leo-2015-en.

OECD/CAF/ECLAC (2013), *Latin American Economic Outlook 2014, Logistics and Competitiveness for Development*, OECD Publishing, Paris, http://dx.doi.org/10.1787/leo-2014-en.

OECD/ECLAC (2012), *Latin American Economic Outlook 2012: Transforming the State for Development,* OECD Publishing, Paris, http://dx.doi.org/10.1787/leo-2012-en.

OECD/IDB (2012), "Follow-up to the Nine Peer Reviews of Competition Law and Policy of Latin American Countries: Argentina, Brazil, Chile, Colombia, El Salvador, Honduras, Mexico, Panama, and Peru", OECD, Paris. Available at: http://www.oecd.org/daf/competition/2012Follow-upNinePeer%20Review_en.pdf.

ProInversión (2015), *Estadisticas Generales* (database), ProInversion (Agencia de Promoción Privada – Perú), www.proinversion.gob.pe.

PwC (2013), *2013 Mining Industry: Doing Business in Peru,* PwC (PricewaterhouseCoopers), Lima, Peru, www.pwc.de/de/internationale-maerkte/assets/doing-business-in-mining-peru.pdf

Rodrigue, J.-P. (2012), "The benefits of logistics investments: Opportunities for Latin America and the Caribbean", *Technical Notes*, IDB-TN-395, Infrastructure and Environment Sector, Inter- American Development Bank, Washington, DC.

Rodrik, D. (2008), "The real exchange rate and economic growth", Harvard University, *Working Papers*, Cambridge, MA.

Rodrik, D. (2004), *Industrial Policy for the 21st Century*, Harvard University, John F. Kennedy School of Government, Cambridge, MA,

SECO (2013), *Peru Country Strategy 2013-2016*, SECO (Swiss Economic Cooperation and Development), Berne, Switzerland, www.eda.admin.ch/content/dam/countries/countries-content/peru/en/Strategie-SECO-Peru-2013-16_en.pdf.

Simoes, A.J.G. and C.A. Hidalgo (2012), "The Economic Complexity Observatory: An analytical tool for understanding the dynamics of economic development", Workshop at the Twenty-Fifth AAAI Conference on Artificial Intelligence, August, 2011, Cambridge, MA.

Távara J. I., E. González de Olarte and J. M. Del Pozo (2014), "Heterogeneidad estructural y articulación productiva en el Perú: Evolución y estrategias", in R. Infante and J. Chacaltana (eds.) *Hacia un Desarrollo Inclusivo: El Caso del Perú*, ILO/United Nations/CEPAL, Santiago de Chile, pp. 39-96.

Torres, D. (2010), *APEC Forum on Human Resources Development 2010: Peruvian Economy Report*, General Directorate of Micro and Small Enterprises and Cooperatives, Ministry of Production of Peru, 2010, http://buenaspracticas.stps.gob.mx/buenaspracticas/pdf_2011/11_Economy_Report_Peru.pdf

UN (2013), *National Report for the National Voluntary Presentation of Peru to the Economic and Social Council*, UN (United Nations) Economic and Social Council, Geneva, Switzerland, www.un.org/ga/search/view_doc.asp?symbol=E/2013/58.

UNCTAD (2013), *Global Value Chains and Development: Investment and Value Added Trade in the Global Economy,* UNCTAD (United Nations Conference on Trade and Development), United Nations Publication, 2013, http://unctad.org/en/PublicationsLibrary/diae2013d1_en.pdf.

UNDP (2011), *Towards Human Resilience: Sustaining MDG Progress in an Age of Economic Uncertainty*, Bureau for Development Policy, UNDP (United Nations Development Programme), New York, www.undp.org/content/dam/undp/library/Poverty%20Reduction/Towards_SustainingMDG_Web1005.pdf.

USGS (2014), *Mineral Commodity Summaries 2014*, USGS (U.S. Geological Survey), http://minerals.usgs.gov/minerals/pubs/mcs/2014/mcs2014.pdf.

WEF (2014), *The Global Competitiveness Report 2014-2015*, WEF (World Economic Forum), Geneva, http://www3.weforum.org/docs/WEF_GlobalCompetitivenessReport_2014-15.pdf.

World Bank (2015), "Peru", *Doing Business – Measuring Business Regulations* (database), http://www.doingbusiness.org/data/exploreeconomies/peru.

World Bank (2014a), *Doing Business 2015: Going Beyond Efficiency*, World Bank, Washington, DC, www.doingbusiness.org/~/media/GIAWB/Doing%20Business/Documents/Annual-Reports/English/DB15-Full-Report.pdf.

World Bank (2014b), "Innovation as key to diversify the economy in Peru", World Bank website, www.worldbank.org/en/results/2014/08/06/innovation-as-key-to-diversify-the-economy-in-peru.

Chapter 4
Macroeconomic policies for inclusive development

Peru's macroeconomic performance has been extraordinary over the last decade. This performance is in part the result of a very favourable external environment, but is also a consequence of a successful combination of sound fiscal policy and monetary credibility. While the former is based on a fiscal responsibility law, the latter is supported by an inflation targeting regime under a dual monetary system. This is a great achievement: a sound macroeconomic framework provides the foundations for a more competitive economy and greater social equity. However, there is still room for improvement. Peru still has a relatively underdeveloped and inefficient financial market. Also, the high level of dollarisation of the financial system increases the economy's vulnerability to external shocks. Finally, a comprehensive fiscal reform is needed to improve the efficiency and equity of the tax system, and in particular to increase fiscal revenues. A more effective and progressive taxation system will be crucial to finance several structural challenges highlighted in the previous chapters, and to reduce income inequalities in Peru.

Underpinned by better macroeconomic management and an exceptionally favourable external environment, Peru's macroeconomic performance has been strong over the last decade. Between 2004 and 2014, per capita GDP grew by an average of 5% per year – the second highest rate of growth in Latin America – and the average inflation rate was 2.6% per annum (Figure 4.1). The unemployment rate fell to historical lows, down from 9.5 % in 2004 to 6% in 2014, while labour participation rose from 71 to 79% in the same period (see Chapter 2). In sum, the last decade has been, in macroeconomic terms, the best Peru has had in over a century (Seminario and Alva, 2012; Mendoza, 2013).

Figure 4.1. **Peru's macroeconomic performance**

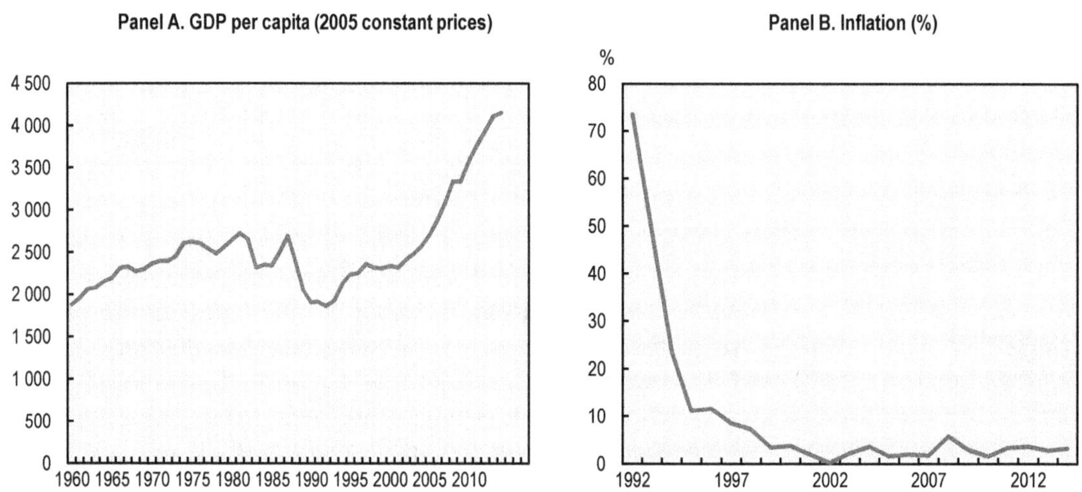

Source: World Bank (2015), *World Development Indicators* (database), Washington, DC, http://data.worldbank.org

StatLink http://dx.doi.org/10.1787/888933265737

Like other Latin American countries, Peru had suffered for many decades from serious political instability, which had a negative impact on economic growth (Chapter 1; Alesina et al., 1996). But the return to democracy and the stabilising political situation have allowed the country to put in place a sound macroeconomic framework as a solid base from which to build stronger economic growth. Key plans in this framework include major changes in the design of Peru's fiscal and monetary policy, which have helped to reduce macroeconomic instability and improve the capacity of policy makers to respond to external shocks, boosting investment and growth.

This chapter presents Peru's macroeconomic performance, and examines the current and structural challenges that the country faces on the macroeconomic front. First, the chapter reviews the factors behind Peru's strong performance in recent years, analyses the short-term economic outlook, and stresses the need for further strengthening the macroeconomic framework in light of a more challenging external environment. Next, this chapter highlights the need for improvement in access to and administration of the financial resources available for supporting inclusive development. These areas correspond to enhancing access to finance, and increasing capacities for domestic resource mobilisation through the taxation system.

Several factors are behind Peru's strong recent performance

The improvements in Peru's conduct of monetary and fiscal policies are reflected in reduced and less volatile inflation, as well as in the lower volatility and less pro-cyclical behaviour of government spending (Figure 4.2). Together these have helped to reduce volatility in GDP growth (Box 4.1). Lower business cycle volatility improves welfare in two ways: 1) it reduces economic uncertainty, thereby fostering investment and boosting economic growth (Hnatkovska and Loayza, 2004); and 2) it reduces income volatility, which can have a strong impact on households' well-being.

Figure 4.2. **Volatility and macroeconomic management in Peru, 1990-2014**

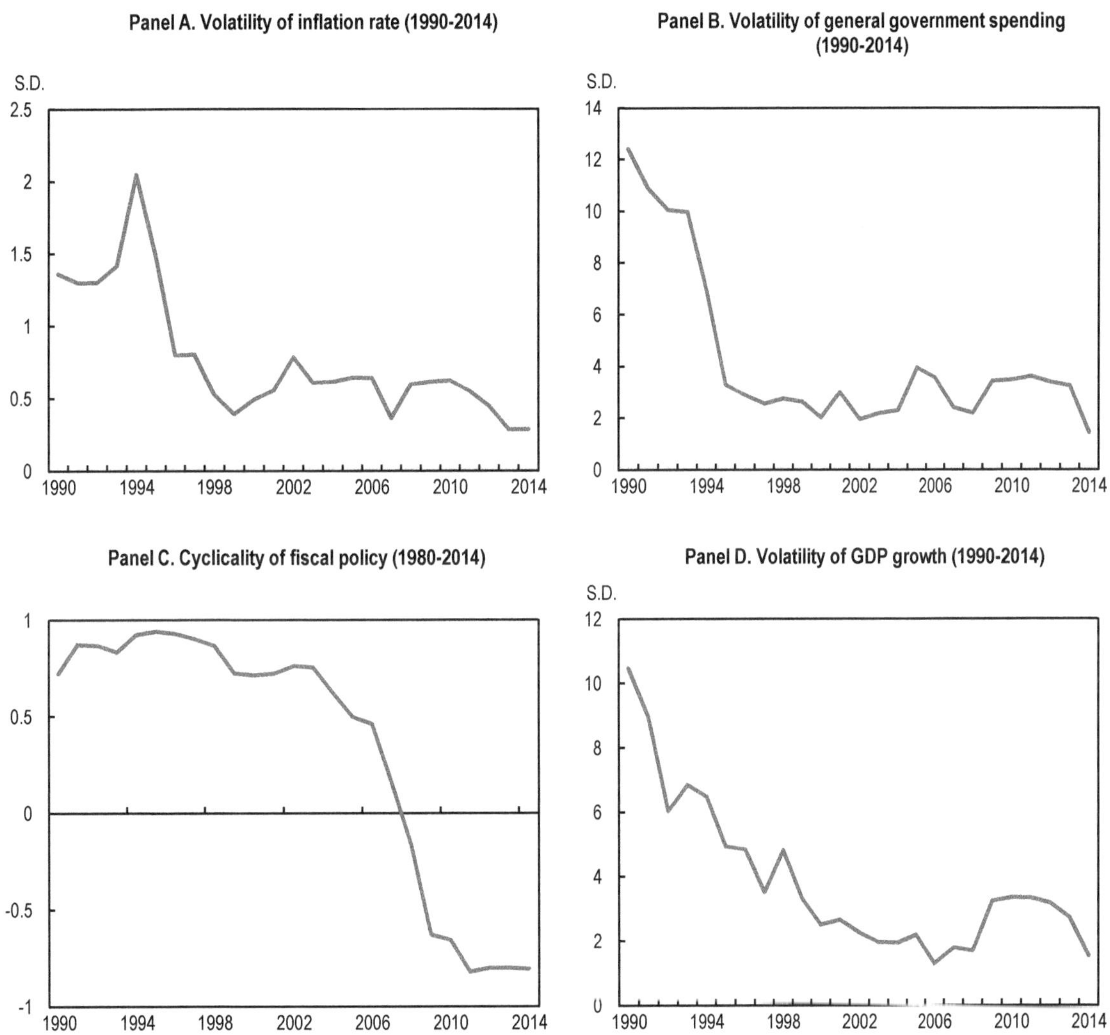

Note: In Panels A, B and D, S.D. refers to standard deviation. Panel C. Correlation coefficient between the cyclical components of real government expenditure and real GDP for a 10-year overlapping window. The cyclical components have been estimated using the Hodrick-Prescott Filter. A positive (negative) correlation indicates procyclical (countercyclical) fiscal policy. Real government expenditure is defined as central government expenditure and net lending deflated by the GDP deflator.

Source: OECD calculations based on World Bank (2015), *World Development Indicators* (database), Washington, DC, http://data.worldbank.org.

StatLink http://dx.doi.org/10.1787/888933265747

Evidence suggests that in Latin America, welfare improvements from lower business cycle volatility can amount to up to 10% of consumption (Loayza et al., 2007). An improved macroeconomic framework is perhaps the most important asset the government has for its conduct of economic policy. Therefore, continuing to strengthen it should be the cornerstone of future policy making and the foundation on which to build a competitive economy and social equity.

Box 4.1. **How have improvements in the macroeconomic framework helped decrease business cycle volatility**

Peru has experienced a dramatic settling down in business cycle volatility over the past 25 years. Indeed, the volatility of real output growth has decreased by around 80% since 1990. What factors contributed to this? This box explores this question. Using a panel of 77 countries, including advanced and emerging economies for the period 1960-2014, the main determinants of business cycle volatility have been estimated. Therefore, using the estimated coefficients from this regression, it has been measured how much each explanatory variable contributed to the decrease in volatility in Peru. The results show that although external factors such as less frequent terms of trade shocks and less volatile capital inflows did contribute to the decline in volatility, improvements in Peru's macroeconomic management played a more important role. In particular, according to the estimations, more than half of the decrease in business cycle volatility in Peru can be explained by more stable fiscal and monetary policies (Figure 4.3).

Figure 4.3. **What were the main drivers of lower business cycle volatility in Peru?**

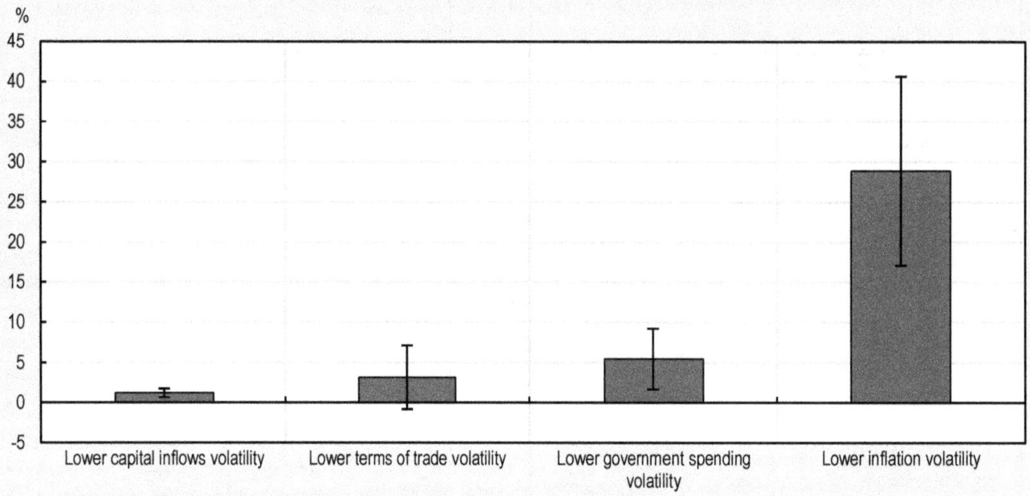

Note: The bars show the contribution of each variable to the decrease in business cycle volatility observed in Peru between 1960 and 2014. Business cycle volatility is measured as the standard deviation of GDP growth in a 5-year rolling window.

Source: OECD calculations based on Olaberría and Rigolini (2009), "Managing East Asia's macroeconomic volatility", *Policy Research Working Paper,* No. WPS 4989, World Bank, Washington, DC.

StatLink *http://dx.doi.org/10.1787/888933265756*

Peru has also benefitted from the exceptional external environment prevalent during the last decade. As one of the largest producers of metals in the world (Chapter 3), Peru benefited immensely from the upswing in commodity prices that started a decade ago, and which, together with record low international interest rates (Figure 4.4), had important macroeconomic implications. First, they provided a strong impulse for GDP growth which, during the last decade, was one of the highest in Latin America. Second, high investment, especially in mining, attracted large capital inflows (Chapter 3). More than two-thirds of these capital flows were in the form of foreign direct investment, lending relative stability to the financing of the current account.

Figure 4.4. **The external conditions influencing Peru**

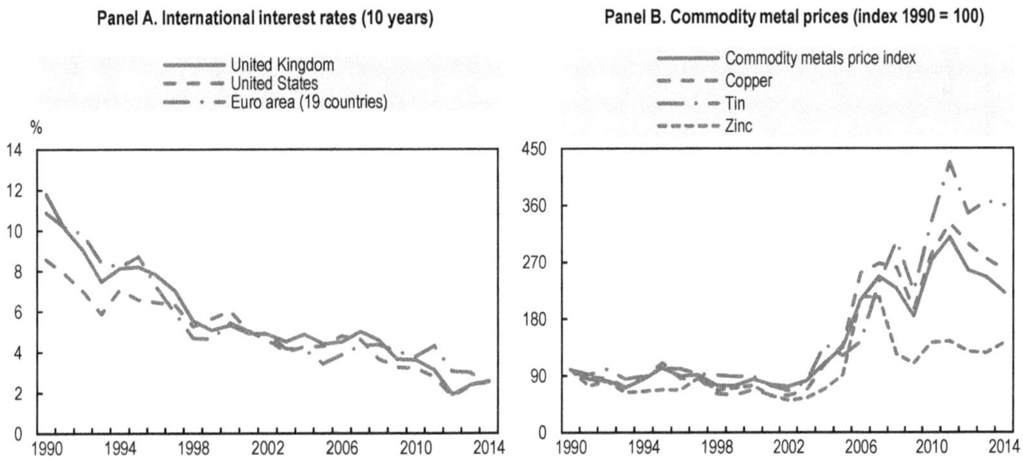

Source: IMF (2014), *World Economic Outlook Database*, International Monetary Fund, Washington DC, http://www.imf.org/external/pubs/ft/weo

StatLink http://dx.doi.org/10.1787/888933265769

After a decade of strong growth, activity is slowing down

The external environment is now shifting, however, as global commodity prices have declined sharply and external financial conditions are expected to tighten. Although commodity prices are still high by historical standards, their significant drop in the last two years has put an end to the so-called commodity super cycle. The widespread view that the decrease in commodity prices has a strong permanent component has affected the investment plans of mining companies. Therefore, the fall in commodity prices has triggered a sharp decline in investment (Figure 4.5). The fall in metal prices in particular has increased uncertainty and undermined domestic confidence. Net capital inflows have also moderated, coming down from 7.5% of GDP in the period 2010-13 to 3% of GDP in 2014.

Domestic demand has weakened. This is partly due to the sharp contraction in private investment, but also because of softer growth in private consumption, which decreased from 6.1% in 2012, to 4.1% in 2014 (Figure 4.6 and Table 4.1). Public expenditure has also suffered, due to problems with fiscal execution at the regional and local government levels. Between 2012 and 2014 it fell from 8.1% to 6.4%. Activity has also been hampered by idiosyncratic shocks to sectors like fishing and mining. These sectors showed negative growth in 2014. As they are important contributors to GDP, economic growth in Peru slowed to 2.4% in 2014 (from an expansion of 6% in 2012 and 5.8% in 2013; Figure 4.6).

Figure 4.5. **Private investment and export prices**

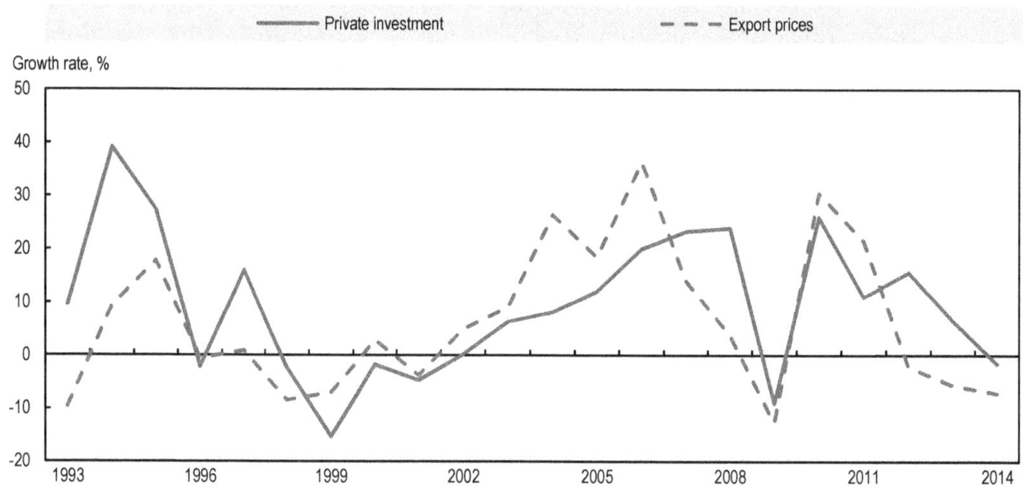

Source: Central Bank of Peru (*Banco de la Reserva del Perú*), http://www.bcrp.gob.pe/estadisticas.html

StatLink http://dx.doi.org/10.1787/888933265779

Economic growth in 2015 is expected to pick up gradually to around 3.4% and could potentially reach 4.3% in 2016. This recovery will be driven by a variety of factors, including:

- The recovery from adverse supply shocks that hit the economy in 2014, such as climatic factors that led to temporary interruptions to mining, fishing and agriculture.
- The opening of new mines and implementation of major infrastructure projects, along with an expected recovery of public investment in infrastructure projects. In particular, the government is expected to spend close to 0.3% of GDP on Lima's Metro (Line 2), and 0.4% of GDP on modernising the *Talara* refinery.
- The planned fiscal stimulus, which is expected to take an expansionary route in 2015 and become neutral in 2016. Various tax measures announced in 2014 are hoped to boost activity in the short and medium term. These measures include cutting the income tax rate for individuals and companies, a reduction in the excise tax on fuels, and simplified regimes for general tax on sales.

Monetary policy is also expected to boost activity. After keeping the policy interest rate at 4.25% for more than two years, the Central Bank cut the rate by 100 basis points and has kept it at 3.25% since January 2015. These cuts were intended to facilitate the recovery of the economy. However, inflation currently stands at the upper limit of the target range, and given the high level of dollarisation of credit and significant currency mismatches on balance sheets, a strong and sharp depreciation could have a systemic impact, seriously damaging activity levels (see the next section). This reduces the scope for further cuts in the policy rate.

Figure 4.6. **Trends in GDP and GDP growth**

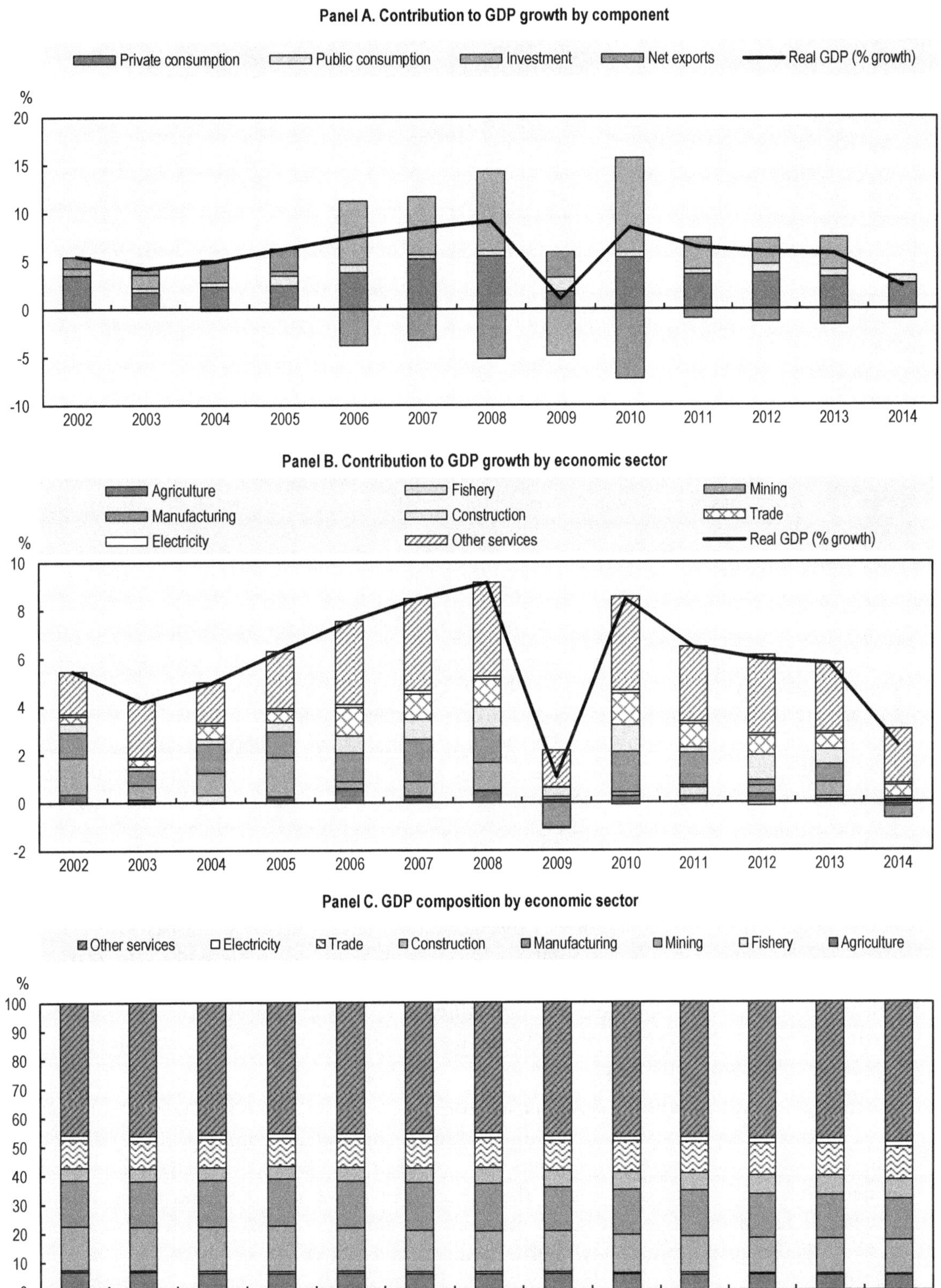

Source: Central Bank of Peru (*Banco de la Reserva del Perú*), http://www.bcrp.gob.pe/estadisticas.html

StatLink http://dx.doi.org/10.1787/888933265785

Table 4.1. **Demand, output and prices: Recent trends and projections in Peru**

	2011	2012	2013	2014	2015	2016
	Current prices in PEN million	Percentage change, volume (prices)				
GDP at market prices	469 854.8	6.0	5.8	2.4	3.6	4.3
Private consumption	281 718.0	6.1	5.3	4.1	4.2	4.5
Government consumption	48 111.0	8.1	6.7	6.4	7.0	6.0
Gross fixed capital formation	120 908.2	10.2	12.1	-3.9	1.0	3.0
Final domestic demand	450 737.2	7.4	7.4	2.0	3.6	4.3
Exports of goods and services	139 336.6	5.8	-2.3	-0.3	3.0	5.0
Imports of goods and services	120 219.0	11.3	3.6	-1.4	2.0	5.0
Net exports[1]	19 117.6	-1.2	-1.7	0.3	0.3	0.1
Memorandum items						
GDP deflator	_	2.1	1.7	2.9	2.0	1.5
Consumer price index	_	2.6	2.9	3.2	2.5	2.0
Unemployment rate	_	6.8	7.5	6.0	6.2	6.0
Current account balance[2]	_	-2.7	-4.4	-4.1	-4.3	-4.5

1. Contributions to changes in real GDP, actual amount in the first column.

2. As a percentage of GDP at market value.

Source: Central Bank of Peru (*Banco de la Reserva del Perú*), www.bcrp.gob.pe/estadisticas.html and OECD projections (June 2015).

The economic environment calls for a stronger and more effective macroeconomic framework

As a small, open economy Peru is highly exposed to external shocks and will, therefore, be significantly affected by the shifting external environment. One important threat to Peru's growth prospects is the deteriorating economic situation in People's Republic of China (China), which has become an increasingly important destination for Peruvian exports (Chapter 3). Lower economic growth in China will hurt Peru through its impact on world metal prices, and hence Peru's terms of trade and economic activity. Estimates suggest that a decrease in China's investment growth by one standard deviation is likely to reduce Peru's terms of trade and GDP growth by about 2 and 0.2 percentage points, respectively (Han, 2014).

Another source of vulnerability is the fact that Peru is a highly dollarised economy. About 40% of Peru's banking system liquidity and 42% of its bank credit to the private sector is denominated in foreign currency. This exposes Peru to changes in external financial conditions which are expected to tighten as the US Federal Reserve starts raising interest rates. Peru's exposure to a US monetary policy shock is larger than that of a typical small, non-dollarised open country.

In sum, shifting external conditions are lowering commodity prices, increasing long-term dollar interest rates, weakening regional currencies and lowering flows of capital to emerging economies. All of these will put pressures on Peru's financial markets and potential growth. As a result, raising the expected revenues and servicing the debt will become more difficult, and tighter financing conditions will affect investment and growth. To better prepare the economy to adjust to the new environment, Peru should reinforce its macroeconomic framework and make sure that banks, governments, businesses and households have solid balance sheets. The sections which follow look at Peru's recent improvements in these dimensions, and suggest areas where further improvements are possible.

The fiscal framework is relatively solid

Fiscal policy responsibility in Peru has gained credibility over the last decade. In the past Peru's public finances were extremely weak and often the cause of financial and economic crises. For instance, the economy operated with fiscal deficits exceeding 10% of GDP during the 1970s and 1980s. High fiscal deficits generated a sharp and unsustainable rise in the government debt-to-GDP ratio: from 29% of GDP in 1980 to 89% in 1990.

In the early 1990s, the government launched a set of constitutional changes that freed up monetary policy to be independent of fiscal policy. For instance, in 1993 Congress passed a law prohibiting the Central Bank from lending to the government. This measure, and the pensions reform of 1992 which helped reduce the large fiscal gap, saw the fiscal deficit rapidly reduce: from 9% of GDP in 1990 to a fiscal surplus of 2% of GDP in 1995 (Figure 4.7). However, by the end of that decade an expansionary fiscal policy combined with the creation of a set of tax exemptions saw the fiscal deficit re-emerge – at almost 3% of GDP.

The Fiscal Responsibility Law, introduced in 1999, has been very effective in strengthening public finances and reducing public debt. Since then, the management of fiscal policy has significantly improved. Between 2002 and 2007 the fiscal deficit was reduced from 2% of GDP to a surplus of 3% (Figure 4.7). Although the international crisis of 2008-2009 prompted the public deficit to rise to 1.3% in 2009, since then the government resumed the downward path of fiscal deficit. Between 2010 and 2013 the government has had fiscal surplus. Consistent with the behaviour of the fiscal deficit, the public debt to GDP ratio also declined sharply over the same period (Figure 4.7).

However, until very recently the fiscal framework lacked a counter-cyclical fiscal policy, contributing to relatively high volatility in government spending. The Fiscal Responsibility Law helped stabilise debt dynamics, but did not contribute much to reduce the high degree of cyclicality of public spending, keeping macroeconomic instability at a relatively high level. Indeed, when measured by the correlation between the change in the cyclical component of government expenditures and the output gap, Peru, like many other emerging economies, has historically displayed a high level of pro-cyclicality (Frankel et al., 2013).

In October 2013 Congress approved a new macro-fiscal framework incorporating medium-term fiscal objectives and introducing counter cyclicality into the budget planning process by focusing on the structural balance. The implementation of this policy has been associated with more counter-cyclical behaviour of the fiscal balance (Alberola et al., 2015). The new framework outlines a stronger regulatory structure with a more comprehensive spending rule, the creation of an independent body to contribute to the technical analysis of fiscal and macro policy, and corrective actions in cases of breaches of the fiscal rule. It also defines the scope of public expenditure coverage for national government and sub-national governments, and simplifies and strengthens their macro-fiscal frameworks when it comes to monitoring, provision of support and corrective actions. This marked a good step forward; since then, Peru has followed a fiscal rule that has a structural (i.e. cyclically-adjusted) fiscal balance as its target.

Figure 4.7. **Fiscal debt and public borrowing, 1990-2014**

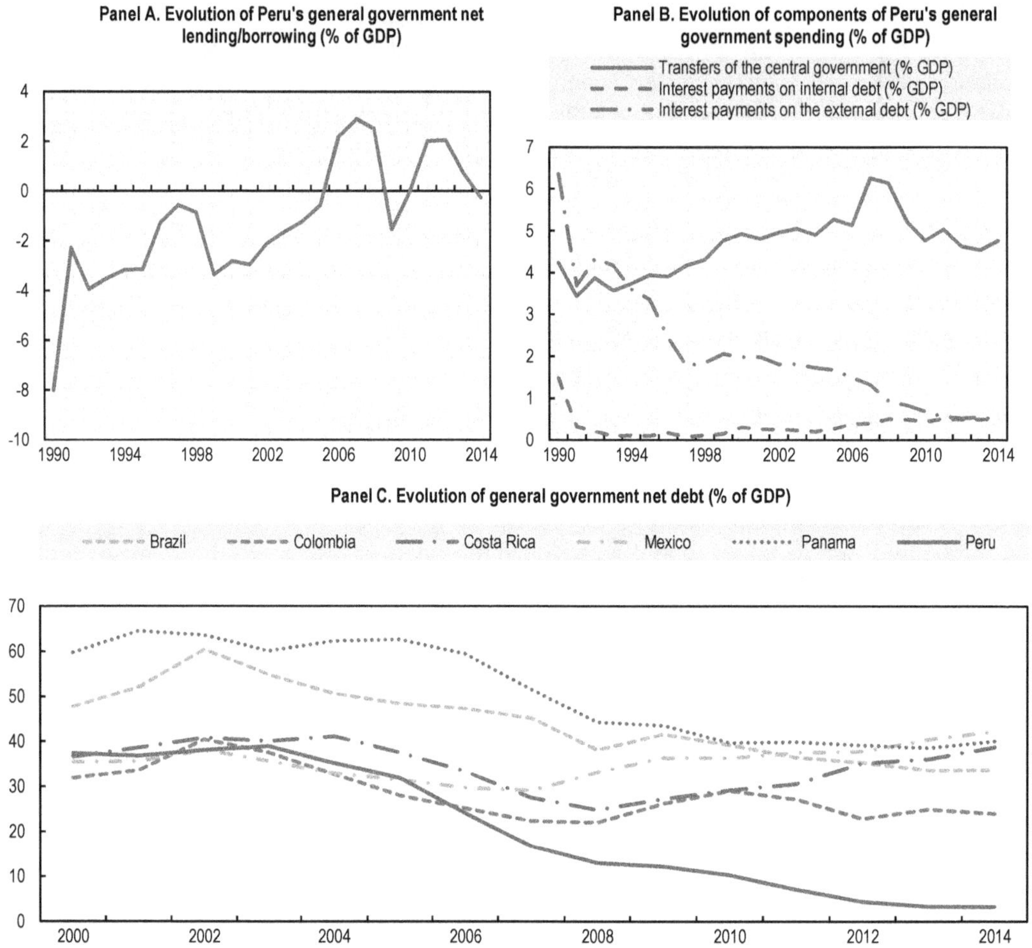

Source: Central Bank of Peru (*Banco de la Reserva del Perú*), http://www.bcrp.gob.pe/estadisticas.html and IMF (2014), *World Economic Outlook Database*, International Monetary Fund, Washington DC, http://www.imf.org/external/pubs/ft/weo.

StatLink http://dx.doi.org/10.1787/888933265792

Another strong point is that the decision-making process in the fiscal and budgetary frameworks is relatively well designed. The Ministry of Economy and Finance has made significant improvements through the Public National Investment System (Chapter 5). In addition, fiscal transparency has been enhanced by frequent and efficient fiscal reporting, such as the latest Multiannual Macroeconomic Framework (MEF, 2015). Fiscal reporting and statistics classify information according to international standards. Budgeting practices also operate according to advanced standards. The budget covers the general government, although with few exceptions, such as the Peruvian National Oil Company (PeruPetro). The strategic plan (covering 3 to 10 years) includes detailed and comprehensive medium-term macroeconomic and fiscal projections thanks to the Multiannual Macroeconomic Framework and the fact that the Multiannual Budget Plan baseline projections allow for a two-year outlook.

However, relatively weak evidence-based decision making is affecting the ability to achieve strategic outcomes in the short and medium term. There is a gap between the planned and executed budget since changes to the initial budget commonly occur. The executed budget exceeded by more than 6% of initial budget in 2013.[1] In addition, there is a lack of appropriate regulations to monitor and better control multi-annual investment projects. Finally, there is no independent evaluation of the government's fiscal performance, despite frequent and significant changes to the fiscal forecasts and targets in the past.

Tax policy needs to do more to target development and equality

A key challenge for Peru is to improve its tax policy so as to turn revenues into a more effective tool for economic and social development. The current tax system does not raise sufficient revenues to finance the provision of the services needed to stimulate inclusive and sustainable economic growth. More revenues need to be raised to finance investment in education and skills (Chapter 2), infrastructure, and innovation (Chapter 3). In the context of the emergence of the middle class, there is a need to provide more and better quality of public services. Social expenditure and infrastructure needs will also require more revenue in the near future. To achieve this objective, it is essential that Peru consolidates the fiscal legitimacy achieved through the public governance improvements (Chapter 5).

In recent years, Peru has taken steps to strengthen its fiscal policy framework and improve its tax revenues. Firstly, Peru has improved the management of its natural resource incomes, thanks to a fiscal rule that helped to reduce the volatility of public expenditure following changes in commodity prices. In addition, public debt at national and sub-national levels remains low, guaranteeing the solvency of the state. In particular, sub-national public debt represents only around 2% of GDP. Secondly, tax revenues as a share of GDP increased by more than 6 percentage points between 1990 and 2013 to reach 18.3% of GDP in 2013. This considerable increase, which is similar to other Latin American countries, is mainly driven by the robust economic growth of recent years and improvements in the tax administration. The most significant increase was in taxes on income and profits, which rose by close to 7 percentage points in the period 1990-2013, much higher than the Latin American average in the same period (less than 2 percentage points).[2]

However, tax revenues in Peru are still low compared to benchmark, OECD and Latin American countries (see Annex 1.A1 of Chapter 1 for a description of benchmark countries). While tax revenues represented 18.3% of Peru's GDP in 2013, the average share in Latin American and OECD countries was 21.3% and 34.1%, respectively (OECD/ECLAC/CIAT/IADB, 2015). Fiscal resources are also lower than in all benchmark countries (Figure 4.8).

The bulk of Peru's fiscal revenues are raised by central government: close to 87% of total tax revenues in 2012 (similar to 88.2% of GDP in 1995). This is much higher than the OECD average for unitary countries (62.9% of GDP in 2012).

Redistributive mechanisms, such as taxes and social transfers, do little to reduce income inequalities in Peru. The impact of taxes and transfers on reducing inequalities remains well below that of some other countries in the region (Figure 4.9). This is directly linked to the ineffectiveness of direct transfers, which largely involve in-kind transfers for free or subsidised government services in education and health (Lustig and Higgins, 2013). The effectiveness indicator of social expenditure (i.e. the ratio between the variation of the Gini index and the size of direct transfers as a percentage of GDP) is very low, with only Bolivia performing below Peru within the group of countries portrayed in Figure 4.9 (Lustig and Higgins, 2013). Moreover, while in Peru inequalities only decline by 2 percentage points after taxes and transfers, in OECD economies they decline by more than 15 percentage points (OECD/ECLAC, 2012). Improvements in fiscal legitimacy at national and sub-national levels are fundamental to increase progressivity and tax revenues in Peru.

Figure 4.8. **Tax revenues as percentage of GDP, 2013**

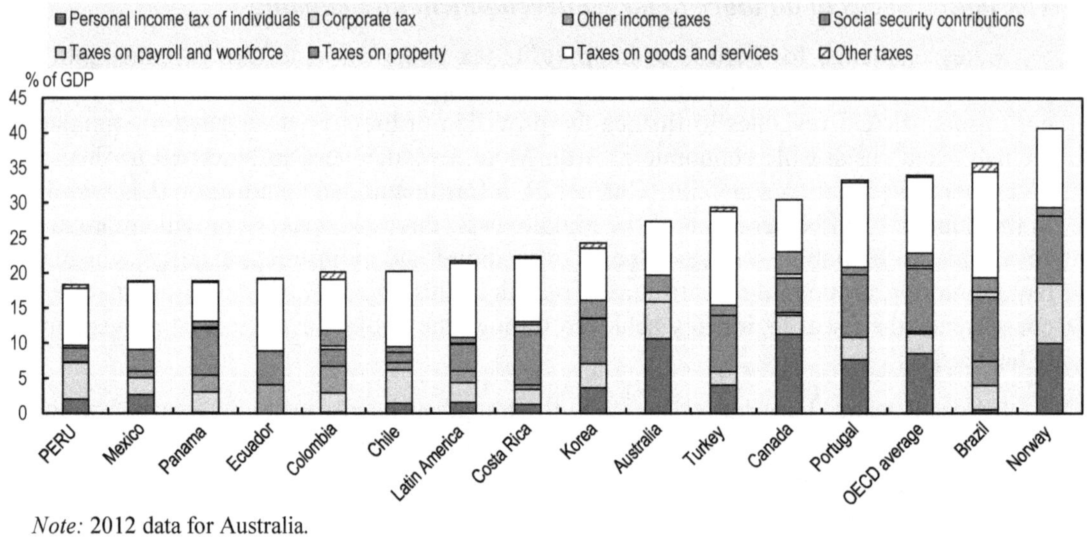

Note: 2012 data for Australia.

Source: OECD/ECLAC/CIAT/IADB (2015), *Revenue Statistics in Latin America and the Caribbean*, OECD Publishing, Paris, http://dx.doi.org/10.1787/rev_lat-2015-en-fr.

StatLink http://dx.doi.org/10.1787/888933265804

Figure 4.9. **Impact of taxes and transfers on income distribution**

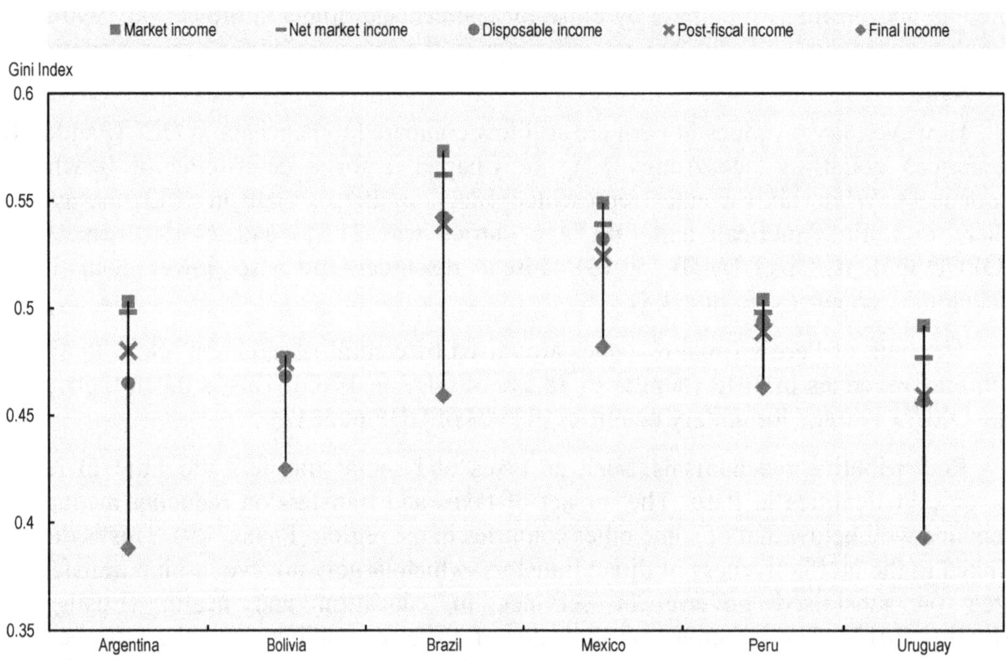

Source: Lustig et al. (2013), "The impact of taxes and social spending on inequality and poverty in Argentina, Bolivia, Brazil, Mexico, Peru and Uruguay: An overview", *CEQ Working Paper*, No. 13, CEQ.

StatLink http://dx.doi.org/10.1787/888933265812

In particular, the prevalence of indirect taxation over direct taxation affects progressivity in Peru. Taxes on goods and services (indirect taxes) represent close to 45% of all taxes. While similar to the average for Latin American economies (50%), this share is high compared to the OECD average (32.8%). Furthermore, a key component of the taxes on goods and services is the Value Added Tax (VAT), which increased from 1.5% of GDP in 1990 to 6.8% in 2013. That increase was impressive even in a Latin American context (involving a 3.7 percentage point change over the same period, to 6.2% of GDP in 2013).[3] In 2011-12, the government reduced the tax rate from 19% to 18% in order to reduce exposure to VAT (ECLAC, 2013). However, VAT as a share of GDP has remained constant in recent years. The limited share of the most progressive tax (income tax) does not offset the non-progressiveness of the VAT (Barreix et al., 2011; Jaramillo, 2013). Indeed, direct taxes, and in particular personal income taxes, remain low. While personal income taxes represent close to 25% of total taxes in OECD economies on average, in Peru they only represent 11%, a slightly higher proportion than in Latin American countries (7% of GDP; OECD/ECLAC/CIAT/IADB, 2015). In addition, the absence of an inheritance tax undermines the progressivity of the taxation system.

Some taxation items could be tapped to increase inclusive growth. For instance, tax expenditure represents close to 12% of total tax revenues and has remained higher than 2% of GDP in recent years. Although this is lower than in other Latin American benchmark countries as a proportion of GDP, such as Chile (5%), Colombia (3.5%) and Mexico (5.9%), this represents a loss of revenues (Gómez Sabaíni, Jiménez and Rossignolo, 2012). Also, the current tax system does little to stimulate green growth. Revenue from environmentally related taxes currently amounts to less than 0.6% of GDP, which is significantly below the OECD average of 1.6% of GDP (Figure 4.10). Although Peru has started to charge a fuel duty, a remaining challenge is to adopt a more comprehensive tax system that promotes environmental-related tax revenues to improve environmental policy instruments and to raise tax revenues.

Some distortions in the taxation system could be a bottleneck for competitiveness. A high corporate tax rate affects the dynamism of an economy. Evidence shows that corporate taxes are the most harmful for growth (Johansson et al., 2008). In particular, the negative effect of corporate taxes is particularly pronounced for firms that are catching up with the technological frontier (Schwellnus and Arnold, 2008). This could be the case of some firms in Peru. In addition to the corporate tax, firms have to pay a tax on dividends at 4.1% if their earnings are not re-invested. The recent effort to gradually reduce the corporate tax rate from 30% in 2014 to 26% in 2019 is tackling this key obstacle to investment and formal employment creation. This would move the tax rate towards the OECD average (about 25%). Another possible source of distortion is a financial transactions tax applied to every operation carried out within the financial system, as is also applied in other countries in Latin America. This tax could affect financial inclusion in Peru (Choy, 2013; Coelho, 2009). However, the level of revenues raised by this tax remains below 0.5% of GDP, lower than the Latin America (1.6% of GDP) and OECD averages (1.2% of GDP).

Figure 4.10. **Revenues from environmentally-related taxes**

% of GDP; 2013 or latest available year

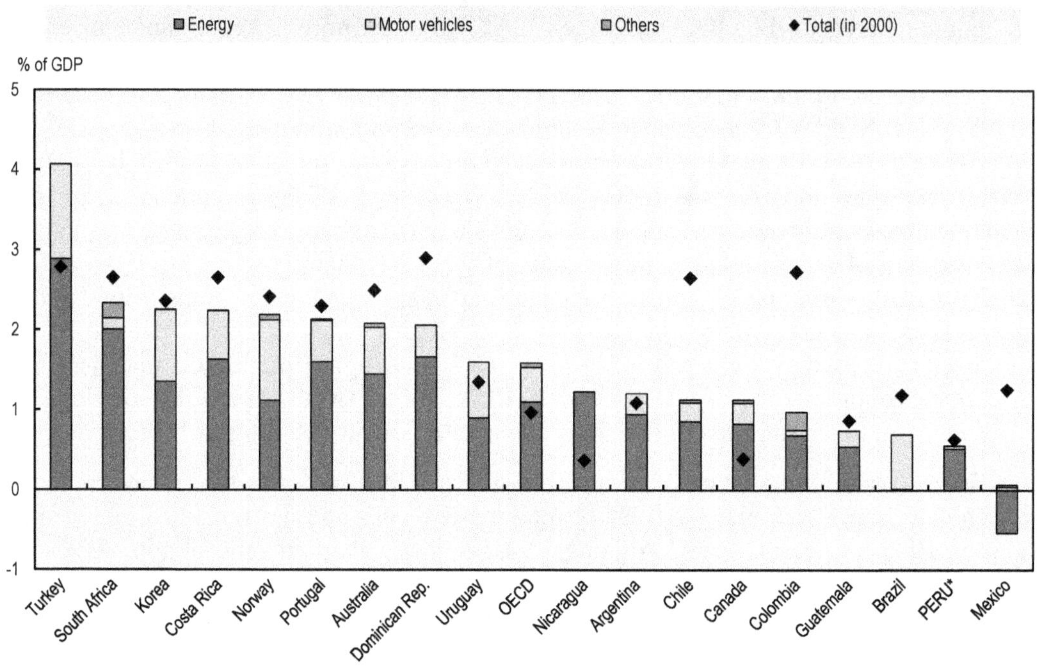

Note: * 2012 data. OECD represents the OECD weighted average.

Source: *OECD Database on Instruments Used for Environmental Policy* (available at http://www2.oecd.org/ecoinst/queries/Default.aspx).

StatLink http://dx.doi.org/10.1787/888933265826

Tax evasion should be tackled in order to increase fiscal space in Peru. Evasion hinders development and inclusive growth and undermines the overall sense of fairness on which the taxation system should be based (Carrasco, 2010). Although it is difficult to estimate tax evasion, studies show that Peru is one of the Latin American economies with the highest levels of tax evasion. In particular, estimated evasion rates for VAT and income taxes are close to 38% and 48%, respectively (Gómez-Sabaini and Jiménez, 2012). Beyond the tax structure, better information systems, and increased transparency and integrity in tax administration operations are fundamental for tackling tax evasion. Moreover, in an international context it is important to ensure that profits are taxed in the country where economic activities generating the profits are performed and where value is created. Like in other developing and emerging markets, base erosion and profit shifting (BEPS) is of major significance for Peru due to its heavy reliance on corporate income tax, particularly from multinational enterprises. Further involvement of Peru in this OECD work in the framework of the Country Programme would help to minimise base erosion and profit shifting.

Peru's tax administration office SUNAT is relatively inefficient compared to its peers' administration offices. For instance, in Peru between 2006 and 2010, aggregate administration costs per 100 units of net revenue collected were higher than 1.5, while in Latin American and OECD economies, this ratio was below 1.5 and 1, respectively (OECD/IDB, 2014). Part of this performance can be explained by the tasks allocated to SUNAT. In contrast to most of the Latin American economies (Argentina and Brazil also being exceptions), SUNAT is also in charge of administering social security contributions

(Corbacho et al., 2012). However, more efforts to include information and communication technologies and better human resources in tax collection would help decreasing the efficiency gap with OECD economies.

Peru's strong monetary policy needs to continue reducing financial dollarisation

Peru's sound monetary policy framework has helped to reduce inflation, supporting strong economic growth. Average inflation in Peru fell from over 100% at the beginning of the 1990s to an average of 2.6% between 2002 and 2014. The conduct of monetary policy during the last two decades can be split into two different periods. The first span, from 1990 to 2002, was one of gradual disinflation. During this period, monetary policy in Peru was implemented through a monetary target framework that used the annual growth rate of the monetary base as an intermediate target and also included instruments such as foreign exchange intervention and high reserve requirements for deposits in foreign currency. The success in disinflation during this period can be attributed to the efficient co-ordination of macroeconomic policies, with a build-up of credibility and a reduction in the consolidated public debt. Low levels of public debt have kept sovereign spreads low, helping to sustain a sharp reduction in monetary policy rates since 2000. The co-ordination between fiscal and monetary policies became the basis of the sound institutional framework that Peru has today.

Since 2002, the monetary framework has been characterised by targeting under a dual monetary system. Indeed, Peru's inflation targeting framework has a particular design, as it is the only central bank in the world to implement the framework within a highly dollarised financial system. The inflation target is 2%, with a tolerance band ranging from 1% to 3%. But the framework requires the central bank to actively intervene in the foreign exchange market to smooth out exchange rate fluctuations and build international reserves as a self-insurance mechanism against negative external shocks. Since 2008, reserve requirements have been used as an active monetary control tool to moderate the impact of capital flows on domestic credit conditions in both domestic and foreign currency.

Dollarisation distorts the transmission mechanism of monetary policy and increases liquidity and solvency risks within the financial system. Because of the high degree of dollarisation in the financial system, the Central Bank of Peru has to intervene frequently in the foreign exchange market to reduce exchange rate volatility and accumulate international reserves to prevent balance sheet effects. In a financially dollarised economy, the interest rate setting also has to take into account how financial dollarisation affects the transmission mechanism of monetary policy. The central bank addresses this issue by explicitly taking into account the impact of dollarisation on credit market conditions and on the dynamics of the exchange rate and inflation (Winkelried, 2013). Dollarisation reduces the impact of monetary policy on inflation and real activity, since a large depreciation not only typically generates a positive impact on exports, but also triggers a negative impact on the financial position of firms with currency mismatches. In sum, the role of credit in the transmission of monetary policy is relatively weak, but would improve if Peru reduced its levels of dollarisation.

In Peru the exchange rate channel is more important than the interest rate channel for keeping inflation under control. Evidence suggests that the interest rate pass-through is rather weak, as is the overall transmission to output and inflation (Acosta-Ormaechea and Coble, 2011). The main issue with financial dollarisation is that it magnifies the reaction of financial intermediaries to sharp movements in the exchange rate. Therefore, a key challenge for the central bank in keeping inflation under control is to avoid sharp depreciations of the exchange rate such as those driven, for example, by a sudden stop in capital inflows.

The solid and healthy financial sector could be still more efficient and accessible

Peru's regulatory framework for its financial system is now strong, following key improvements:

- The inclusion of a countercyclical component in the non-performing loans.
- At 10%, bank regulatory capital to risk-weighted assets is above the Basel ratio of 8%, and is similar to other Latin American countries.
- In addition to the inclusion of liquid and operational risks in banks' assessments, Peru has improved the measure of capital in the solvency ratio. A countercyclical component is included and high concentration in specific business activities requires additional capital from banks to meet their bank regulatory capital to risk-weighted assets ratio.
- The institutional framework of the *Superintendencia de Banca, Seguros y AFP* (SBS) is strong. Despite the Superintendent being appointed by the executive, the Superintendence of Banks, Insurances and Pensions is not subordinated to any ministry, and has autonomy in the regulation and supervision of the financial system.

Overall, the financial system is in a solid position. While credit risk indicators (in particular those related to loans to the retail segment) increased slightly during 2014 as a consequence of lower economic growth, financial institutions took corrective measures. Thanks to the strong regulatory framework explained above, the solvency of the financial system remains good. Banks in Peru account for almost 90% of the assets of the financial system and their solvency and liquidity indicators remain strong. Non-performing loans and credit risk indicators are relatively low. For instance, as of 2014, Peru's bank regulatory capital to risk-weighted assets ratio was 14.4%, above that of Australia, Portugal and Argentina (Figure 4.11).

Despite increases in domestic credit to the private sector over the last decade, access to finance remains low, responding in part to the structural challenges of the Peruvian economy. In the wake of the 1998-2000 emerging markets crisis, credit to the private sector contracted from its peak of 30% of GDP in 1999 to 18% of GDP in 2004. It has since increased – to more than 31% of GDP in 2013. However, this is still very low compared to the OECD average (above 150% of GDP), and some Latin American economies, such as Chile (100% of GDP), Brazil, Colombia and Costa Rica (Figure 4.12, Panel A). To increase investment going forward, access to finance needs to increase and real interest rates need to go down. Borrowers in Peru pay an average annual real interest rate of 18% in 2013, which is significantly higher than in most countries (Figure 4.12, Panel B).

Figure 4.11. **Peru's banking system**

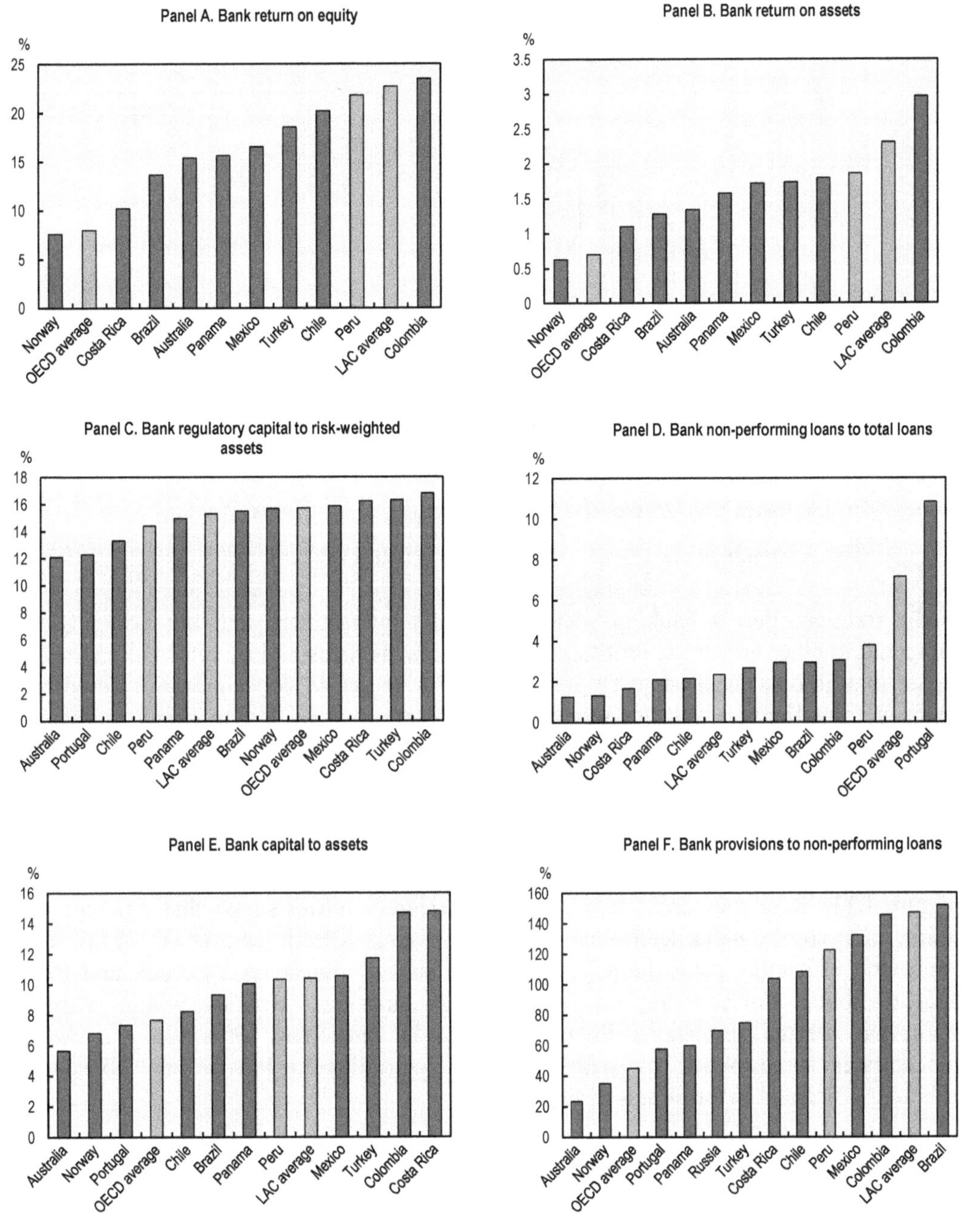

Note: Bank return on equity is the annualised net income before taxes as a percentage of the value of capital. Bank return on assets is the annualised net income before taxes as a percentage of the value of assets. Bank regulatory capital to risk weighted assets is the total regulatory capital after supervisory deductions, as defined by the Basel Committee on Banking Supervision and national supervisory guidance, as a share of risk weighted assets. Bank provisions to non-performing loans are the total specific loan-loss provisions as a percentage of total non-performing loans.

Source: IMF Financial Soundness Indicators (http://fsi.imf.org/Default.aspx).

StatLink http://dx.doi.org/10.1787/888933265834

Figure 4.12. **Access to credit and cost of finance in Peru (2013)**

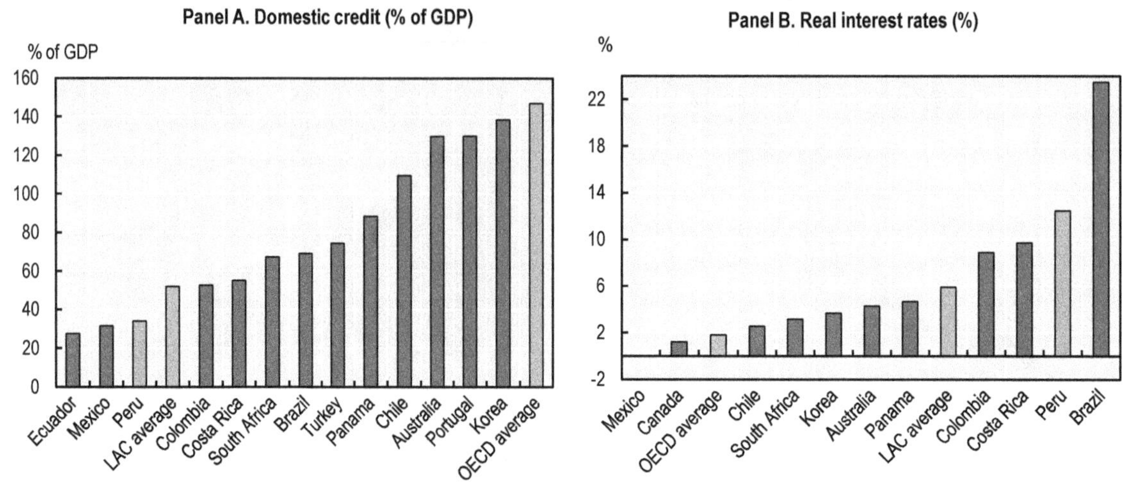

Source: World Bank (2015), *World Development Indicators* (database), Washington, DC, http://data.worldbank.org.

StatLink http://dx.doi.org/10.1787/888933265840

In addition, Peru's banking sector is highly concentrated and not very efficient compared to other countries. Profitability indicators, as measured by return to capital, are higher than in other economies (Figure 4.13). The degree of concentration of credit and deposits from financial entities remains high, responding in part to previous financial crises. In particular, close to 80% of the market share is retained by only four banks in Peru. The Herfindahl-Hirschman Index (HHI) in lending (corporate, large enterprises, medium enterprises) and on mortgages shows a relatively high level of concentration: at between 1 500 and 2 500 (Financial Stability Report, 2014).[4] Estimates of cost efficiency and market contestability show that efficiency in Peru's banking system is relatively low (Figure 4.13). Recent evidence from Latin American countries shows that efficiency and competition are the main determinants of interest rates (Chortareasa et al., 2012). Thus, improving efficiency could be a key driver of lower interest rates (Brock and Rojas-Suárez, 2000). Furthermore, concentration of business activities within a public institution creates distortions in the market. In particular, *Banco de la Nación* concentrates some public payments, such as subsidies to low-income households, affecting efficiency in the access to finance.

The cost of and access to finance could also be influenced by regulatory requirements. Peru's banks are required to hold reserve requirements, and the central bank makes extensive use of them. This requirement, although necessary to main stability in a financially dollarised economy, can distort efficient asset allocation by banks. High reserve requirements generate efficiency costs that affect the degree of financial development and can keep real interest rates relatively high. The fact that the central bank decreased the reserve requirement in domestic currency from 30% in 2013 to 6.5% in June 2015 is good news in this regard. To reduce financial dollarisation, the central bank has also increased reserve requirements in foreign currency to close to 70%.

Figure 4.13. **Peru's efficiency in the banking system**

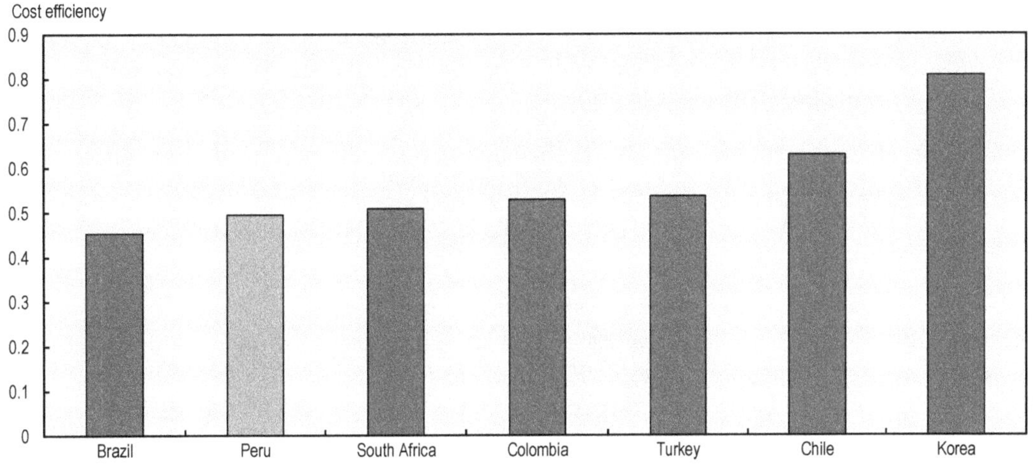

Note: Cost efficiency is a measure of the relative distance from the efficient frontier. It ranges between 1 for a fully efficient and 0 for a fully inefficient firm. The selection of benchmark countries (Annex 1.A1 of Chapter 1) is based on data availability.

Source: Daude and Pascal (2015), "Efficiency and contestability in the Colombian banking system", *OECD Economics Department Working Papers*, No. 1203, OECD Publishing, Paris, http://dx.doi.org/10.1787/5js30twjgm6l-en.

StatLink *http://dx.doi.org/10.1787/888933265858*

The tax on financial transactions (discussed above) could also harm access to formal credit markets if the tax administration office increases this tax in the future. Representing only 0.5% of GDP and a taxation rate of only 0.005%, it is not currently perceived as a binding constraint to access to finance. This tax is levied on transactions in national or foreign currency for any entry or exit of money in accounts in financial companies, and operations that convey cash payments, regardless of the medium used. Furthermore, it may create barriers to competition by exempting transactions within the same institution of the same holder.

Finally, a key aspect affecting the effectiveness of the financial system is the efficiency of the judicial sector. The process for addressing disputes is long and costly (Chapter 3). The lack of contract enforcement and delays in obtaining collateral affect the cost of financing for households and firms.

Important efforts are being made to increase access to finance by maintaining the stability of the financial system; these should move forward:

- Current financial education initiatives by the public and private sectors are familiarising households from low socio-economic backgrounds with financial activities in order to increase their access to finance. These initiatives are welcome and should be expanded.
- Retail companies known as *corresponsales bancarios* are working in partnership with the banking system to provide access to finance to households living in areas without retail bank offices. This helps reduce banks' operational costs. The number of households using these *corresponsales* has been increasing – from 12 395 in 2010 to 38 552 in 2014.

- Recent initiatives in the regulatory framework are promoting mobile banking. These are welcome as they enhance access to finance in remote areas.
- Efforts are being made to adapt scoring and risk analysis to informal firms and workers; these should be stepped up as they can reduce fixed costs and enhance access to finance for these actors.
- To guarantee the stability of the financial system, the inclusion of the supervision of *cooperaciones financieras* at the SBS should reduce the solvency risks of these institutions and would improve the information on the activities of these institutions.

Finally regarding private fixed income market, many Peruvian corporations have been issuing debt instruments in the international market. Renewing them could be harder given the tighter financial conditions. However, as a share of total assets, the debt levels of these corporations has remained relatively stable over the last five years because they have used the emissions in international markets to finance investment projects or to replace other liabilities. Thus, companies have used the proceeds from the bond issue on the international market to pay bank short and medium term domestic debts, thus helping to lengthen the maturity of companies' liabilities (Central Bank of Peru, 2014). In sum, tighter financial conditions will increase the cost of financing abroad for Peruvian corporations, but should not be a source of financial turmoil.

Macro-prudential policies should continue to reduce vulnerabilities to the external environment

Peru's external position has improved significantly over the last decade, although it has recently deteriorated due to weak export performance and lower terms of trade. The current account went from a deficit of around 8% of GDP in 1995 to a surplus of 3% of GDP in 2007 (Figure 4.14). Indeed, this strong external position in the wake of the 2008-09 financial crisis helped Peru weather the turmoil relatively easily. However, since 2010 the current account deficit has increased to around 4% of GDP. This has been driven by deteriorating terms of trade, while export volumes fell and import volume growth remained strong, in particular after 2012.

A potential sharp reversal of capital flows can be an important risk. So far the current account deficit has been easily financed by a bonanza of capital inflows (Figure 4.14). Net capital inflows into Peru have amounted to around 8% of GDP every year, on average, over the last five years, well above the regional average of 5% (Figure 4.15). This bonanza can be explained by both domestic and global factors. Domestically, as discussed above, strong growth of GDP and improved macroeconomic fundamentals attracted large amounts of investment, particularly in mining activities. Meanwhile, the extremely low interest rates in advanced economies generated a flood of financial inflows into emerging economies, including Peru. However, these conditions are changing as international financial conditions are expected to tighten. Evidence suggests that countries like Peru, with large current account deficits and relatively low external assets, may suffer more from a sudden and sharp hike in long-term interest rates in the United States (Olaberría, 2014). In the past, sharp increases in US interest rates have created severe volatility in asset prices and a sudden drying up of capital flows into Latin America, leading to financial crises (Reinhart and Reinhart, 2009).

Figure 4.14. **Trends and comparisons in Peru's current account, 1980-2013**

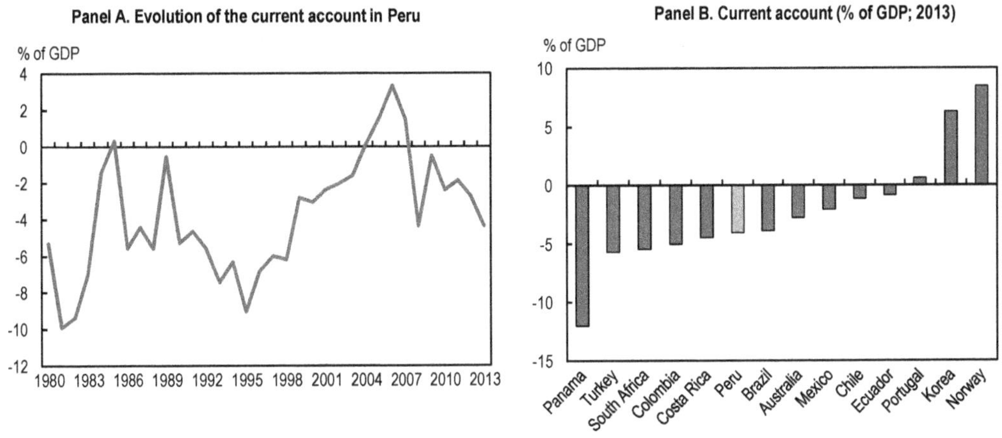

Source: IMF (2015a), *World Economic Outlook April 2015: Uneven Growth, Short- and Long-Term Factors*, IMF, Washington, DC, www.imf.org/external/pubs/ft/weo/2015/01/.

StatLink http://dx.doi.org/10.1787/888933265868

A decrease in capital flows and asset prices could dramatically affect the real economy. In Peru housing prices have been increasing fast, largely following the evolution of net capital inflows and credit in foreign currency (Figure 4.15). Evidence shows that there is a strong link between cycles of capital inflows, credit and asset prices and housing prices (Jara and Olaberría, 2013). When large capital inflows enter an economy the demand for houses increases and prices rise, thereby increasing the economy's access to credit – as houses are the collateral for loans. Increases in credit lead to new rounds of capital inflows that can evolve into a boom in housing prices. This involves a sort of circular process in which higher housing prices make the financial conditions of the economy seem sounder than they actually are, promoting more borrowing and pushing prices even higher. Indeed, the circular process between capital flows and asset prices is stronger in economies which, like Peru, have underdeveloped financial markets, relatively low quality of institutions and are highly dollarised (Olaberría, 2012). In these conditions, the risk is that if capital inflows dry up, the whole circular process can reverse. The result can be great pain, as falls in housing prices reduce the value of collateral, triggering margin calls and causing domestic credit flows to collapse. The financial shock can quickly reverberate within the real economy if firms that cannot finance their working capital cut back on employment and investment.

So far, the risks due to external shocks are being contained. The real effective exchange rate is broadly in line with fundamentals (IMF, 2015b), and the level and composition of Peru's international investment position have improved over the last decade. This is because the negative international investment position has halved since the early 2000s and the composition of foreign liabilities has shifted significantly into non-debt items (Figure 4.16). Also, net international reserves remain comfortable, according to various metrics. Peru does not maintain exchange restrictions or multiple currency practices, and its macro-prudential measures enhance financial stability.

Figure 4.15. **House prices, capital flows and credit growth in Peru**

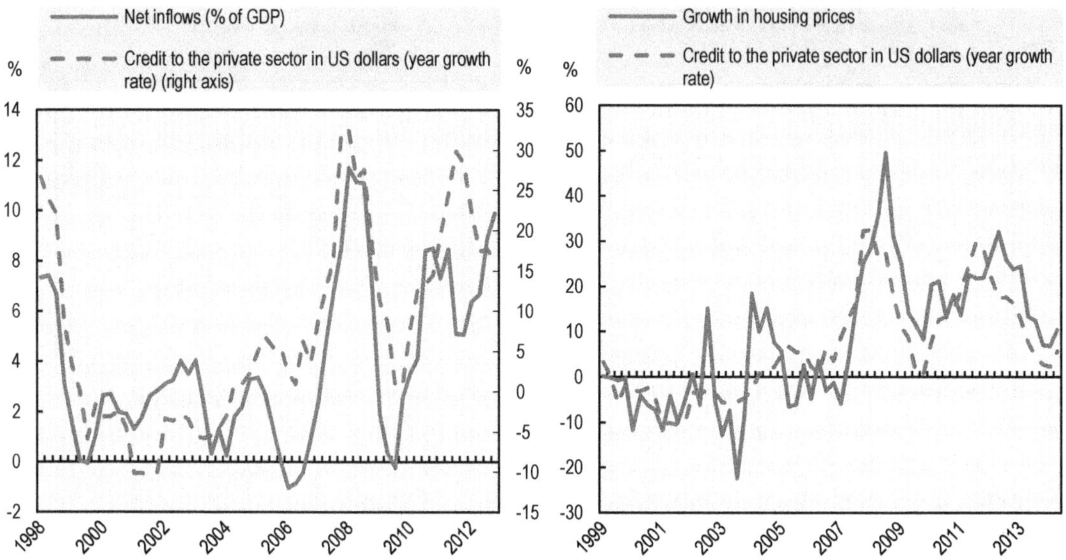

Source: Central Bank of Peru (*Banco de la Reserva del Perú*), http://www.bcrp.gob.pe/estadisticas.html and IMF (2014), *World Economic Outlook Database*, International Monetary Fund, Washington DC, http://www.imf.org/external/pubs/ft/weo.

StatLink http://dx.doi.org/10.1787/888933265872

Figure 4.16. **Peru's international investment position, 2000-14**

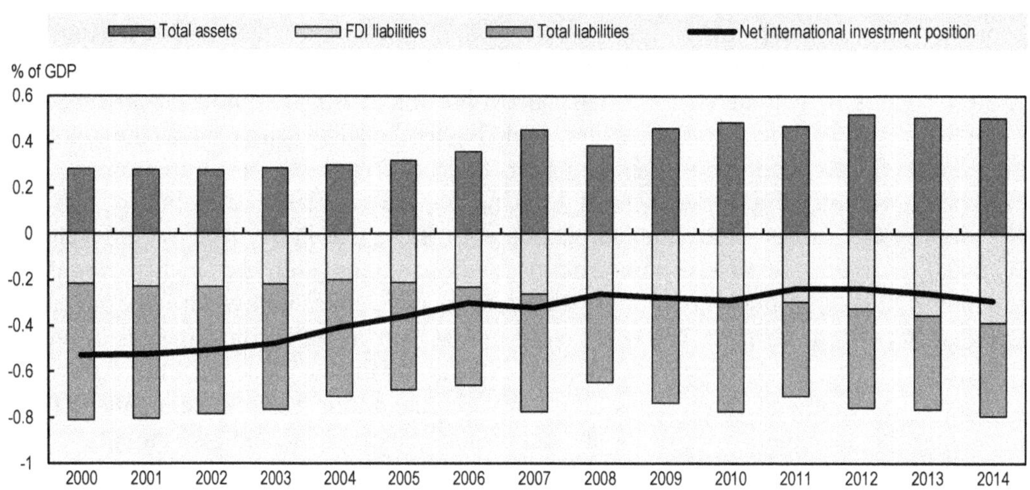

Source: Central Bank of Peru (*Banco de la Reserva del Perú*), http://www.bcrp.gob.pe/estadisticas.html

StatLink http://dx.doi.org/10.1787/888933265880

The Central Bank has been using a range of macro-prudential tools to contain financial vulnerabilities. For example, the use of reserve requirements has allowed the Central Bank to induce the necessary tightening of monetary policy necessary to offset spillover coming from the quantitative easing policies implemented by the Federal Reserve and European Central Bank. In particular, reserve requirements have been used to offset the impact of capital inflows on credit. Furthermore, to encourage banks to internalise the risk of granting dollar-denominated loans, Peru's Central Bank sets higher reserve requirements on foreign currency obligations than on domestic currency obligations. The use of differentiated reserve requirements has helped Peru create a foreign exchange liquidity buffer to reduce systemic liquidity risks, given that the Central Bank cannot act as lender of last resort in foreign currency. To some extent, this has been useful to flatten the credit cycles generated by the capital inflow bonanza, reducing their expansionary effects on domestic credit and maintain stability in the short run. However, as discussed above, reserve requirements imply an important cost in terms of efficiency, so their effects on long-term growth could be positive thanks to a lower financial dollarisation.

Going forward, the Central Bank should strengthen policies to reduce the level of financial dollarisation, while at the same time preventing unnecessary impediments to capital mobility. This will help Peru reduce its vulnerabilities to external shocks and, at the same time, improve the transmission of monetary policy, allowing more room for the exchange rate to fluctuate. Maintaining exchange rate flexibility is a very useful way of cushioning the economy against external shocks. For instance, when the current account deteriorates, or capital inflows decline, the Central Bank will be able to allow the currency to depreciate to absorb the shock. Currently, the Central Bank cannot do that because the typical expansionary effect of the exchange rate channel after the implementation of a policy easing measure is considerably reduced by the high level of financial dollarisation. Only when financial dollarisation is sufficiently low will the expansionary net export effect of currency depreciation be larger than the balance sheet effect.

Conclusions

A credible macroeconomic framework has been crucial for increasing economic stability and boosting economic growth in Peru. Initiated in the 1990s, it has improved the country's monetary and fiscal stances remarkably. The adoption of an inflation-targeting regime to increase stability in the monetary front and the implementation of a fiscal rule to avoid volatility in the public finances contributed to boosting investment and improving consumers' confidence.

However, some risks remain on the macroeconomic front as external conditions become less favourable. Deterioration in commodity prices and economic conditions in China, coupled with increases in US interest rates should affect Peru's balance of payments. Any decline in the current account deficit or a drying up of capital flows and FDI would affect Peru's external solvency. Macro-prudential policies to continue the de-dollarisation of the Peruvian economy will be fundamental to minimising risks of instability in the Peruvian economy (including the housing market).

Access to finance remains low and is affecting both entrepreneurship and inclusiveness. Despite domestic credit to the private sector increased over the last decade, it remains low at less than 35% of GDP. Several factors should be behind this low level of access to finance. These include high levels of work informality and Peru's banking sector is highly concentrated and not very efficient compared to other countries. Also, the cost and access to finance could be influenced by regulatory requirements and inefficiencies in the judicial system. Efforts to increase access to finance are being adopted and should continue.

The fiscal responsibility efforts should be accompanied by improvements in the taxation system to support inclusive development in Peru. The current tax system does not raise sufficient revenues to finance the provision of services that can stimulate inclusive and sustainable economic growth. Furthermore, the tax system does little to reduce inequality and to promote a green economy. Major bottlenecks related to these challenges are the imbalance between direct and indirect taxes, the lack of progressivity in the taxation system, the large tax expenditures as proportion of total tax revenues, and the low level of environment-related taxes.

Notes

1. Based on information provided by the Ministry of Economy and Finance.

2. Like other countries in the region, Peru has recently increased taxation on all labour and capital income. In particular, the abolition of exemptions on interest and capital gains and the expansion of the tax to cover dividends helped to increase the tax revenues.

3. In the case of Peru, the sustainable growth of VAT-type taxes has more than compensated for the reduction in taxes on international trade and in selective taxes on goods and services (i.e. excise taxes).

4. The Herfindahl-Hirschman Index (HHI) can range from close to 0 to 10 000. It approaches zero when a market is occupied by a large number of firms of relatively equal size and reaches its maximum of 10000 points when a market is controlled by a single firm. According to the US Department of Justice, the agencies generally consider markets in which the HHI is between 1 500 and 2 500 points to be moderately concentrated, and consider markets in which the HHI is in excess of 2 500 points to be highly concentrated.

References

Acosta-Ormaechea S. and D. Coble (2011), "Monetary transmission in dollarized and non-dollarized economies: The cases of Chile, New Zealand, Peru and Uruguay", *IMF Working Paper,* No. WP/11/87, IMF (International Monetary Fund), Washington, DC.

Alberola, E., I. Kataryniuk, A. Melguizo and R. Orozco (2015), "Fiscal policy and the cycle in Latin America: The role of financial conditions and fiscal rules", Banco de España Working Paper Series, forthcoming.

Alesina, A., S. Ozler, N. Roubini and P. Swagel (1996), "Political instability and economic growth", *Journal of Economic Growth,* Vol. 1(2), pp. 189-211.

Barreix A., M. Bès and J. Roca (2011), "El IVA Personalizado: Aumentando la recaudación y compensando a los más pobres", Instituto de Estudios Fiscales, Documentos No. 8/2011, available at: http://www.ief.es/documentos/recursos/publicaciones/documentos_trabajo/2011_08.pdf

Brock, P. and L. Rojas-Suárez (2000), "Interest rate spreads in Latin America: Facts, theories, and policy recommendations", in P. Brock and L. Rojas-Suárez (eds.), *Why So High? Understanding Interest Rate Spreads in Latin America*, IDB (Inter-American Development Bank), Washington, DC, pp. 1-38.

CAF (2012), *Finanzas Públicas para el Desarrollo: Fortaleciendo la Conexión entre Ingresos y Gastos*, CAF (Development Bank of Latin America), Bogota, Colombia, www.caf.com/media/4249/RED2012.pdf.

Carrasco, C.M. (2010), "Instrumentos y técnicas para la medición de la evasión", *Temática Tributaria series,* No. 7, Inter-American Centre for Tax Administrations (CIAT).

Central Bank of Peru (2014), *Financial Stability Report 2014*, Central Bank of Peru, Lima.

Chortareasa, G.E., J.G. Garza-García and C. Girardoneb (2012), "Competition, efficiency and interest rate margins in Latin American banking", *International Review of Financial Analysis,* Vol. 24, September 2012, pp. 93-103.

Choy, M. (2013), "Avances en la inclusión financiera en el Perú", *Revista Moneda*, Issue 155, pp. 26-30.

Coelho, I. (2009), "Taxing bank transactions. The experience in Latin America and elsewhere", paper presented at the Third International Tax Dialogue (ITD) Conference, Beijing, 26-28 October.

Corbacho, A., V. Fretes Cibils and E. Lora (eds.) (2012), *More than Revenue: Taxation as a Development Tool*, IDB, Washington, DC.

Dancourt, O. (2012), "Reglas de política monetaria y choques externos en una economía semi-dolarizada", *Working Paper*, No. 346, Departamento de Economía de la PUCP, Lima, Peru.

Dancourt, O. and W. Mendoza (2009), "Perú 2008-2009: Del auge a la recesión. Choque externo y respuestas de policía macroeconómica", in O. Dancourt and F. Jiménez (eds.), *Crisis Internacional: Impactos y Respuestas de Política Económica en el Perú*, Fondo Editorial – PUCP, Lima, Peru.

Dancourt, O. and W. Mendoza (1999), "Los dos canales de transmisión de la política monetaria en una economía dolarizada", *Working Paper*, No. 162, Departamento de Economía de la PUCP, Lima, Peru.

Daude, C. and J. Pascal (2015), "Efficiency and contestability in the Colombian banking system", *OECD Economics Department Working Papers*, No. 1203, OECD Publishing, Paris, http://dx.doi.org/10.1787/5js30twjgm6l-en.

ECLAC (2013), *Fiscal Panorama of Latin America and the Caribbean: Tax Reform and Renewal of the Fiscal Covenant*, ECLAC (Economic Commission for Latin America and the Caribbean), Santiago de Chile.

Frankel, J.A., C. Vegh and G. Vuletin (2013), "On graduation from fiscal procyclicality", *Journal of Development Economics*, Vol. 100(1), pp. 32-47.

Gómez Sabaíni, J.C. and J.P. Jiménez (2012), "Tax structure and tax evasion in Latin America", *Macroeconomics of Development Series*, No. 118 (LC/L.3455), ECLAC, Santiago de Chile.

Gómez Sabaíni, J.C., J.P. Jiménez and D. Rossignolo (2012), "Imposición a la renta personal y equidad en América Latina: Nuevos desafíos", *Macroeconomics of Development Series*, No. 119 (LC/L.3477), ECLAC, Santiago de Chile.

Han, F. (2014), "Measuring external risks for Peru: Insights from a macroeconomic model for a small open and partially dollarized economy", *IMF Working Paper*, No. WP/14/161, IMF, Washington, DC.

Hnatkovska, V. and N. Loayza (2004), "Volatility and growth", *Policy Research Working Paper Series,* No. 3184, World Bank, Washington, DC, http://dx.doi.org/10.1596/1813-9450-3184.

IMF (2015a), *World Economic Outlook April 2015: Uneven Growth, Short- and Long-Term Factors*, IMF, Washington, DC, www.imf.org/external/pubs/ft/weo/2015/01/.

IMF (2015b), "Peru 2015 Article IV Consultation", IMF Country Report, No. 15/133, IMF, Washington, DC.

Jara, A. and E. Olaberría (2013), "Are all capital inflows associated with booms in house prices? An empirical evaluation", *Working Papers,* No. 696, Central Bank of Chile, Santiago.

Jaramillo M. (2014), "The incidence of social spending and taxes in Peru", *Public Finance Review*, Vol. 42(3), pp. 391-412, May.

Johansson, A., C. Heady, J. Arnold, B. Brys and L. Vartia (2008), "Taxation and economic growth", *OECD Economics Department Working Paper,* No. 620, OECD Publishing, Paris, http://dx.doi.org/10.1787/241216205486.

Loayza, N., R. Rancière, L. Serven and J. Ventura (2007), "Macroeconomic volatility and welfare in developing countries", *World Bank Economic Review,* Vol. 21(3), pp. 343-357.

Lustig, N. and S. Higgins (2013), *Commitment to Equity Assessment: Estimating the Incidence of Social Spending, Subsidies and Taxes: Handbook*, CEQ (Commitment to Equity).

Lustig, N. et al. (2013), "The impact of taxes and social spending on inequality and poverty in Argentina, Bolivia, Brazil, Mexico, Peru and Uruguay: An overview", CEQ Working Paper, No. 13, CEQ.

MEF (2015), "Marco Macroeconómico Multianual 2016-2018", Ministry of Economics and Finance, Lima, Peru.

Mendoza, W. (2013), "Milagro peruano: ¿Buena suerte o buenas políticas?", *Economía,* Vol. 36(72), pp. 35-90.

OECD/ECLAC/CIAT/IADB (2015), *Revenue Statistics in Latin America and the Caribbean*, OECD Publishing, Paris, http://dx.doi.org/10.1787/rev_lat-2015-en-fr.

OECD/ECLAC (2012), *Latin American Economic Outlook 2012: Transforming the State for Development*, OECD Publishing, Paris, http://dx.doi.org/10.1787/leo-2012-en.

OECD/IDB (2014), *Government at a Glance: Latin America and the Caribbean 2014: Towards Innovative Public Financial Management*, OECD Publishing, Paris, http://dx.doi.org/10.1787/9789264209480-en.

Olaberría, E. (2014), "US long term interest rates and capital flows to emerging economies", *OECD Economics Department Working Papers,* No. 1155, OECD Publishing, Paris, http://dx.doi.org/10.1787/5jz0wh67l733-en.

Olaberría, E. (2012), "Capital inflows and booms in assets prices: Evidence from a panel of countries", *Working Papers,* No. 675, Central Bank of Chile.

Olaberría, E. and J. Rigolini (2009), "Managing East Asia's macroeconomic volatility", *Policy Research Working Paper,* No. WPS 4989, World Bank, Washington, DC.

Reinhart, C.M. and V.R. Reinhart (2009), "Bonanzas de flujos de capital: Una mirada que abarca el pasado y el presente", *Ensayos sobre Política Económica*, Vol. 27(59), pp. 188-250.

Rossini, R., Z Quispe and D. Rodríguez (2013), "Flujo de capitales, política monetaria e intervención cambiaria en el Perú", *Revista Estudios Económicos*, Vol. 25, pp. 39-50.

Schwellnus, C. and J. Arnold (2008), "Do corporate taxes reduce productivity and investment at the firm level?: Cross-country evidence from the Amadeus Dataset", *OECD Economics Department Working Papers,* No. 641, OECD Publishing, Paris, http://dx.doi.org/10.1787/236246774048.

Seminario, B. and N. Alva (2012), "El PIB, tres siglos pasados y media centuria venidera", in B. Seminario, C. Sanborn and N. Alva (eds.), *Cuando Despertemos en el 2062: Visiones del Perú en 50 Años*, Universidad del Pacífico, Lima.

Winkelried, D. (2013), "Modelo de proyección trimestral del BCRP: Actualización y novedades", *Revista Estudios Económicos*, Issue 26, pp. 9-60.

World Bank (2015), *World Development Indicators* (database), Washington, DC, http://data.worldbank.org.

Chapter 5
Good governance and effective state capacities in Peru

Peru should enhance its governance and state capacity to prioritise and effectively implement the policies highlighted in the preceding chapters. Better governance is not an end in itself but a means to achieve the policy objectives needed to boost inclusive development. In particular, tackling corruption should both increase the trust citizens have in their government and build state legitimacy. The governance of the judiciary and legislature should improve, while central government requires better co-ordination and enhanced leadership to drive long-term reforms. Much has been done to integrate the private sector in expenditures and investments, but better management of the process is needed to avoid inefficiencies and unexpected fiscal costs. At the regional level, the allocation of public resources does not contribute to reducing sub-national disparities, and local governments require more capacity to improve their policy making. Although the environmental institutional framework has improved in recent years, implementation of public policies to foster environmental sustainability remains weak.

Peru is a unitary presidential state comprising three branches (legislative, executive and judicial), plus autonomous organs, control institutions and an electoral organisation. The executive branch exercises the government administrative functions of the state and includes all public authorities at sub-national levels (departments, provinces and districts). It is chaired by the President of the Republic. In addition, the Presidency of the Council of Ministers co-ordinates national policies with different ministries, civil society and the private sector to create a participative and transparent framework to boost the processes of modernisation, decentralisation, governance, and social and economic inclusion in Peru.

Peru has adopted key reforms to improve governance and citizens' participation in recent years. At the central government level, its public investment framework (*Sistema Nacional de Inversión Pública*), fiscal framework projections and budgeting process are more effective and transparent. In addition, information technology is better used to enhance transparency, integrity and the efficiency of the procurement. The regulatory and institutional frameworks for public-private partnerships offer better processes to prioritise, implement and monitor private investments. At the sub-national level, the 2002 decentralisation process and subsequent regulations have enhanced local participation, and local responsibility for expenditure. Recent reforms have provided environmental authorities with greater institutional capacity in attempt to boost sustainable green growth.

However, negative perceptions of Peru's institutions among the population remain; these could be tackled through a number of policies. Specifying better the roles of central government institutions will be essential for improving the effectiveness and co-ordination of public policies in order to boost legitimacy and build confidence. A long-term strategic framework comprised of appropriate checks and balances over public expenditures and investments would increase business confidence and improve the way institutions are perceived. Better interactions horizontally – between different ministries and agencies of the central government – and vertically – with departments and provinces – are key to achieving more effective public policies. Furthermore, the current multi-level governance lacks an appropriate methodology for boosting regional development and tackling regional inequalities. One area specifically affected by these institutional weaknesses is the environment.

This chapter discusses four key dimensions needed to improve the effectiveness of public policies in Peru. First, it analyses the role of the central government and, in particular, its capacity to co-ordinate and monitor horizontal policies in Peru. Second, it considers how private-sector involvement in investments is governed and the need for further improvements in procedures related to public-private partnerships, public procurement and Works for Taxes (*Obras por Impuestos).* Third, given the regional socio-economic disparities in Peru, it examines the need to improve the allocation of resources to sub-national authorities and to increase capacity building at local level. Finally, it focuses on the institutional capacity of the environmental sector, which requires effective co-ordination horizontally (across central government), vertically (at multiple levels of governance) and with private actors (mainly legal and illegal mining firms).

A weak institutional framework undermines state legitimacy

Peru's poor institutional framework is affecting state legitimacy. For instance, corruption is as a distorting factor affecting the quality, composition and productivity of physical capital, and undermining the benefits of investment. In this context, corruption can be perceived as a cost to entrepreneurs and to citizens in general. It can affect public investment policies, and challenge private investment by creating a negative business climate for the private sector. More generally, institutions that are perceived as ineffective in achieving their goals, non-transparent in how they act and unaccountable for their results undermine social cohesion, hampers collective action to achieve shared objectives, and reduce the well-being of individuals and communities.

Trust in institutions is a key challenge in Peru

Lack of trust in existing institutions is a crucial concern in Peru. Confidence in institutions is a key pillar of the governance dimension in the OECD well-being framework discussed in Chapter 1. Several institutions in Peru suffer from lack of public confidence. Compared to the benchmark countries (described in Annex 1.A1 of Chapter 1), few citizens in Peru trust in institutions such as the national government and the judicial system (Figure 5.1). Corruption is considered the second most important problem in Peru after delinquency (INEI, 2014). Corruption is perceived to be widespread, with 82% of Peruvians believing it to occur within businesses and 89% throughout the government (Gallup Organisation, 2015). More than 60% of citizens have not complained about cases of corruption because they believe it would be useless or even cause them problems. This perception persists at the sub-national level in some departments. For instance, more than 95% of citizens of Madre de Dios, Apurímac, Huánuco, Callao and Tumbes perceive their governments to lack integrity. In Callao and Tumbes, more than 80% of their citizens report having bribed public servants (CAD, 2013). Building a national and sub-national environment in which people are confident in their government will enhance incentives for entrepreneurship, job creation and well-being of individuals.

Figure 5.1. **Confidence in institutions in Peru (2014)**

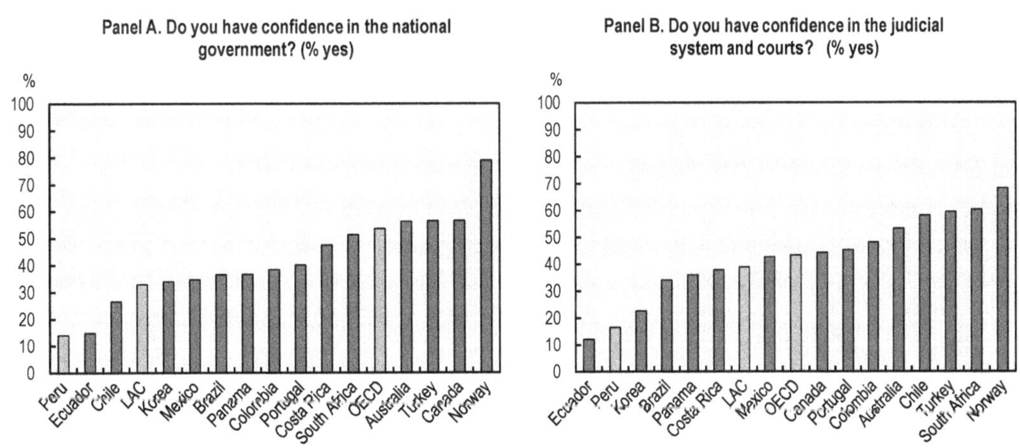

Source: Gallup Organisation (2015), *Gallup World Monitor* (database).

StatLink *http://dx.doi.org/10.1787/888933265894*

In recent years, Peru has approved several policies to enhance public administration and reduce corruption (World Bank, 2012). A key reform initiated in the early 2000s helped to enhance public servants' responsibilities and increase sanctions (PCM, 2012). It also improved the quality and professionalism of public administration. The Criminal

Procedure Code, implemented in 2009-10, contributed to enhancing the sector's efficiency and transparency (World Bank, 2012). Institutions offering public services can now share information technology systems. For instance, linking social services ministries and judicial institutions was a step towards better access to justice and boosted anti-corruption policies. Greater transparency and monitoring by the public procurement agency (*Organismo Supervisor de Contrataciones del Estado,* OSCE) strengthened these activities and reduced the possibilities for corruption. A Public Sector Integrity Review is currently being carried out in Peru, within the framework of the OECD Country Programme, to analyse and provide recommendations in further policies to fight against corruption.

Despite certain progress, Peru faces a number of barriers to moving towards transparent and open government to fighting corruption alongside the private sector and civil society. According to meetings with experts from private sector and non-governmental organisations, only a few public institutions are considered to be free of corruption. These include the Ministry of Economy and Finance; the Central Bank of Peru; the Superintendency of banks, insurance companies and pension funds; and the competition authority INDECOPI. Ineffective red tape increases the probability of public servants being bribed to accelerate procedures in Peru (Yamada and Montero, 2011). Although the number of procedures and the time needed to complete them have been reduced, this number remains high compared to OECD and some benchmark countries (Chapter 3). Peru is also facing higher risks from illegal activities, such as drug production and trafficking, which are often facilitated by the bribery of public servants in. This is in particularly the case for transportation and control authorities (Pedagrio, 2014). For instance, the share of Peruvians who lack confidence in the police has increased from 58% in 2002 to close to 80% in 2013.[1]

In that context, strong trust networks are essential to reduce corruption. In social groups where trust is low, as is the case of Peru, there is greater cause for corruption (Yamada and Montero, 2011). In such cases, a vicious circle results in which the incentive for an individual to be corrupt depends on the collective reputation of the group to which they belong (Tirole, 1996). Consequently, it may not be in the interest of individuals to be honest when the institutions they work for have a reputation for being corrupt.

A weak judiciary is powerless in the fight against corruption

The ineffectiveness in courts and in the judiciary system is also increasing corruption in Peru. Higher workloads are causing delays to judicial procedures, providing greater incentive for litigants to engage in corruption activities (Rose-Ackerman, 2007; Salazar and Ramos, 2007). Low levels of education and low wages also render judges prone to corruption (Sánchez Urribarrí, 2008; Hammergren, 2007). Widespread inefficiencies and corruption in the judiciary affect economic activity. In particular, the ineffectiveness of the legal system, and the low probability of being either detected or punished, have an impact on corruption (Andvig and Moene, 1990).

There are several institutions in Peru to fight against corruption. These institutions include the Attorney General (*Ministerio Público*), the General Comptroller and the Prosecutor against Corruption (*Procuraduría Pública Especializada en Delitos de Corrupción)*. The Attorney General is responsible for conducting investigations and judicial actions in defence of public interests. The transparency and efficiency of this institution are affected by a lack of experts and the fact that several provincial prosecutors are appointed discretionally. In addition, corruption cases at the highest level have reinforced its lack of legitimacy.[2] The General Comptroller is the ruling body of the National Control System, in charge of supervising and auditing the proper use of the goods and resources of the state. Ineffectiveness in this institution results from a lack of prevention and dissuasion of public servants, as well as from the poor internal control mechanisms within other public administrations (Panfichi and Alvarado, 2011). The Prosecutor against Corruption lacks an institutional framework to prioritise corruption cases, and is short of specialised human resources due to its restricted budget (Simon and Caro, 2012). Peru needs a better balance between punishment and effective decision processes for public servants to create appropriate incentives for their activities.

The legislative branch and the decentralisation process fail to impose adequate accountability on the executive

The legislative branch does not contribute enough to the fight against corruption. In addition to its law-making power, the legislature has the power of political control and supervision. In practical terms, it has the power to investigate cases of public interest, including cases of corruption. Similar to other countries in Latin America, the checks and balances the legislature provides over the decisions of the executive remain limited (Dayton-Johnson et al., 2011). This implies that it is not necessarily in the interests of individual congressmen to increase their supervision over the executive, limiting the quality of the control they can exert (Panfichi and Alvarado, 2011). This results in a lack of efficiency among the parliamentary commissions in charge to investigate public cases. Furthermore, citizens consider Congress the most corrupt institution in Peru.[3]

Corruption remains a key challenge at sub-national level. In the 1990s, before the decentralisation process began, weak control institutions and a centralised executive without checks and balances affected corruption in Peru (Morris and Blake, 2009). The decentralisation process initiated in 2002 has not achieved its objective of bringing accountability closer to citizens. The judicial system has not improved as much as desired, and Peru is lagging behind other countries in the region in strengthening the rule of law at the sub-national level. Corruption cases persist at local levels and in administrations that interact directly with citizens. Around 65% of corruption incidences happen at the level of regional governments (Arbizu, 2014). Better management of public resources at the sub-national level is fundamental to enhancing transparency of public institutions in Peru (see section below on sub-national policies).

Poor co-ordination and implementation of public policies hamper central government

In all countries, the centre of government (CoG) should play a key role in ensuring the quality, co-ordination and monitoring of public policies at the executive level. The CoG is the body or group of bodies that provides direct advice to the head of the government and ministers. More precisely, it supports quality decision making by the head of government, provides cross-government policy co-ordination and monitoring of the government policy implementation. Apart from their traditional role of serving the executive from an administrative perspective, CoGs are now playing a more active role in policy development and co-ordination across OECD countries. The extended definition of the CoG does not only include the presidency or its equivalent, but also comprises key strategic partners, such as the ministry of finance or the ministry of planning. Depending on a country's particular institutional makeup, several actors can play an important role in CoG co-ordination. Additionally, central agencies responsible for coherent human resources policies, e-government policies and regulatory policies across different departments can also contribute to reinforcing cross-government co-ordination.[4]

Peru lags behind benchmark countries in the co-ordination of public policies. One flaw in Peru's centre of government set-up is the lack of co-ordination of public policies in the country. Despite efforts to increase dialogue among different institutions in recent years, the lack of collaboration and co-ordination among ministries and within the administration is an obstacle to effective policy making and implementation (Figure 5.2). This poor performance compared to benchmark countries can be explained by a number of factors, such as weakness in the prioritisation and implementation phases for policies involving several ministries. This includes environmental policies (see section below), and other key policies considered in previous chapters (e.g. skills and education in Chapter 2, and innovation and infrastructure in Chapter 3).

Figure 5.2. **Perceptions of co-ordination among public institutions, 2012**

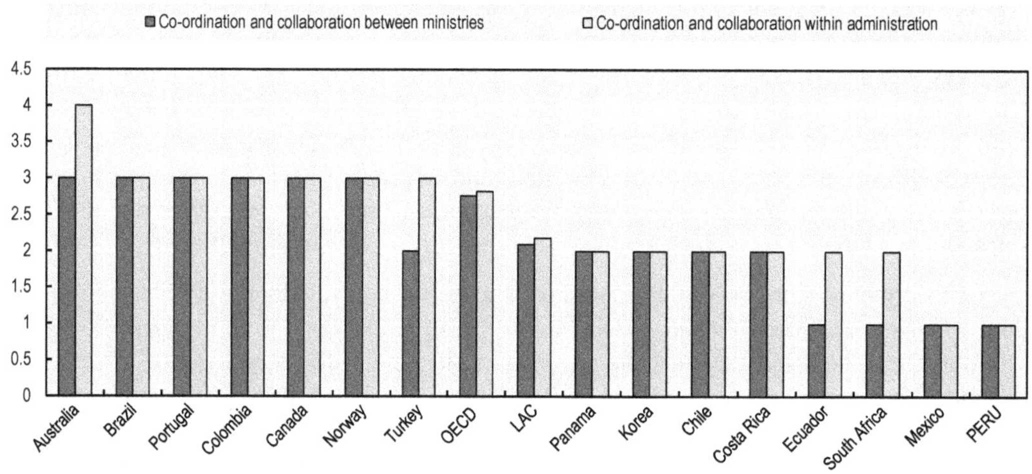

Note: 0 represents very little co-ordination and 4 strong co-ordination. The Institutional Profiles Database provides an original measure of countries' institutional characteristics through composite indicators built from perception data. The perception data were gathered through a survey completed by country/regional Economic Services (*Services économiques*) of the French Ministry for the Economy and Finance and the *Agence Française de Développement*'s offices.

Source: IPD (2012), "2012 governance data", *Institutional Profiles Database*, www.cepii.fr/institutions/EN/ipd.asp.

StatLink http://dx.doi.org/10.1787/888933265902

The centre of government in Peru faces challenges related to leadership, co-ordination and long-term implementation of policies. It is composed of the Presidency of the Council of Ministers (PCM) including the National Centre for Strategic Planning (CEPLAN), and the Ministry of Economy and Finance. To increase the effectiveness of public policies to reduce inequalities and boost productivity, CoGs need to offer vision, leadership and innovation. In Peru, this is especially difficult as the country faces high levels of political and public-sector fragmentation. In addition, the lack of enforcement of a National Development Plan in the long term puts pressure on the strategic policy-making capacity of the state and its service delivery capacity. In that context, there is a lack of co-ordination of public policies in the medium and long term. In the period 2000-15, there were 20 different Presidents of the Council of Ministers, representing close to 6 appointments per presidential mandate. This high turnover is primarily explained by political and corruption scandals (even those originating outside the PCM).

It affects the stability and legitimacy needed to move forward with reform, and to reinforce the PCM's strategic role in supporting the quality and co-ordination of the decision-making process. In addition, although CEPLAN has the technical capacity to undertake research and analysis, little is done at the executive level to promote the adoption and implementation of these studies. Indeed, the president of CEPLAN's governing board is not a member of the Council of Ministers, and CEPLAN does not have the capacity to take the lead in adopting or executing specific projects.

Peru also displays little capacity for strategic foresight to improve evidenced-based decision making. Strategic foresight refers to a long-term period (exceeding ten years) including planning scenarios. Development plans prepared by different ministries overlap and sometimes show lack of co-ordination. For instance, in the past few years, the executive has released numerous national plans, such as the Productive Diversification National Plan (from the Ministry of Production), the National Strategic Development Plan (CEPLAN) and the National Strategic Export Plan (Ministry of Trade). A key challenge for Peru will be to create a National Development Plan, defined at the CoG, discussed with different public and private actors, and integrated with the public investment framework. A single plan could facilitate the legitimacy of a long-term agenda, while the current multiplicity of plans reduce the coherence within the executive and may affect their overall credibility with civil society and the private sector. Furthermore, these plans are not approved by Congress and are not necessarily linked with the Multi-Annual Investment Plan defined by the executive.

There have been significant improvements in the Public National Investment System at the Ministry of Economy and Finance (MEF) but they need to be better co-ordinated with other public institutions. There is today greater fiscal transparency in the short and medium term thanks to the Multi-Annual Macroeconomic Framework and the Multi-Annual Budget Plan (Chapter 4). In addition, public investment projects are subject to cost-benefit analyses and their procurement follows competitive tenders. Recent improvements in the information available and technologies used for tracking public investment are increasing investment transparency. All direct public investment projects are subject to the national framework for public investment (*Sistema Nacional de Inversion Pública,* SNIP), defined and monitored by the MEF. All projects costing more than PEN 10 million must have feasibility studies, including cost-benefit analyses, and the express approval of the project by the MEF.

The OECD Country Programme with Peru undertakes detailed analyses and considers recommendations on the functioning of the public governance and the regulatory framework in Peru. Better public governance and regulatory practices are fundamental to Peru's development agenda. In that context, the OECD Country Programme includes the Public Governance Review, the Review of Regulatory Reform Policies and the implementation of best international practices in Regulatory Impact Analysis. These studies support Peru to develop and implement good governance and regulatory practices, and to achieve better social, economic and environmental objectives.

Private-sector involvement brings benefits but also governance challenges

In order to avoid unexpected fiscal costs and to enhance the effectiveness of its public policies, Peru has improved the regulatory and institutional framework for private-sector involvement in recent years. However, challenges remain in three areas of private-sector involvement: 1) public-private partnerships; 2) *Obras por Impuestos* or Works for Taxes; and 3) public procurement.

Despite impressive improvements, regulation of public-private partnerships could still be more effective

Faced with growing demand for infrastructure to promote economic development and guarantee further fiscal sustainability, Peru has used private participation to help finance projects. The private sector can provide expertise, innovation, lower costs and higher quality; a competitive auction process can result in the selection of the most efficient operator as well as the optimal price, given that competition takes place before firms commit to invest (Guasch, 2004). Since the 1990s public-private partnerships and concession contracts have been widely used to develop major infrastructure projects in Peru. Government officials adopted this approach with the aim of consolidating public finances after the profound economic crisis of the 1980s (Chapter 1).

The framework for private-sector involvement is improving

Overall, the legal framework for concessions in Peru is relatively clear and comprehensive, offering incentives to attract both local and international private investors. Since 1991 the executive introduced the regulation of private initiatives for investment and the participation of public entities such as ministries and sub-national authorities in the pre-implementation evaluation, design and approval of projects (Decrees Nos. 662 and 757).

The legislation on public-private partnerships in Peru has improved as institutional knowledge has grown, supported by international and domestic training and assistance. The 1996 Public Works Concession Law, followed by the 2008 Regional and Local Public Investment with Private Participation Law, introduced more flexibility to the contract structure, improved the project cycle for concessions and simplified the means by which the government can attract investment.

From 2014 Peru has addressed the barriers to creating more sustainable public-private partnerships in infrastructure (Law No. 30167). This has demonstrated growing political support for these projects. It improved the framework for such partnerships, creating a national register of contracts. It also made it possible to present private initiatives directly to ProInversión, the national agency responsible for private investment promotion, and opened the development of applied research and technological innovation projects to public-private partnership projects.

Peru has also increased its capacity to plan and oversee partnerships. It has strengthened the capacity of the public sector to manage them, particularly in the electricity-generation sector, where planning and oversight for private investment have been significantly streamlined (EIU, 2015). In 2014 Peru was ranked third behind Chile and Brazil out of 19 countries in Latin America and the Caribbean in the Infrascope ranking, which assesses the capacity of countries in Latin America and the Caribbean to carry out sustainable public-private partnerships in infrastructure. This was mainly due to its score on operational maturity from the growing number of recently developed projects (17 since mid-2012). These projects helped build capacity throughout the public sector (EIU, 2015).

In the transport sector, three public institutions primarily determine the institutional design of public-private partnerships. The Ministry of Transport and Communications acts as the public counterpart to the concessionaires. It participates in the prioritisation and design of projects and is in charge of the technical regulation of the transport sector. The national agency responsible for private investment promotion (ProInversión) promotes projects to national and international investors, and designs, executes and manages their auctioning. Finally, the supervisory institution of investments on public transport infrastructure (*Organismo Supervisor de la Inversión en Infraestructura de Transporte de Uso Público*, OSITRAN) supervises and regulates contracts and adjusts tariffs (Flor and Rojas, 2007).

Poor planning, prioritisation and co-ordination can drive up costs

Although the institutional framework of public-private partnerships is fairly complete, the current distribution of responsibilities between agencies can complicate overall co-ordination. Inefficiencies occur when the agencies responsible for providing a service are not involved in managing the concession through the whole life cycle. Without such a life-cycle approach to contract management, ambiguities can arise over the allocation of responsibility for addressing irregularities. In addition, OSITRAN's oversight role is undermined by its involvement in contract management during construction and operation (Bitran et al., 2013).

Weaknesses in the prioritisation and planning phases can also cause inefficiencies in public-private partnership projects. Ex-ante feasibility studies and value-for-money evaluations could help solve difficulties at these stages. However, the institutional framework supporting value-for-money analysis in Peru remains weak. Delays and inefficiencies in the processes of environmental and land licensing as well as consultation with local actors affect the timing and certainty of concession contracts. Peruvian authorities are already discussing these aspects to improve the regulatory framework of public-private partnership projects.

As with other Latin American countries, Peru has had to renegotiate concessions, which can increase the total cost of public-private partnership projects. The performance of concessions is determined by the contract, and regulatory and institutional design. However, flaws in the design of concession contracts have caused excessive costs in Latin America (OECD/ECLAC, 2012). In the case of Peru, out of a sample of 15 national road concession contracts signed from 1994 to 2010, 11 were renegotiated at least once. These renegotiations led to a total of 53 changes and extra costs of over USD 300 million, and added 9 years to the concessions' terms (Bitran et al., 2013). Nevertheless, compared to other Latin American countries, Peru has experienced only a modest amount of renegotiation, partly due to its well-conceived concession designs.

Poor past performance highlights the need to better account for the risks associated with public-private partnerships in the fiscal framework. While ProInversion's selection process has improved its efficacy in recent years, these partnerships must be included in the reporting of fiscal risks to limit the chances of unexpected costs from renegotiations.

***Obras por Impuestos* is innovative, but may need greater supervision**

In order to increase the efficiency of investments in Peru, the government delegates infrastructure investment to private firms in exchange for tax credits. Despite steady growth and increases in tax revenue received by local governments in mining areas, mining communities still lack basic services (see section below). In 2008, the Peruvian government designed a mechanism called *Obras por Impuestos,* or Works for Taxes, with the objective of accelerating and improving the quality of public investments. This mechanism allows private firms to finance physical infrastructure and maintenance expenditures which are the responsibility of local governments in exchange for future tax credits.

This type of policy secures local government support and aims to increase the efficiency of infrastructure investments. For local governments with limited capacity to carry out capital investment, *Obras por Impuestos* plays a key role in the execution of investment and the delivery of public goods at sub-national level. This mechanism appears to have benefitted regional and local governments by increasing the execution of infrastructure projects, accelerating local infrastructure, using the know-how of private companies to increase the quality of their investments, and enhancing the reputation and image of local governments by helping them to reach their goals and objectives.

However, this policy also means that private sector is taking up the role of the public sector in the execution of public services. A key challenge therefore is to provide the appropriate checks and balances within these projects. The main risk associated with allowing private firms to replace the local and regional authorities in the provision of public infrastructure is how far these investments are aligned with the priorities needed to promote local development.

The regulatory and institutional framework for public procurement has advanced in recent years

The experience of many OECD countries has been that procurement is particularly vulnerable to corruption because of the financial interests at stake and the volume of business opportunities for suppliers. Public procurement in Peru represents close to 50% of total government expenditures, a higher percentage than in other countries in Latin America. For instance, in countries such as Brazil, Chile, Colombia and Mexico, public procurement does not exceed 30% of total expenditure. Furthermore, it has been concentrated in central government operations (OECD/IDB, 2014).

The institutional framework for public procurement has improved considerably over the past seven years. The Law on Public Procurement – *Ley de Contrataciones del Estado (Decreto Legislativo 1017, 2008)* – and subsequent decrees have helped to improve the regulatory framework for public procurement procedures. The executive also enhanced the institutional framework for public procurement by replacing CONSUCODE (*Consejo Superior de Contrataciones y Adquisiciones del Estado*) with the OSCE (*Organismo Supervisor de las Contrataciones del Estado*). Peru's public procurement regulations allow for open and competitive tenders for projects above PEN 11 500 (equivalent to USD 3 500 as of August 2015) with additional requirements depending on project size. One of the main benefits has been improvements in transparency, attributed to greater use of information and technology in the public procurement process. All information regarding individual projects and procurement processes is available on a web portal administered by the OSCE. In that sense, the creation of the platform SEACE (*Sistema Electrónico de Contrataciones del Estado*) may help to increase efficiency and reduce cases of bribery around public procurement.

However, more could still be done to increase the effectiveness of public procurement in Peru. First, the full implementation of a value-for-money approach instead of a unique criteria based on pricing would more appropriately define the assets acquired by the state. Second, increasing the number of private firms participating in public procurement would bolster competition. This could be done by improving procurement procedures, such as the methods of payment.

Given the importance of public procurement in Peru in comparison with other countries in the region, and the need to build the evidence to inform policy making and improve service delivery, the OECD Country Programme includes an OECD Public Procurement Review.

Policies at sub-national level have not improved equity and productivity across all regions

The decentralisation process needs improvements to boost economic performance in Peru. Co-ordination problems with central government, weak sub-national institutions, political fragility at the regional level and an inefficient allocation of resources have affected the effectiveness of the decentralisation process. Key policies, in areas such as education, infrastructure and innovation have not necessarily been prioritised or properly implemented by sub-national governments. In that context, the institutional framework of public policy implementation has not contributed enough to boost productivity and reduce regional disparities.

Peru is divided into three levels of regional government: departments, provinces and districts, making it the only Latin American economy to have a local government system with two sub-levels: provinces and districts. Peru has 25 departments (including Lima and Callao), 196 provinces and 1 853 municipal districts.

In the past three decades, the regional framework has undergone three transitions between centralised and decentralised governments. The 1979 Constitutional Act moved Peru from military dictatorship to democracy. This act started the decentralisation process by giving Peruvian municipalities resource-management responsibilities. In 1980, the first political cycle of local elections followed. Before the 1980s, 80% of fiscal transfers to sub-national authorities went to Lima and Callao, and the decentralisation process widened transfers to other local authorities. However, the limited capacity of some municipalities, particularly those located in rural areas, has hindered their ability to exploit this new regime and foster local development in Peru (Muñoz, 2010).

During the 1990s, Peru reverted to a centralised government after the regional governments elected in 1989 and 1990 were dissolved (Contreras, 2004). During this period under President Fujimori, Peru started a process that re-centralised the economy. Regionally elected governments were eliminated and central government took on most of the regional leadership by concentrating resources and functions in the Ministry of the Presidency. In 1993 the new constitution eliminated the distinction in competences between the provincial and district authorities. This removed the pre-eminence of the provinces over the district authorities (Muñoz, 2005).

The current sub-national framework was initiated in 2002 in a new process of decentralisation, with constitutional reforms aimed at increasing the fiscal resources and political power of sub-national governments. The main focus of the decentralisation process was to increase fiscal transfers through two key components: the Municipal Compensation Fund (*Fondo de Compensación Municipal*, FONCOMUN) and commodities revenues. FONCOMUN transfers resources based on compensatory mechanisms defined by socio-economic and demographic criteria. The main revenues of sub-national governments obtained from commodity exploitation are *canon* and royalties.[5] In line with some OECD economies, royalties are based on companies' profits, while *canon* represents 50% of the corporate tax from mining companies (the other half is retained by the central government). These revenues should be spent on capital investment.[6]

Addressing regional inequalities for sustainable inclusive growth

Regional disparities in Peru remain high in comparison with OECD economies, as we have seen in Chapter 2. As with other Latin American economies, there are large differences in per capita income levels between departments. These are greater than the average regional differences within OECD economies – regional inequality in Peru is 18 percentage points higher than the OECD average, using the Gini coefficient of GDP per capita to measure disparities (Figure 5.3). Lack of data on GDP per capita at the provincial and district levels makes it difficult to compare inequality at these levels with OECD economies.

Figure 5.3. **Regional income disparities in Peru**

Gini index of inequality of GDP per capita (2012 or latest available data)

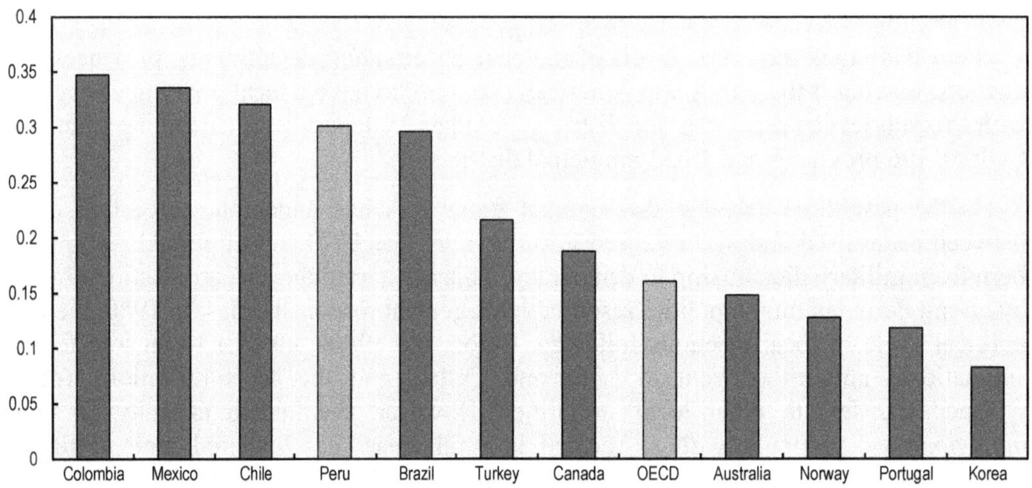

Note: The figure refers to each country's main political divisions (TL2 regions). For instance, states in the United States and departments in Peru. 2013 data for Peru; 2012 data for Australia, Canada, Chile, Colombia, Korea and Mexico; 2011 data for Brazil, Norway, Portugal and Turkey.

Source: OECD calculations based on data provided by INEI (National Institute of Statistics) and *OECD Regional Database*, www.oecd.org/gov/regional-policy/regionalstatisticsandindicators.htm (accessed on 19 March 2015).

StatLink *http://dx.doi.org/10.1787/888933265917*

Regional differences in poverty have also increased in Peru and have become a spatial challenge. While poverty reduction in Peru has been impressive overall (Chapter 2), disparities between rural and urban areas have increased. Monetary poverty fell by more than 70% between 2004 and 2013 in Lima, while in traditionally poor rural areas, such as Sierra and Selva, poverty rates fell by less than 40% and 50% respectively. While the poor represented close to 13% of Lima's population in 2013, the proportion was close to 53% in Sierra and 43% in Selva.[7]

Most of the discrepancies in regional GDP between Lima and the rest of Peru are due to low labour productivity (Figure 5.4). Differences in labour productivity between departments have remained almost constant over the past decade, with the main exception being commodity-producing regions, where highly productive commodity sectors have emerged which created little employment (Chapter 3). This is the situation in Moquegua, a department in which mining is important thanks to its copper resources (a key actor in this department is the firm Southern Copper Corporation) and to a lesser extent gold and silver. Analysis of total factor productivity corroborates the differences in labour productivity across regions (Céspedes et al., 2014).

Figure 5.4. **The sources of real income disparities across regions, 2013**

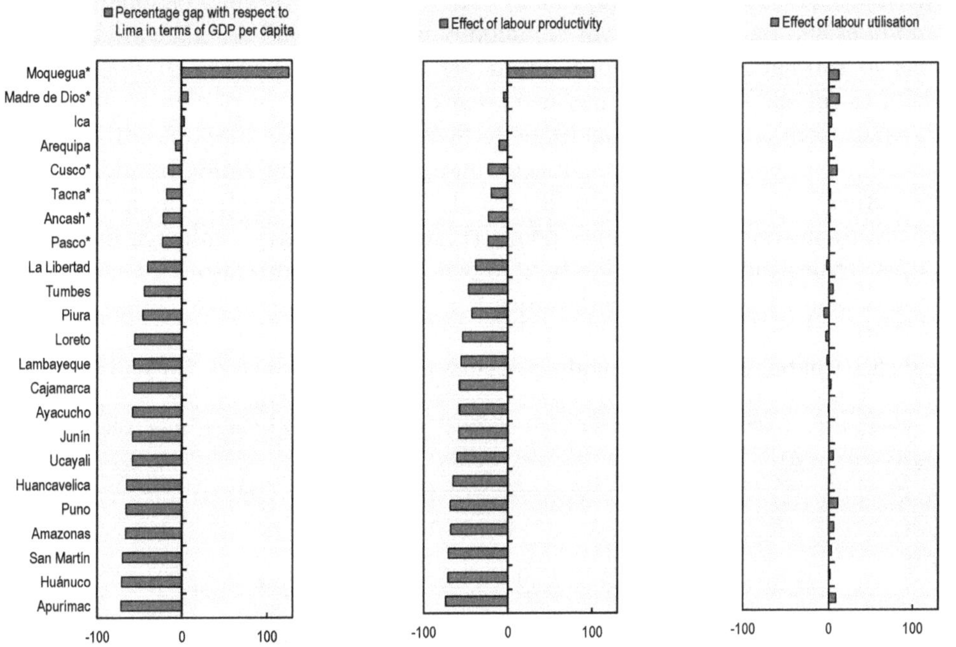

Note: * denotes departments in which the mining sector represents more than 30% of total 2013 GDP (Ancash, Cusco, Madre de Dios, Moquegua, Pasco and Tacna).

Source: OECD calculations based on data provided by INEI (National Institute of Statistics).

StatLink http://dx.doi.org/10.1787/888933265928

Furthermore, regions with low levels of productivity suffer from a variety of deficiencies. Informality remains high in these less-developed regions with low labour productivity (Chapter 2). Performance in education and health, two sectors which are the responsibility of the sub-national authorities, is also very poor in some municipalities. Access to, and quality of, education differ considerably across departments and between rural and urban areas. While close to 36% of the students in primary schools in urban areas have the capacity to read and interpret a text, this share is less than 7% in rural areas. In urban areas this proportion has increased by more than 15 percentage points in the last five years, but it has not increased at all in rural areas.[8] There are similarly disappointing differences in health care services and health outcomes (Chapter 2).

In some departments in Peru, basic needs are still going unmet and people lack access to some services. Departments such as Amazonas, Huancavelica, Loreto, Pasco, San Martin and Ucayali show high levels of unmet basic needs.[9] Despite some improvements in the last five years, these departments are not meeting at least one of the five basic needs for more than 30% of their inhabitants. In contrast, the figures for Arequipa, Ica, Lima, Moquegua, and Tacna are less than 15% of inhabitants. Other indicators, such as access to finance and other business services, exacerbate the differences in GDP per capita. For instance, while Lima contributes around 50% of Peru's GDP, it receives more than 70% of loans whereas Huánuco received only 0.1% of the loans despite contributing more than 1.1% of GDP.[10]

Sub-national governments face crucial challenges in Peru

Commodity-based transfers exacerbate inequality

Commodity-based transfers have been volatile in recent years, requiring counter-cyclical resource management. The volatility of international prices for commodities and the uncertainty of commodity production in Peru have affected revenue streams to sub-national authorities. From the early 2000s, commodity-based regional transfers to sub-national authorities increased considerably. In particular, from 2001 to 2005, funds from *canon* increased by more than 150%. After 2005 these fiscal transfers amounted to more than 1.0% of GDP, and represented close to 1.45% of GDP on average in the period 2010-2014. Between 2012 and 2014, these transfers, as a percentage of GDP, fell by nearly 0.5 percentage points (Figure 5.5). A key challenge therefore is to adopt fiscal rules and a stabilisation fund to better manage these resources and to even out revenue streams to sub-national authorities.

Figure 5.5. **Contribution of commodities sectors to regional transfers, 2004-14** (% of GDP)

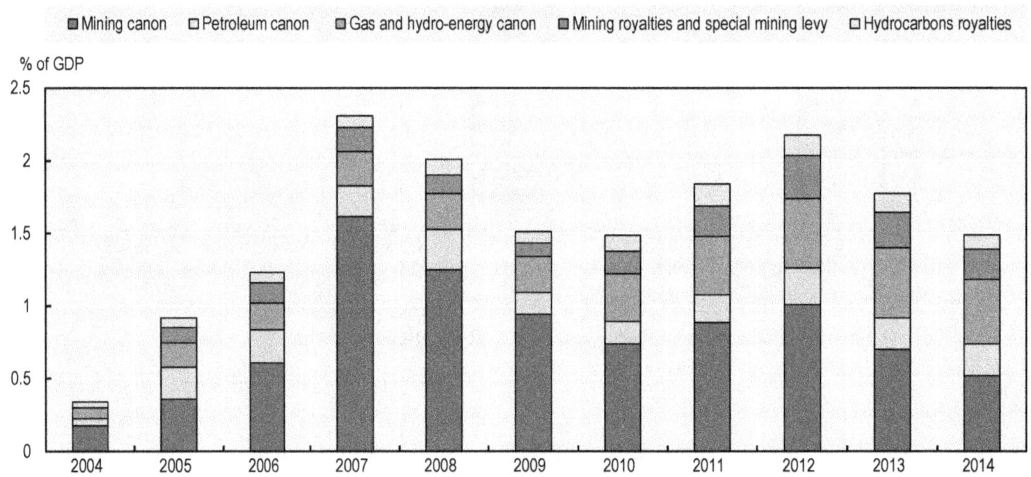

Note: The *canon* and royalties are transfers of natural resources. *Canon* is distributed exclusively to the sub-national governments where the minerals are extracted. Royalties are based on companies' profits and *canon* represents 50% of the corporate tax from mining companies.

Source: SUNAT – Superintendencia Nacional de Aduanas y de Administración Tributaria (http://www.sunat.gob.pe/) for mining royalties; PERUPETRO (http://www.perupetro.com.pe/) for hydrocarbon royalties (accessed 15 June 2015); and Ministry of Economy and Finance (2015), "Consulta de Transferencias a los Gobiernos Nacional, Regional, Local y EPS", Transparencia Económica website, http://apps5.mineco.gob.pe/transferencias/cuadros/Hoja1_1.aspx for *canon* data.

StatLink http://dx.doi.org/10.1787/888933265936

Commodity-based transfers have been largely allocated to the regions producing raw materials, exacerbating regional disparities. The *canon* and royalties are mainly distributed to the sub-national governments where the raw materials are extracted. The fiscal transfers based on commodities per capita received by Cusco and Moquegua alone are greater than those obtained by 15 departments in Peru put together. Just 5 out of the 25 departments receive more than half of the total resources (Figure 5.6). Nor do these fiscal resources target the poorest regions. Indeed, they are negatively correlated with the level of unmet basic needs the departments have.[11] For instance, commodity-based transfers to Moquegua are 8 times higher than those to Loreto and 12 times higher than those to Amazonas. However, while only 1.2% of the population in Moquegua has at least one unmet basic need, while the figure is 24% in Loreto and 15% in Amazonas.

Therefore, a key challenge is to improve the allocation of commodity-based transfers according to the level of development of Peruvian departments. Similar to the case of Colombia before the 2011 Royalties Reform, there is a need to increase the diversification of these resources across the regions (OECD, 2013). Resources should to be efficiently allocated by accounting for specific department needs according to their socio-economic challenges, and by supporting governance capacity at the sub-national level (see below).

Figure 5.6. **The mismatch between regional commodity transfers (2014 data) and basic needs (2013 data)**

Transfers per capita (in PEN)

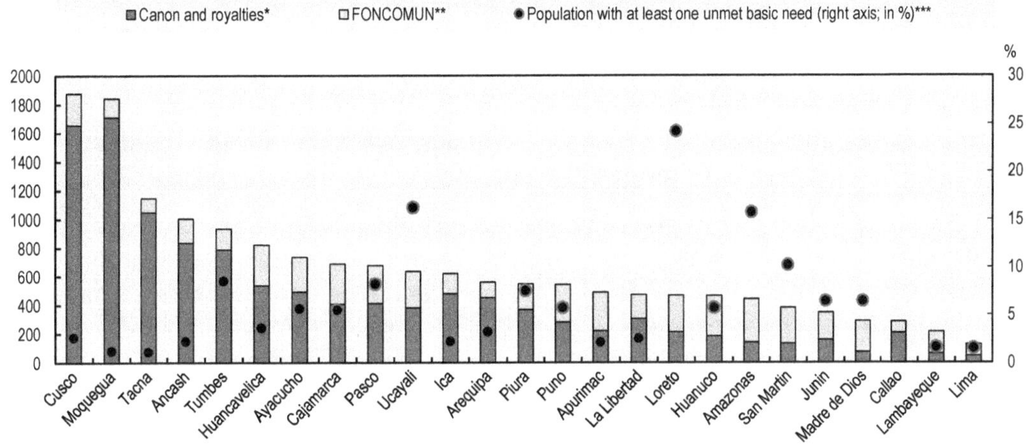

Notes: * See Figure 5.5 for the definition of *canon* and royalties. Customs are also included. ** FONCOMUN is the Municipal Compensation fund. This fund seeks to promote investment at the municipal level with a redistributive objective. It prioritises the poorest municipalities, particularly in rural areas and marginal urban areas. *** The components of Unmet Basic Needs are: quality of the house, non-overcrowding of the house, access to sanitary services, school attendance, and economic dependency. No data for Callao.

Source: OECD calculations based on National Households Survey Data (ENAHO – Encuesta Nacional de Hogares) from INEI (National Institute of Statistics) for unmet basic needs (http://www.inei.gob.pe/estadisticas/indice-tematico/sociales/). SUNAT – Superintendencia Nacional de Aduanasy de Administración Tributaria (http://www.sunat.gob.pe/) for mining royalties; PERUPETRO (http://www.perupetro.com.pe/) for hydrocarbon royalties; and Ministry of Economy and Finance (2015), "Consulta de Transferencias a los Gobiernos Nacional, Regional, Local y EPS", Transparencia Económica website, http://apps5.mineco.gob.pe/transferencias/cuadros/Hoja1_1.aspx for FONCOMUN and *canon* data (accessed on 15 June 2015).

StatLink http://dx.doi.org/10.1787/888933265947

Sub-national governments lack the capacity to govern effectively

Given the limited institutional capacity of the sub-national authorities, better co-ordination with central government is needed to improve the effectiveness of regional public expenditures. The fiscal transfer system lacks the appropriate co-ordination between different levels of government needed for efficient resource allocation. In practice, a discretionary framework at the vertical level defines the allocation of resources.[12] This is highly relevant given that some of Peru's districts are small (nearly

60% of districts have less than 5 000 citizens), and do not necessarily have the management capacity to spend fiscal resources appropriately.

The poorest municipalities have limited capacity, preventing them from establishing an effective development agenda. Local governments lack the human resources and experience to fulfil their roles, resulting in poor management of municipal public services. In addition, red tape and procedural complexities affect the efficiency of decision-making processes. Some authorities do not follow regulatory frameworks because they lack knowledge of the complete legal process required to adopt and implement policies (Muñoz, 2005). Sub-national authorities require effective support from the central government to improve the efficiency of expenditures from regional transfers. For instance, when public-private partnerships are envisaged at sub-national level, support from OSITRAN would be useful to avoid inefficiencies in the involvement of the private sector.

Furthermore, fiscal transfers are not accompanied by a clear definition of the responsibilities of different levels of government. First, the institutional framework lacks internal controls and checks and balances on decisions taken by mayors.[13] Second, the hierarchical framework between provinces and district authorities is unclear. This dual system at the municipal level, unique to Latin America, creates conflicts over responsibilities and sources of revenue (Muñoz, 2005).

Peru needs to improve its co-ordination between the allocation of commodity-based fiscal transfers and other sources of revenue. *Canon* and royalties are spent solely on capital investment at the regional level. This rigidity creates a misallocation of resources (Del Valle, 2013). This is particularly evident in the weak co-ordination between capital investment and current expenditure at the regional level. If investments are to function well, capital expenditures have to be planned over a multi-annual framework that includes maintenance and current expenditures.

Transfers to local authorities do not necessarily ensure efficiency gains for local institutions. Efficiency can be measured by the inputs that could be saved while still obtaining the same output or services (e.g. in the areas of education, health, and transport). *Canon* and FONCOMUN transfers have a negative impact on the efficiency of municipal districts (Muñoz, 2010). Further mining transfers have only positive short-term effects, such as an increase in temporary public employment, which are explained in part by the strategic behaviour of local politicians (Maldonado, 2015). Indeed, an increase in transfers helps to boost public expenditure at sub-national level but does not help to improve the quality of this expenditure. Sub-national authorities with higher *canon* revenues did not improve their performance for some social indicators, suggesting inefficiencies in spending (Sanguinetti, 2010; Arreaza and Reuter, 2012). Furthermore, in 2014 most of the departments involved in misappropriation of public funds have received sizeable transfers from *canon* and royalties (Korinek, 2015). In contrast, policy dialogue with local actors through the Local Co-ordination Council (a proxy for civil participation in local government decisions) improves the efficiency of local institutions (Herrera and Francke, 2007).

The fragility of political parties affects the effectiveness of public policies. Peru has a large number of political parties at the local level. For instance, in the 2010 sub-national elections, more than 180 political organisations were registered in the departmental elections, 250 in the provincial elections and 550 in the district elections. Most of these political organisations are local parties; national political parties only made up around 10% of the total political organisations at sub-national level. Furthermore, the small regional political organisations succeeded in taking power in more than 50% of the departmental and local (i.e, provincial and district) governments.[14] This political fragmentation affects co-ordination both horizontally across local governments and vertically, between levels of government. Decentralisation in a context of weak national political parties and unstable regional political organisations has thus worsened the effectiveness of public policies at the regional level. For instance, political fragmentation and weak political parties, combined with the fact that there is no second round for municipal elections, mean mayors often do not have the political support to legitimise their decisions (Muñoz, 2005). This limits their overall effectiveness and the ability to implement their policies.

Weakness in the planning of public policies of political parties limits the efficiency of sub-national expenditures, particularly those at the provincial level. Traditional national political parties have not succeeded in improving local efficiency; on average, their efficiency of public expenditures is lower than mayors elected by local parties. This is evident after controlling for other factors such as those concerning fiscal, demographic and socio-economic conditions (Muñoz, 2010). These national parties are least efficient and effective in the poorest rural areas, where strong and transparent candidates are most needed. Furthermore, fragile local alliances sometimes disappear just after an electoral period (Zavaleta, 2014). This affects the planning and prioritisation of policies at sub-national level.

Urban planning is a key priority for developing sustainable cities in Peru

Urban planning and organisation are pressing challenges in Peru. In recent decades, Peru has faced large rural migration outflows, mainly towards urban centres in coastal regions, primarily Lima. This was coupled with a process of demographic transition. While in 1972 the urban population was approximately 8 million, in 2007 that population has grown to nearly 21 million, according to the last census by the National Institute of Statistics (INEI). Lima's growth has been even more striking. Its population now exceeds 9 million, close to 30% of the total population and 43% of the urban population in Peru. Its population has grown by more than 130% over the past 50 years, while the country as a whole has grown by less than 100% in the same period. Similar to other countries in Latin America, Peru's urban population, at nearly 80%, is a larger share of the total population than the average for Africa (47%), Europe (73%) or the world (54%).[15] Furthermore, a significant increase in urbanisation is predicted for Peru over the next 35 years, presenting challenges in urban planning (Figure 5.7). Further growth of the cities will require innovative policies to ensure equal quality of public services to all citizens. In that context, a better linkage between urban and rural development policies is needed to avoid pressures on cities, and improve well-being in Peru.

The process of decentralisation granted local governments important competences in terms of urban planning. Local governments manage urban planning, they form plans for local development in co-ordination with the local community and they approve mechanisms for community participation and auditing of municipal action. The regulations also emphasised the engagement of civil society in decision-making processes. The central government drafts the national and sectoral plans, by taking into account regional and local plans. Cities are also in charge of the management of certain public services such as public transport and traffic, housing and urban renovation, social programmes, and waste management.

Figure 5.7. **Urban population in Peru, 1950-2050**

% of population

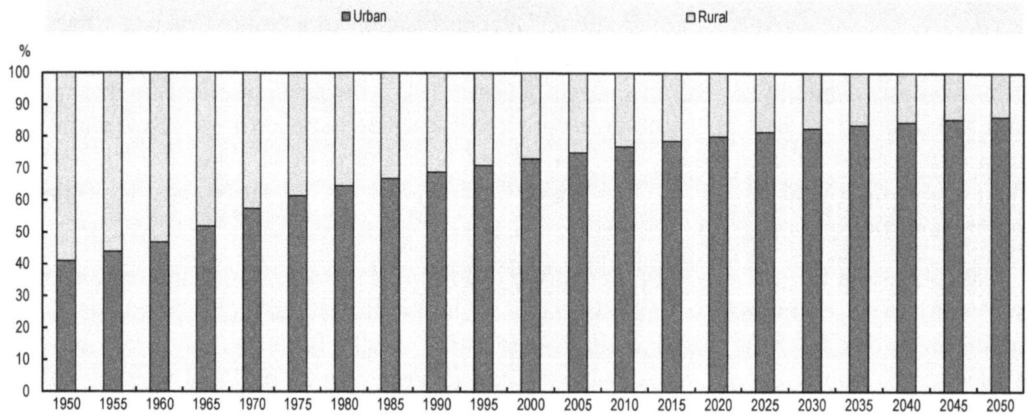

Source: United Nations (2015), *World Urbanization Prospects: 2014 Revision, Population Division*, Department of Economic and Social Affairs, United Nations, New York, http://esa.un.org/unpd/wup/.

StatLink http://dx.doi.org/10.1787/888933265954

At the national level, the central government prepared a National Plan for Urban Development for 2006-2015 (Ministry of Housing, Construction and Sanitation, 2006). These plans traditionally cover long periods (the previous covered the period 1974-1990) in order to identify medium and long-term objectives. The latest plan responds to the need for both better-structured cities with their nearest urban areas, and more strategic city planning. To respond to the process of urbanisation, the plan covers four principles: 1) governance and governability; 2) connectivity and communications; 3) specialisation, productive articulation and innovation; and 4) sustainability and competitiveness.

The plan's development is intertwined with the establishment of other national reforms such as the housing plan and the municipal and regional urban development plans. Some of the most significant objectives include increasing the institutionalisation and human capital of local and regional governments, boosting connectivity within and between cities, promoting cities' economic development by exploiting competitive advantages and fostering private sector investment, targeting land regularisation, constructing and improving pre-existing housing, and expanding access to water and sewage.

Lima has its own urban development plan which recognises future challenges from increasing urbanisation, but there are barriers to its implementation. PLAM 2035 (*Plan Metropolitano de Desarrollo Urbano Lima y Callao 2035*) is a renewal of the city's 1993-2010 plan, and comprises an extensive framework for future development (Municipality of Lima, 2014). It outlines strategies to address concerns including the distribution of urbanisation zones and public transport reform and backs plans to increase the city's urban density through more than 200 specific infrastructure projects. Some of these projects have already been presented to the *Sistema Nacional de Inversion Pública* (SNIP). The plan also considers unifying the transport authority for Lima and Callao into a single authority. The biggest challenge of the plan is to gather sufficient political support to carry out its long-term policies. Since the plan was developed and approved by a former local government, and aims to adopt long-term perspective, a key challenge is to enhance and maintain dialogue between different political parties to implement these policies and develop more effective urban planning methodology.

Transport policies remain a key component of the urbanisation process in Peru. The number of vehicles in Lima alone has increased substantially, from 776 000 in 2000 to approximately 1.4 million in 2012. Peru has followed a similar pattern to other Latin American countries, with significant expansion of the car fleet among people with relatively low incomes, and slow development of the motorcycle fleet. This pattern poses challenges regarding the development of public transportation in order to avoid rapid increases in private motorisation and pollution in Peruvian cities (Box 5.1).

The socio-economic challenges Peru faces at sub-national level require more effective public policies. To tackle these challenges and improve decision making, Peru needs to improve its territorial statistics and the management of public finances at the sub-national level. This will be crucial to boosting rural development through the management of natural resources, and to fostering urban development and competitiveness. Underlying these challenges is the need for better co-ordination between central and sub-national authorities. As these areas represent a binding constraint for inclusive development in Peru, the OECD Territorial Review will be a key review in the context of the OECD Country Programme.

Box 5.1. **Public transport, private car ownership and potential pathways of CO_2 emissions in Peruvian cities**

Peruvian policies towards urban transport infrastructure and services have recently aligned with other countries in the region. Large Peruvian cities began developing their systems later than other metropolitan areas of Latin America. Recent investments in bus rapid transit, subway and suburban rail aim to meet increasing travel demand while keeping the mode shares of public transport high. The Ministry of Transport and Communications recently published a comprehensive investment plan up to 2025 for large urban areas in Peru. The main focus of the plan is to promote greater mobility while improving territorial access.

Projections for car and motorcycle ownership in Lima suggests that levels will rise from 2030 onwards if the expected increase in economic growth is not accompanied by greater investment in public transport infrastructure. A recent study of Latin American cities explored various potential pathways for the development of mobility as a function of the implementation of the transport investment and land use policies adopted (OECD/ITF, 2015). The study focuses on cities with populations of over 500 000. Peruvian cities show moderate levels of urban sprawl (with the highest sprawl observed in Argentine cities and the lowest in Colombian ones). Rapid motorisation is expected as households with increasing disposable income prioritise car and, more recently, motorcycle ownership. More intensive investment in roads will only increase growth of car ownership in the longer term, by relieving the current constraints on car use caused by congestion. Accelerated investment in public transport will be the only approach to significantly alter the trend towards private motor transport (Figure 5.8). The study found that poor public transport provision is the strongest incentive for car and motorcycle use. It also stresses the importance of transport policies on vehicle ownership rates.

Box 5.1. **Public transport, private car ownership and potential pathways of CO_2 emissions in Peruvian cities** *(cont.)*

Figure 5.8. **The influence of public transport policies on car and motorcycle ownership in Peruvian cities**

Car and motorcycle ownership per 1 000 inhabitants in cities over 500 000 inhabitants (2010-50)

Panel A. Passenger cars

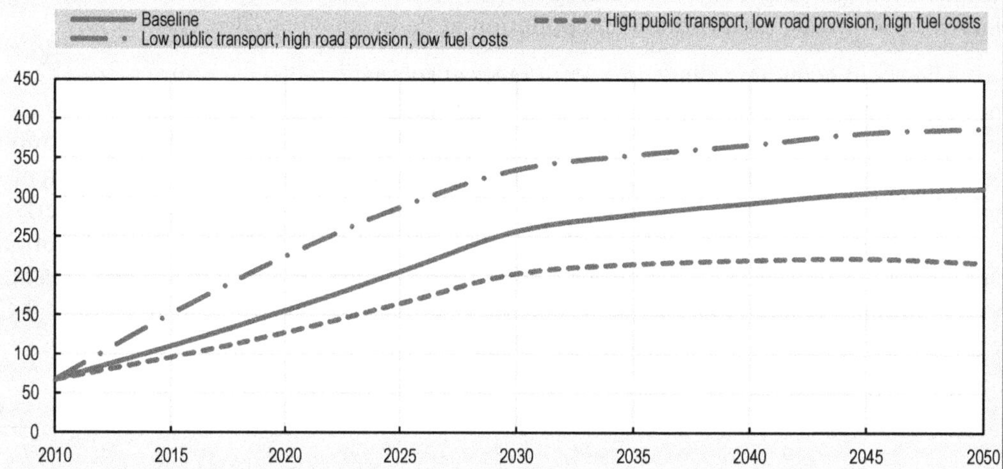

Panel B. Motorcycles

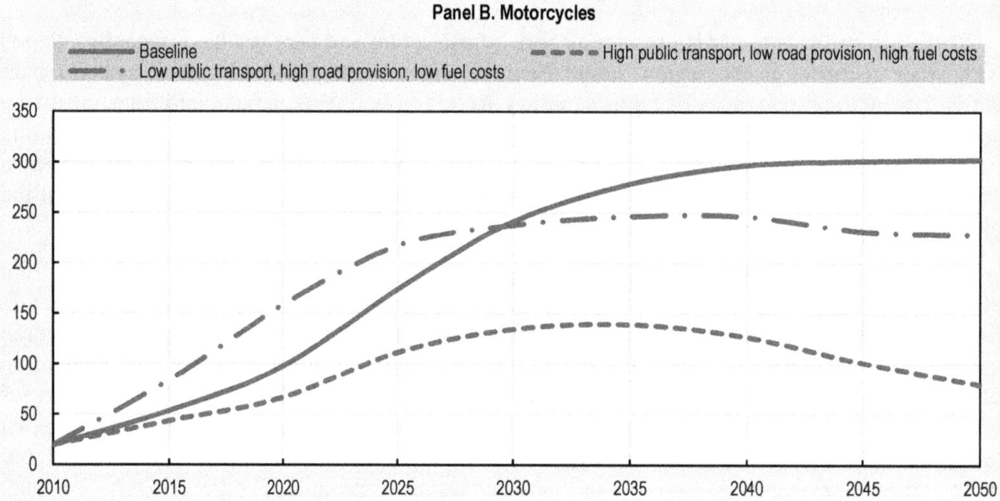

Source: OECD calculations based on OECD/ITF (2015), *ITF Transport Outlook 2015*, OECD Publishing, Paris, http://dx.doi.org/10.1787/9789282107782-en.

StatLink http://dx.doi.org/10.1787/888933326596

Trends in car and motorcycle use largely determine the transport-related emission levels of local air pollutants and CO_2. The report explored outcomes from three CO_2 emission scenarios: 1) low investment in public transport, high road provision and low fuel costs; 2) high investment in public transport, low road provision and high fuel costs; and 3) baseline levels of public transport investment, road provision and fuel costs. It showed the significant effect of private mobility on overall CO_2 emissions in large Peruvian cities (Figure 5.9). This highlights the importance of aligning policies to reduce CO_2 emissions and local pollutants with transport policies at the city level. The development of well-designed public transport would reduce environmental damage in Peruvian cities.

Box 5.1. **Public transport, private car ownership and potential pathways of CO_2 emissions in Peruvian cities** *(cont.)*

Figure 5.9. **The influence of car-oriented vs public transport-oriented policies on CO_2 emissions in Peruvian cities, 2010-50**

Cities over 500 000 inhabitants

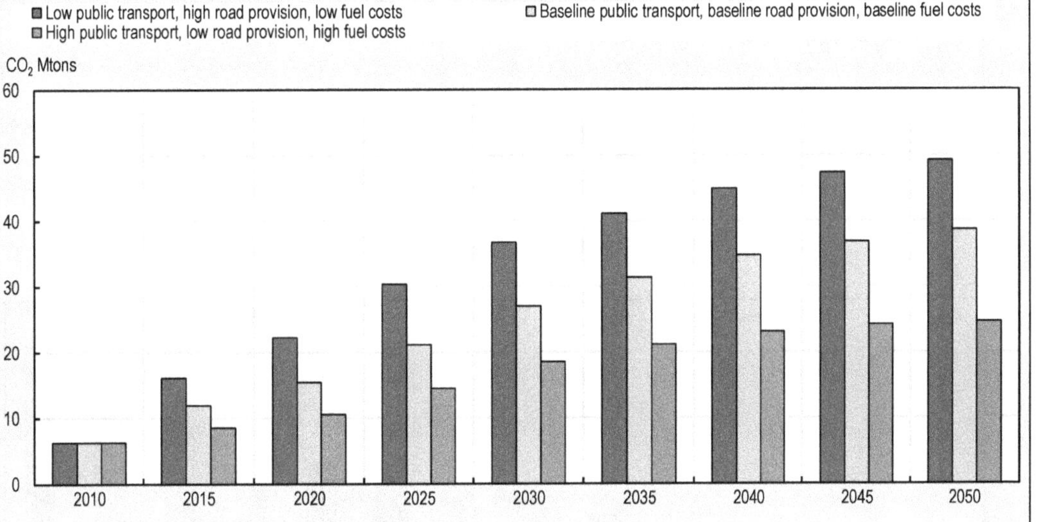

Note: Mtons refers to millions of metric tons.

Source: OECD/ITF (2015), *ITF* Transport *Outlook 2015*, OECD Publishing, Paris, http://dx.doi.org/10.1787/9789282107782-en.

StatLink http://dx.doi.org/10.1787/888933265970

Environmental risks should drive improvements in Peru's environmental policy

Peru faces a range of environmental risks, including climate change. Environment is a key pillar for the well-being of all (Chapter 1). The effects of climate change are estimated to lower potential GDP by 4.3 percentage points (CAN, 2008) by 2025, and could further generate a loss of 6 percentage points of potential GDP by 2050 (Vargas, 2009). GDP losses at between 11.4% and 15.4% over the period 2010-2100 (IDB/UNECLAC, 2014) are forecasted according to a recent estimate released in December 2014 at the 20th Conference of the Parties to the United Nations Framework Convention on Climate Change (UNFCCC-COP 20) in Lima. Fishing, livestock in the high Andes and agriculture would be most affected by climate change in Peru.[16] In terms of land use, Peru has lost close to 3.0% of its forest area in the last two decades, which contrasts with the slight increase of forest cover in the OECD area, but it is lower than the deforestation rate in other Latin American economies (Figure 5.10, Panel A). Another environmental indicator is the level of air pollution by particulate matter, the air pollutant that most commonly affects people's health. Concentrations of particulate matter less than 10 micrometres in size (PM_{10}) have been measured at 63 micrograms per cubic metre ($\mu g/m^3$) in Peruvian cities, which is high by OECD standards and exceeds Peru's own ambitious target and World Health Organization (WHO) air quality guideline of 20 $\mu g/m^3$ (Figure 5.10, Panel B).

Figure 5.10. **Environmental risks in Peru and benchmark countries**

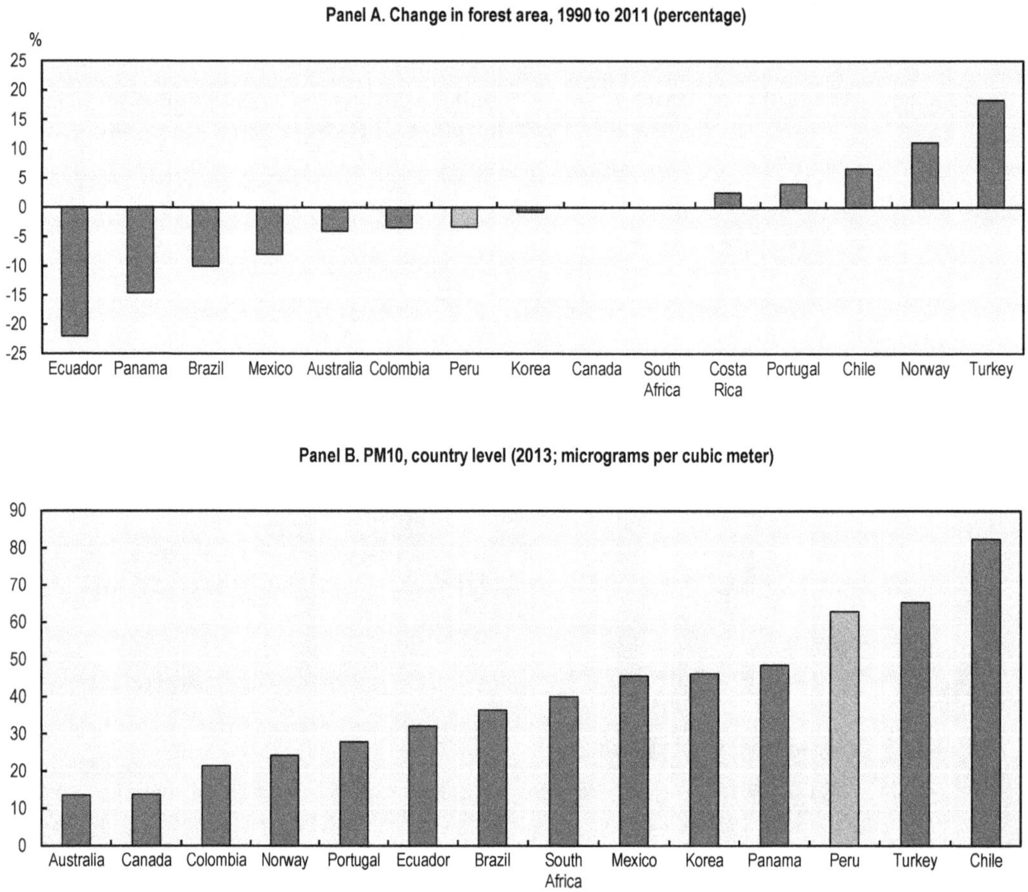

Note: HDRO calculations based on data on forest and total land area from Food and Agriculture Organisation (FAO) (http://faostat.fao.org/site/377/default.aspx#ancor).

Source: HDRO (2014), *Human Development Statistical Tables, Human Development Report Office* (database), New York, http://hdr.undp.org/en/data (Panel A), and World Bank (2015), *World Development Indicators* (database), Washington, DC, http://data.worldbank.org (Panel B).

StatLink http://dx.doi.org/10.1787/888933265982

By international comparison, Peru appears to be ahead in regulating air pollution by sulphur dioxide (SO_2), another key pollutant affecting human health. This results from a stepped approach in 2014 to align the air quality standard (24-hour mean) for sulphur dioxide to the WHO guideline of 20 $\mu g/m^3$ (WHO, 2006).[17] However, the private sector argued that environmental quality standards had been set too high for Peru's level of development (Zubieta, 2014). Indeed, the new standard is proving difficult for some sectors (e.g. metal processors) to achieve in the short-term. In that context, three cities have been given more time to comply.[18] This is consistent with WHO recommendations to move gradually towards full compliance.

The institutional framework for environmental protection has been strengthened

The Peruvian government created the Ministry of Environment (MoE) in 2008 out of the National Council for Environment to tackle environmental challenges and increase environmental legitimacy. By raising the council to ministerial status, the government gave environmental policy more political leverage. The ministry's overarching mission is to promote environmental conservation to ensure a sustainable, responsible, rational and ethical use of natural resources, and the environment that sustains them. It also contributes to social, economic and cultural development in harmony with the environment.[19]

A key mandate of the MoE is to enhance coherence between environmental policies and other sectoral policies. A multi-sectoral commission was created in 2012 to develop regulations and policy proposals aimed at improving environmental and social conditions under which economic activities take place, especially from extractive industries.[20] Proposals are discussed in a multi-sectoral commission composed of the ministries of Agriculture, Culture, Economy and Finance, Energy and Mining, Environment (which serves as the secretariat of the commission), Health, Production, Development and Social Inclusion, and chaired by the Presidency of the Council of Ministers. Several tasks have been allocated to the MoE. Its lead roles include: formulate, supervise and evaluate national environment policy; ensure compliance with environmental standards; coordinate implementation of national environmental policy with sectors, regional governments and local governments; and, provide technical support to regional and local governments (Comisión Multisectorial, 2012).

Six bodies assist the MoE in accomplishing its mission (Ministry of Environment, 2015a). Three of them focus on providing information in the areas of meteorology and hydrology, geophysics, and biodiversity in the Peruvian Amazon. The other three are more oriented towards management and policy execution and include the Environmental Evaluation and Inspection Agency (OEFA), the National Service of Protected Natural Areas (SERNANP), and the National Service of Environmental Certification for Sustainable Investments (SENACE).[21]

SENACE was created in 2012, and reviews and approves detailed and semi-detailed environmental impact assessments (EIA, *Estudios de Impacto Ambiental*) for high-impact and medium-impact public, private or mixed capital investment projects.[22] Different ministries have been in the process of transferring their competences on their respective subject to this new institution. As this process has not finished yet, SENACE is not fully operating today. EIAs are carried out during project planning. SENACE approval of EIA reports is required to obtain operating permits. The projects subject to EIA are mainly in the fields of agriculture, energy, mining, construction and certain types of industrial production. EIAs estimate the environmental impacts of such activities and propose actions for the project holder to mitigate them. Smaller projects simply require a declaration of environmental impact (DIA, *Declaración de Impacto Ambiental*). In that case, the parties involved are either the ministries in charge of the relevant sector or regional and local governments.[23]

Yet, the implementation and legitimacy of environmental policies are challenging

In recent years, measures to promote investments have focused on reducing environmental regulatory burdens. Prior to 2013, amendments to an EIA were not regulated and followed an ad-hoc process. Since 2013, the procedure to amend EIAs and to operate on public land has been expedited.[24] In particular, the government has given investors the possibility of amending EIAs by presenting technical reports. As a result, investors do not have to initiate a new administrative proceeding to amend an EIA, which could take up to a year. Prior to 2013, obtaining investment permits over public land was difficult, onerous and time-consuming. Today, investors can request easements from the Superintendence of National Properties (SBN), which is a much more expeditious approach to obtain required rights over vacant public land. Moreover, Law N°30230, enacted in July 2014 to promote and revitalise investments in Peru, lowers by half the maximum fines for the three-year period 2014-16, but excludes the most serious of environmental violations.[25] Furthermore, this law strips the government of its ability to quickly create reserve zones, hindering the expansion of protected natural areas.[26] The law also reduces to 45 days the time allotted to governmental entities for reviewing EIAs, and civil servants are subject to sanctions for failing to meet the deadline.[27]

Other measures have been approved to reduce red tape and the multiplicity of government bodies required to approve investment projects. Fast track processes for EIAs and environmental permits have been approved through Law N°30327 (enacted in May 2015).[28] Also, investment projects can now obtain "global environmental certification" (GEC), which combines EIA and environmental permitting (Box 5.2). In addition, procedures, responsibilities and deadlines for granting easements in vacant public land have been clarified in Law N°30327. The law also shortens the process of land expropriation for major infrastructure projects (e.g. highways, electricity transmission lines).[29] These recent measures to promote investment require effective and adequate implementation to guarantee the legitimacy of environmental policy in Peru.

Box 5.2. **Greening investments through the global environmental certification (GEC)**

The GEC's first step is to approve the EIA terms of reference and the EIA baseline (i.e. the part of the EIA that describes the state of the environment in the project area). The baseline must be approved simultaneously by the National Forestry and Wildlife Service (SERFOR) for impacts on forest areas, the Ministry of Production (PRODUCE) when it regards fishing and SERNANP in relation to protected areas. To speed up the EIA process, projects located in the same geographical area can share the same baseline. The Ministry of Environment estimated that publicly sharing baseline studies could cut the time needed to draw up EIAs by almost a year.

Acting as a single window, SENACE then integrates the EIA approval with the granting of up to 14 environmental permits by the Ministry of Agriculture and Irrigation (National Water Authority (ANA) and SERFOR); the Presidency of the Council of Ministers (Supervisory Agency for Investment in Energy and Mining or OSINERGMIN); the Health Ministry (General Directorate of Environmental Health or DIGESA); and the Peruvian Coastguards (DICAPI). SENACE facilitates simultaneous (rather than sequential) issuance of environmental permits in a range of activities, such as for water abstraction, building water supply infrastructure, wastewater discharge, and deforestation (for purposes other than timber harvest). The GEC approval procedure must be completed within 150 days from the submission of the draft EIA.

Law N°30327 considerably strengthens SENACE powers in managing EIAs by supervising the nomination of experts in charge of reviewing EIAs and by coordinating formally dispersed environmental permitting. The law's effectiveness will largely depend on providing SENACE with the necessary means to perform these additional functions.

Mining brings conflicts as well as rewards

Mining activities play a major role in the Peruvian economy and are also the largest contributor to socio-environmental conflicts in Peru, accounting for close to 70% of the total (Defensoría del Pueblo, 2015). Many of these conflicts are fuelled by actual or perceived risks of environmental degradation, as well as distributive issues between the mining company and local communities (Dargent and Muñoz, 2012). For instance, the Camisea project to exploit reserves of natural gas in the Peruvian Amazon was delayed 20 years after environmental and social concerns escalated. The project is located near the Urubamba River, home to several indigenous communities and one of the world's most biodiverse regions. Also, the Conga mining project in Cajamarca was suspended in 2011 after violent community protests about risks to water resources.

Environmental problems associated with mining include air emissions of sulphur dioxide, particulate matter and heavy metals and spillage of toxic chemicals used to extract minerals. Encroachment of protected areas is also a concern: fifteen protected areas are threatened by illegal mining (Ministry of Environment, 2015c). In Madre de Dios (Peruvian Amazon), 20 000 hectares of forest have been destroyed between 1999 and 2012, and the area affected by informal alluvial gold mining has increased by 400%. Alluvial gold mining has also produced mercury contamination. In Puerto Maldonado, Madre de Dios' main city, 60% of the fish consumed exceed levels of mercury deemed acceptable by WHO, and 78% of adults have hair mercury levels three times higher than the maximum allowable limits (Ministry of Environment, 2015b).

Illegal mining has been identified as a major health and environmental concern. Illegal mining is present in virtually all regions of the country, closely related to changes in international gold prices. It is estimated on average to account for more than 20% of gold exports, generate some USD 1 billion annual profits and evade taxes by USD 300 million (Ministry of Environment, 2015c). Several attempts have been made to simplify the complicated and lengthy formalisation process. Campaigns to promote formalisation have been combined with direct regulatory measures to address illegal mining. According to the MoE, nearly all of the estimated 70 000 informal miners came forward to declare their intent to achieve full formalisation.

Lack of effective socio-environmental management in the mining industry hinders Peru's sustainable development objectives. It has had significant negative impacts in terms of social unrest as well as political and financial instability. Investors have faced uncertainty over continued access to mineral resources.

Good environmental policies require the effective involvement of public and private actors in both planning and implementation. Furthermore, Peruvian authorities should ensure that environmental regulations should be both powerful and efficiently administered at the same time. A forthcoming UNECLAC/OECD Environmental Performance Review, as part of the OECD Country Programme, will provide more in-depth analysis of Peru's environmental policies, including measures to promote green growth.

Conclusions

Good governance and effective state capacities are two key pillars for development in Peru. They are fundamental to increasing the effectiveness of public policies in areas such as education and skills, environment, infrastructure, and innovation. Promoting inclusive and sustainable development in Peru will require closing gaps in terms of both the quality and quantity of expenditure in these areas. A long-term strategic framework that allows for a more effective role of the centre of government, and better co-ordination among different levels of government (i.e. between different ministries and agencies of the central government, and with sub-national authorities) are essential for achieving medium and long-term development objectives in Peru.

Inefficiencies hinder the governance of public policies in Peru, and not just in the executive branch. First, Peru needs to increase the efficiency and transparency of the judicial sector. Second, the legislative branch lacks the capacity to administer checks and balances on the executive and is thus perceived as a source of ineffective policies in Peru.

Significant efforts have been deployed to better leverage the private sector for expenditure and investment, but greater transparency and accountability are required to avoid inefficiencies and unexpected fiscal costs. Although the regulatory and institutional frameworks for public-private partnerships have continuously improved, adjustments are still needed in areas such as environmental permits and land acquisitions to avoid delays and renegotiation of contracts. In addition, the *Obras por Impuestos* programme should be accompanied by a fully-realised set of checks and balances within the sub-national and central governments. Finally, tracking spending and implementing value-for-money analysis in the first stages of the procurement process would improve public procurement.

Several means should be considered to tackle regional disparities and enhance socio-economic development at the sub-national level. First, the allocation of commodity-based fiscal transfers at sub-national level needs to be improved. Second, sub-national governments will need to strengthen their capacity to spend resources more strategically, according to local socio-economic needs. In that context, the central government will need to support and co-ordinate better with sub-national authorities in order to avoid persistent public expenditure inefficiencies in Peru.

Finally, environmental regulations can be both powerful and efficiently administered at the same time. Although the regulatory and institutional frameworks for environmental policy have improved in recent years, Peru continues to experience difficulties in implementing policies to foster sustainable growth and preserve the environment. More can be done. It is necessary to strengthen environmental risk management, including stakeholder co-ordination, in setting environmental objectives and assessing the instruments to achieve them more cost effectively. This would also facilitate conflict resolution in the mining sector.

Notes

1. Furthermore, while more than 41% of the households trusted in the police in 2002, this had fallen by more than 20 percentage points in 2013 (INEI, 2014).

2. The most recent case happened in May 2015 where the Attorney General was dismissed by Congress for misconduct such as covering up for a corrupt ex-governor of a mining province.

3. Based on Proética (2013).

4. See http://www.oecd.org/gov/cog.htm for further OECD analysis of the role of Centre of Government.

5. In contrast, the special mining levy (*gravamen especial a la minería*) is a fiscal revenue of the central government. This *gravamen* is a voluntary and temporary surcharge that mining companies pay by virtue of agreements they have made with the government. It is only applicable to firms with valid stability contracts signed before 2011 and those that agreed to the application of this levy with the Peruvian government (Korinek, 2015).

6. See SUNAT – *Superintendencia Nacional de Aduanas y de Administración Tributaria* – website (http://www.sunat.gob.pe/) for more details on how royalties are calculated.

7. Data based on the National Households Survey Data (ENAHO, *Encuesta Nacional de Hogares*) from INEI (http://www.inei.gob.pe/estadisticas/indice-tematico/sociales/), accessed on 15 July 2015.

8. Based on information from the Ministry of Education (Resultados de la Evalución Censal de Estudiantes, 2007-2011).

9. The concept of unmet basic needs in Peru is defined by INEI and comprises: quality housing, non-overcrowding of housing, access to sanitary services, school attendance and lack of economic dependency.

10. Based on information from the *Superintendencia de Banca, Seguros y AFP*.

11. Using data at the department level, the correlation between the amount of fiscal transfers per capita and the percentage of the population with at least one unmet basic need is -0.32.

12. See Muñoz (2008) for concrete examples on the lack of clarity in the tasks among different levels of government and political fragmentation in the Puno department.

13. In particular, mayors have discretional power in the municipal councils, affecting the existence of internal control at the municipal level.

14. More precisely, these regional political parties governed during the period 2010-14 in 14 regional governments, 112 provincial regions, and 845 districts (see *Jurado Nacional de Elecciones* website http://portal.jne.gob.pe/default.aspx).

15. Data based on United Nations (2015).

16. See http://www.cepal.org/en/pressreleases/climate-change-peru-seen-affecting-fishing-high-andes-livestock-and-agricultural.

17. The standards in Peru were 365 μg/m^3 in 2001 and 80 μg/m^3 in 2009 (Supreme Decrees 003 -2008 –MINAM and 074-2001-PCM).

18. These places are the coastal city of Ilo, the highland town of La Oroya, and Arequipa, Peru's second-largest city.

19. Legislative Decree N° 1013 of 14 May 2008 which approves the establishment, organisation and functions of the Ministry of Environment.

20. Supreme Resolution N° 189-2012-PCM.

21. More precisely, the OEFA is in charge of the evaluation, supervision, inspection and sanctioning on environmental matters.

22. Law N° 29968 on the creation of SENACE, available at: http://www.peru.gob.pe/docs/PLANES/14284/PLAN_14284_2014_Norma_creacion_SENACE.pdf

23. See Law N° 27446, Supreme Decree 002-2009-MINAM on environmental impact assessment (EIA), available at: http://www.minam.gob.pe/wp-content/uploads/2013/10/Ley-y-reglamento-del-SEIA1.pdf, and http://www.minam.gob.pe/seia/ entidades-que-participan-en-la-certificacion-ambiental/ regarding the institutions participating in EIAs.

24. Supreme Decrees 054-2013-PCM and 060-2013-PCM.

25. Law N° 30230 establishes tax measures, simplifies procedures and permits for the promotion and revitalisation of investments in the country, available at: http://www.minem.gob.pe/minem/archivos/file/Mineria/LEGISLACION/2014/JULIO/LEY30230.pdF

26. As is the case for establishment of a protected natural area, reserve zones creation must now be approved by Supreme decree (issued by the executive/signed by the President) and not any longer by ministerial resolution (issued by the Minister of agriculture).

27. This contravenes the 50-day deadline prescribed by the National Environmental Impact Assessment Law (N° 27446) for detailed EIAs.

28. Law N° 30327 to promote investment for economic growth and sustainable development.

29. However, provisions on easement and expropriation do not apply to lands and territories of indigenous.

References

Alvarado, S. (2015), "Estudios de Impacto Ambiental: cuatro voces, tres empresas, una sola tarea", *Gestión*, April, http://gestion.pe/economia/estudios-impacto-ambiental-cuatro-voces-tres-empresas-sola-tarea-2130458.

Andvig, J. and K. Moene (1990), "How corruption may corrupt", *Journal of Economic Behaviour and Organization*, Vol. 13(1), pp. 63-76.

Arbizu, J. (2014), "El espiral de la corrupción en el Perú", *Argumentos – Revista de Análisis y Critica*, Vol. 8(3), http://revistaargumentos.iep.org.pe/wp-content/uploads/2014/12/arbizu_julio2014.pdf.

Arreaza, A. and A. Reuter (2012), "Can a mining windfall improve welfare? Evidence from Peru with municipal level data", *CAF Working Papers*, No. 2012/04, CAF, Caracas.

Bitran, E., S. Nieto-Parra and J.S. Robledo (2013), "Opening the black box of contract renegotiations: An analysis of road concessions in Chile, Colombia and Peru", *OECD Development Centre Working Papers,* No. 317, OECD Publishing, Paris, http://dx.doi.org/10.1787/5k46n3wwxxq3-en.

CAD (2013), "Corrupción en gobiernos regionales 2013", *Boletín CAD*, No. 161, CAD (Ciudadanos al Día).

CAN (2008), *El Cambio Climático no Tiene Fronteras: Impacto del Cambio Climático en la Comunidad Andina*, Secretaria General de la Comunidad Andina (CAN), Lima, Peru, www.comunidadandina.org/public/libro_cambioclimatico1.pdf.

Catalan Herrera, P. and P. Francke Ballve (2007), "Análisis de la eficiencia del gasto municipal y de sus determinantes", *CIES, Pontificia Universidad Católica del Perú, edición Julio 2007*, Lima.

Céspedes, N., M. Aquije, A. Sanchez and R. Vera-Tudela (2014), "Productividad sectorial en el Perú: Un análisis a nivel de firmas", *Revista Estudios Económicos*, Issue 28, Banco Central de Reserva del Perú, pp. 9-26.

Comisión Multisectorial (2012), *Ejes Estratégicos de la Gestión Ambiental*, Report from the Multisectorial Commission, www.minam.gob.pe/wp-content/uploads/2013/06/EJES-ESTRATEGICOS-DE-LA-GESTION-AMBIENTAL.pdf.

Contreras, C. (2004), "Centralismo y descentralización en la historia del Perú independiente", in C. Contreras (ed.), *El Aprendizaje del Capitalismo: Estudios de Historia Económica y Social del Perú Republicano*, Instituto de Estudios Peruanos, Lima, pp. 273-305.

Dargent, E. and P. Muñoz (2012), "Peru 2011: Continuities and changes in politics without parties", *Revista de Ciencia Política*, Vol. 32(1), pp. 245-268.

Dayton-Johnson J., J. Londoño and S. Nieto-Parra (2011), "The Process of Reform in Latin America: A Review Essay", *OECD Development Centre Working Papers*, No. 304, OECD Publishing, Paris, http://dx.doi.org/10.1787/5kg3mkvfcjxv-en.

Defensoría del Pueblo (2015), "Reporte de conflictos sociales", N° 134, www.defensoria.gob.pe/modules/Downloads/conflictos/2015/Reporte-Mensual-de-Conflictos-Sociales-N-134-Abril-2015.pdf.

Del Valle, M. (2013), "Ingresos Fiscales por Explotación de Recursos Mineros e Hidrocarburos en Perú", Resumen de Políticas, BID (Banco Interamericano de Desarrollo), http://publications.iadb.org/bitstream/handle/11319/1512/RRNN_Peru.pdf.

EIU (2015), *Evaluating the Environment for Public-Private Partnerships in Latin America and the Caribbean: The 2014 Infrascope*, EIU (Economist Intelligence Unit), www.fomin.org/en-us/Home/Knowledge/Publications/idPublication/137450.aspx.

Flor L. and O. Rojas (2007), "¿Existe regulación por incentivos en las concesiones viales?: El caso peruano", *Revista de la Competencia y la Propiedad Intelectual*, Vol. 3(5), pp. 141-172.

Gallup Organisation (2015), *Gallup World Monitor* (database).

Guasch J.L. (2004), *Granting and Renegotiating Infrastructure Concessions: Doing it Right*, World Bank, Washington, DC, http://elibrary.worldbank.org/doi/abs/10.1596/0-8213-5792-1.

Hammergren, L. (2007), "Fighting judicial corruption: A comparative perspective from Latin America", in *Global Corruption Report 2007: Corruption in Judicial Systems*, Transparency International/Cambridge University Press, pp. 138-146.

Herrera, P. and P. Francke (2007), "Análisis de la eficiencia del gasto municipal y de sus determinantes", Informe final de Investigación, CIES – PUCP, Lima.

IDB/UNECLAC (2014), *La Economía del Cambio Climático en el Perú*, Banco Interamericano de Desarrollo (IDB), Comisión Económica para América Latina y el Caribe (UN-ECLAC), http://repositorio.cepal.org/bitstream/handle/11362/37419/S1420992_es.pdf?sequence=1

INEI (Instituto Nacional de Estadística e Informática) (2014), *Módulo de opinión: Gobernabilidad, Democracia y Transparencia*, Encuesta Nacional de Hogares, INEI, Lima.

IPD (2012), "2012 governance data", *Institutional Profiles Database*, www.cepii.fr/institutions/EN/ipd.asp.

Korinek, J. (2015), "Managing the Minerals Sector: Implications for Trade from Peru and Colombia", OECD Trade Policy Working Paper, Paris (forthcoming).

Maldonado S. (2015), "The Political Effects of Resource Booms: Political Outcomes, Clientelism and Public Goods Provision in Peru", Mimeo, University of California, Berkeley, https://stanislaomaldonadodotorg1.files.wordpress.com/2015/05/resource-curse-and-political-support-042915.pdf

Ministry of Economy and Finance (2015), "Consulta de transferencias a los gobiernos nacional, regional, local y EPS", Transparencia Económica website, http://apps5.mineco.gob.pe/transferencias/cuadros/Hoja1_1.aspx.

Ministry of Environment (2015a), "Misión y vision", Ministry of Environment website, www.minam.gob.pe/?el-ministerio=mision-y-vision.

Ministry of Environment (2015b), "Los efectos de la minería illegal", Ministry of Environment website, www.minam.gob.pe/mineriailegal/los-efectos-de-la-mineria-ilegal/.

Ministry of Environment (2015c), "Una historia de devastación", Ministry of Environment website, www.minam.gob.pe/mineriailegal/una-historia-de-devastacion/.

Ministry of Environment (2011), *Plan Nacional de Acción Ambiental, PLANAA- PERU 2011-2021*, 2nd Edition, Lima.

Ministry of Housing, Construction and Sanitation (2006), *Plan Nacional de Desarrollo Urbano: Territorio para Todos. Lineamientos de Politica de Desarrollo Urbano 2006-2015*, Ministry of Housing, Construction and Sanitation, Lima, Peru, http://eudora.vivienda.gob.pe/OBSERVATORIO/destacados2/PlanNacionalDesarrolloUrbano20062015.pdf.

Morris, S. and C. Blake (2009), "Political and analytical challenges of corruption in Latin America", in S. Morris and C. Blake (eds.), *Corruption and Democracy in Latin America*, University of Pittsburgh Press, Pittsburgh.

Municipality of Lima (2014), *Plan Metropolitano de Desarrollo Urbano Lima y Callao 2035,* Volumes 1, 2 and 3, Municipality of Lima.

Muñoz, P. (2010), "¿La Política Importa? Los Determinantes Políticos de la Eficiencia del Gasto Municipal", CIES, SER (Asociación Servicios Educativos Rurales), Lima, www.cies.org.pe/es/investigaciones/descentralizacion-y-modernizacion-del-estado/la-politica-importa-los-determinantes.

Muñoz, P. (2008), "La incertidumbre de la política regional. Estudio sobre la articulación entre el gobierno regional y los gobiernos locales de Puno (2003-2007)", Asociación SER/Oxfam, Lima.

Muñoz, P. (2005), *El Diseño Institucional Municipal 1980-2004 y sus Implicancias para las Zonas Rurales*, SER (Servicios Educativos Rurales (SER), Lima.

OECD (2013), *OECD Economic Surveys: Colombia 2013: Economic Assessment*, OECD Publishing, Paris, http://dx.doi.org/10.1787/eco_surveys-col-2013-en

OECD/ECLAC (2012), *Latin American Economic Outlook 2012: Transforming the State for Development,* OECD Publishing, Paris, http://dx.doi.org/10.1787/leo-2012-en.

OECD/IDB (2014), *Government at a Glance: Latin America and the Caribbean 2014: Towards Innovative Public Financial Management*, OECD Publishing, Paris, http://dx.doi.org/10.1787/9789264209480-en.

OECD/ITF (2015), *ITF Transport Outlook 2015*, OECD Publishing, Paris, http://dx.doi.org/10.1787/9789282107782-en.

Panfichi, A. and M. Alvarado (2011), *Corrupción y Gobernabilidad,* CIES (Consorcio de Investigación Económica y Social), Pontificia Universidad Católica del Perú, Lima.

PCM (Presidency of the Council of Ministers) (2012), *Plan Nacional de Lucha contra la Corrupción: 2012-2016*, CAN (Comisión de Alto Anticorrupción), Lima, Peru.

Pedagrio. S. (2014), "Corrupción y economía ilegal. El estado: un protector más que un botín", Argumentos – *Revista de Análisis y Critica*, Vol. 8(3), http://revistaargumentos.iep.org.pe/articulos/corrupcion-y-economia-ilegal-el-estado-un-protector-mas-que-un-botin/

Proética (2013), *VIII Encuesta Nacional Sobre Percepciones de la Corrupción en el Perú 2013*, Proética, www.proetica.org.pe/viii-encuesta-nacional-sobre-percepciones-de-la-corrupcion-en-el-peru-2013/

Rose-Ackerman, S. (2007), "Judicial independence and corruption", in *Global Corruption Report 2007: Corruption in Judicial Systems,* Transparency International/Cambridge University Press, pp.15-24.

Salazar, R. and J. Pablo Ramos (2007), "Increased transparency helps curb corruption in Costa Rica", in *Global Corruption Report 2007: Corruption in Judicial Systems,* Transparency International/Cambridge University Press, pp. 190-194.

Sánchez Urribarrí, R. (2008), "Characteristics of the judiciary vs. corruption perception", *Sistemas Judiciales,* 13, pp. 88-99.

Sanguinetti, P. (2010), "Canon minero y decisiones fiscales subnacionales en el Perú", *CAF Working Papers*, No. 2010/01, CAF, Caracas.

Simon, J. and J. Caro (2012), "Procuraduría anticorrupción: Diagnostico actual y propuestas de optimización de su funcionamiento", in Simon and Ramirez (eds.), *La Lucha Contra la Corrupción en el Perú. El Modelo Peruano: La Experiencia de las Procuradurías Anticorrupción*, Griley, Lima, pp. 253-283.

Tirole, J. (1996), "A theory of collective reputations (with applications to the persistence of corruption and to firm quality)", *Review of Economic Studies*, Vol. 63(1), pp. 1-22.

United Nations (2015), *World Urbanization Prospects: 2014 Revision, Population Division*, Department of Economic and Social Affairs, United Nations, New York, http://esa.un.org/unpd/wup/.

Vargas, P. (2009), "El Cambio Climático y sus efectos en el Perú", *Working Paper Series*, No. 2009-14, Banco Central de la Reserva del Perú, Lima.

World Bank (2012), *Country Partnership Strategy for the Republic of Peru for the Period FY2012-FY2016*, World Bank, Washington, DC.

World Health Organization (WHO) (2006), *WHO Air Quality Guidelines for Particulate Matter, Ozone, Nitrogen Dioxide and Sulfur Dioxide, Global Update 2005, Summary of Risk Assessment*, WHO/SDE/PHE/OEH/06.02, WHO, Geneva.

Yamada, G. and R. Montero (2011), "Corrupción e inequidad en los servicios públicos en el Perú", *Working Paper*, No. 87, CIES, Lima.

Zavaleta, M. (2014), *Coaliciones de Independientes: Las Reglas no Escritas de la Política Electoral*, IEP, Lima.

Zubieta, R. (2014), "Estándares ambientales en Perú: ¿son muy exigentes?", *El Comercio*, http://elcomercio.pe/economia/peru/estandares-ambientales-peru-son-muy-exigentes-noticia-1739547.

ORGANISATION FOR ECONOMIC CO-OPERATION AND DEVELOPMENT

The OECD is a unique forum where governments work together to address the economic, social and environmental challenges of globalisation. The OECD is also at the forefront of efforts to understand and to help governments respond to new developments and concerns, such as corporate governance, the information economy and the challenges of an ageing population. The Organisation provides a setting where governments can compare policy experiences, seek answers to common problems, identify good practice and work to co-ordinate domestic and international policies.

The OECD member countries are: Australia, Austria, Belgium, Canada, Chile, the Czech Republic, Denmark, Estonia, Finland, France, Germany, Greece, Hungary, Iceland, Ireland, Israel, Italy, Japan, Korea, Luxembourg, Mexico, the Netherlands, New Zealand, Norway, Poland, Portugal, the Slovak Republic, Slovenia, Spain, Sweden, Switzerland, Turkey, the United Kingdom and the United States. The European Commission takes part in the work of the OECD.

OECD Publishing disseminates widely the results of the Organisation's statistics gathering and research on economic, social and environmental issues, as well as the conventions, guidelines and standards agreed by its members.

OECD DEVELOPMENT CENTRE

The Development Centre of the Organisation for Economic Co-operation and Development was established in 1962 and comprises 27 member countries of the OECD: Austria, Belgium, Chile, the Czech Republic, Denmark, Finland, France, Germany, Greece, Iceland, Ireland, Israel, Italy, Korea, Luxembourg, Mexico, the Netherlands, Norway, Poland, Portugal, Slovak Republic, Slovenia, Spain, Sweden, Switzerland, Turkey and the United Kingdom. In addition, 22 non-OECD countries are full members of the Development Centre: Brazil (since March 1994); India (February 2001); Romania (October 2004); Thailand (March 005); South Africa (May 2006); Egypt and Viet Nam (March 2008); Colombia (July 2008); Indonesia (February 2009); Costa Rica, Mauritius, Morocco and Peru (March 2009); the Dominican Republic (November 2009); Senegal (February 2011); Argentina and Cabo Verde (March 2011); Panama (July 2013); Côte d'Ivoire, Kazakhstan and Tunisia (January 2015); and the People's Republic of China (July 2015). The European Union also takes part in the work of the Centre.

The Development Centre occupies a unique place within the OECD and in the international community. It provides a platform where developing and emerging economies interact on an equal footing with OECD members to promote knowledge sharing and peer learning on sustainable and inclusive development. The Centre combines multidisciplinary analysis with policy dialogue activities to help governments formulate innovative policy solutions to the global challenges of development. Hence, the Centre plays a key role in the OECD's engagement efforts with non-member countries.

To increase the impact and legitimacy of its work, the Centre adopts an inclusive approach and engages with a variety of governmental and non-governmental stakeholders. It works closely with experts and institutions from its member countries, has established partnerships with key international and regional organisations and hosts networks of private-sector enterprises, think tanks and foundations working for development. The results of its work are discussed in experts' meetings as well as in policy dialogues and high-level meetings, and are published in a range of high-quality publications and papers for the research and policy communities.

For more information on the Centre, please see *www.oecd.org/dev.*

OECD PUBLISHING, 2, rue André-Pascal, 75775 PARIS CEDEX 16
(41 2015 06 1 P) ISBN 978-92-64-24326-2 – 2015-02

www.ingramcontent.com/pod-product-compliance
Lightning Source LLC
Chambersburg PA
CBHW061211240926
51846CB00006B/1186